SCOTLAND YARD'S GHOST SQUAD

This book is dedicated to my grandchildren:

Emma Charlotte, Jessica Louise &
Harry Thomas Charles Cowper and Samuel Henry
& Annie Grace Jerreat.

In addition, it is dedicated to the stalwarts who
made up the Ghost Squad:

'Charley Artful', 'The Ferret', 'The Yokel' and 'Nobby'.

SCOTLAND YARD'S GHOST SQUAD

THE SECRET WEAPON AGAINST POST-WAR CRIME

DICK KIRBY

First published in Great Britain in 2011 by
Wharncliffe Local History
an imprint of
Pen & Sword Books Ltd
47 Church Street
Barnsley
South Yorkshire
S70 2AS

ISBN 978 1 84884 451 3

Typeset in 11/13pt Plantin by
Mac Style, Beverley, East Yorkshire

Printed in China through Printworks Int. Ltd.

Pen & Sword Books Ltd incorporates the Imprints of
Pen & Sword Aviation, Pen & Sword Maritime, Pen & Sword
Military, Wharncliffe Local History, Pen and Sword Select, Pen
and Sword Military Classics, Leo Cooper, Remember When,
Seaforth Publishing and Frontline Publishing.

For a complete list of Pen & Sword titles please contact
PEN & SWORD BOOKS LIMITED
47 Church Street, Barnsley, South Yorkshire, S70 2AS, England
E-mail: enquiries@pen-and-sword.co.uk
Website: www.pen-and-sword.co.uk

Contents

Contents

Acknowledgements

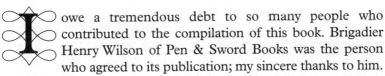owe a tremendous debt to so many people who contributed to the compilation of this book. Brigadier Henry Wilson of Pen & Sword Books was the person who agreed to its publication; my sincere thanks to him. Martin Gosling MBE, the son of one of the book's principal characters, John Gosling, provided me with a splendid foreword and unlimited access to his late father's papers, and for that, his friendship and for being a genial host, I thank him. John Brinnand, the son of one of the other founding members of the Special Duty Squad, Matthew Brinnand, was good enough to provide me with details of his father and other members of his extended family, for which I am most grateful. Jacqueline Ridgwell JP, the niece by marriage of Henry Clark, and Mavis Bidmead, Clark's sister, conspired together to unearth a great deal of information regarding their illustrious relation which they were good enough to make available to me; my profound thanks to them both. Mick Priddle was kind enough to engineer an introduction to Shirley Woodall, the daughter of Percy Burgess, who agreed to make available to me her late father's privately published memoirs, and I am indebted to both of them.

Steve Earl, Robin Gillis and Ken Stone, former members of the Metropolitan Police Museum and Archives Section, and the late Maggie Bird from the Metropolitan Police Records Management Branch were all enormously helpful. Mary Clucas, Ellie Haynes and Suzanna Parry from the Metropolitan Police Library gave much needed help, as did Chris Forester, the editor of *The Peeler* and other periodicals. Karen McCall and Susi Rogol, the past and present editor respectively of the *London Police Pensioner*, have provided massive assistance and encouragement over the years.

More recently, Phillip Barnes-Warden of the Metropolitan Police Historic Collection has been a tower of strength and has worked tirelessly on my behalf. Alan Moss, with his encyclopaedic knowledge of police history provided (as always) tremendous assistance. Pamela Pappé from the Peel Centre Library has also been most helpful. My thanks go to them all.

Bob Fenton QGM, the honorary secretary of the Ex-CID Officers' Association orchestrated the former CID officers who got in touch with me, my son Robert assisted with the background research, and my sons-in-law, Steve Cowper and Rich Jerreat, helped enormously with the computer side of the book; my thanks to all of them.

Over the years, a number of people either assisted me considerably with my research or wrote or spoke to me with some wonderful stories about the men who appear in this book. In alphabetical order, they are: John Beare, Jan Caddey, David Capstick, the late Henry Clark, the late Ivy May Clark, Ben Gosling, Joy Guest, David Hewett, the late Bob Higgins, Steve Holloway, the late Fred Lambert, Julie Milstead, the late George Price, David Pritchard, Leonard 'Nipper' Read QPM, Pete Rogers, Ruth Silburn, Daphne Skillern QPM, Michael Stuart-Moore, GBS, QC, John Swain QPM, 'Dick' West and Victoria Wragg.

My thanks to Martin Gosling, John Brinnand, Mavis Bidmead, Philippa Hewett and Shirley Woodall for providing some of the photographs. Every effort has been made to contact copyright holders and the publishers and I apologise for any inadvertent omissions.

Finally, my thanks to my family, especially my wife Ann, for her love and support during over forty-five years of marriage, as well as my unbounded admiration for her in her courageous fight against cancer.

Any faults or imperfections in the book are mine alone.

Dick Kirby

Foreword
Martin Gosling MBE

R eference to the work of the Special Duty Squad has been made by several crime writers and it is mentioned in the memoirs of some former Metropolitan Police officers, whose knowledge or recollection of events was, perhaps, less than perfect.

However, in this outstanding book Dick Kirby has brought together his own unrivalled insights into the nuances and culture of detective work. These and the fruits of his meticulous research have resulted in a definitive account of what really took place.

His trawl through the deep waters of police practice and the controversial use of informants reveals values and methods of operating that would perhaps be frowned upon in today's world of political correctness and obsessive systems of recording. But the officers of the Special Duty Squad, later known as the Ghost Squad, produced phenomenal results in their campaign against soaring crime in the period following the end of the Second World War.

This is far more than an academic treatise on criminal investigation during a fascinating period in the history of the Metropolitan Police. Mr Kirby takes the trouble to explore the personal and operational backgrounds of the individual CID officers who toiled in difficult circumstances in those hard times. In doing this he brings to life the day to day challenges faced by those who took part – the lack of proper funding that led to inadequate provision of transport, and the inevitable resentments engendered when a successful undercover enterprise was operating in police Divisions that already had their own structures of criminal investigation.

By setting these events against the background of austerity and deprivation that prevailed in those bleak years, Mr Kirby has contrived to imbue his account with a sense of reality that can almost be tasted. The flavour will be even sharper for those of an age to recall those times.

My own memories are shaped by my father, John Gosling, who was the only member of the Squad to have served through the entire period of its existence. As a child I was aware of the uneven hours of his work that inevitably affected the whole family. He would frequently return home well after midnight, only for the household to be woken again later by the telephone ringing in the small hours, summoning him back to confront yet another criminal enterprise. This put some strain on domestic routines and on occasions led to my mother's voice being raised in protest. There were other times when, knowing he had only a few hours respite, my father would simply snatch a short sleep downstairs in an armchair.

Other recollections include occasional visits from one or two ebullient Londoners who were clearly on good terms with my father but who were only much later identified to me as being amongst his coterie of 'snouts'.

The officers who served with the Squad were required to display qualities of tenacity, tact, perseverance and fortitude. These attributes and more were necessary to deal effectively with the criminal cunning, ruthlessness and propensity for violence deployed by many of the law-breakers they faced. The officers worked unholy hours with no prospect of being paid overtime.

The extent of their achievement is vividly described by Mr Kirby who has succeeded in shining a much needed light onto some of the previously obscure and often abstruse aspects of detective work with informers.

Welcome too is an explanation of the most likely reason for the Squad being disbanded at a time when it seemed that its obvious success should have ensured its survival.

Scotland Yard's Ghost Squad is altogether a good read. It will be an important addition to the bookshelves of those who appreciate an authentic and clearly stated account of a fascinating period in the history of criminal investigation.

Martin Gosling
Wingfield, Suffolk

Prologue

Percy Street, London W1, runs between Rathbone Street to the west and Tottenham Court Road to the east. It is a fairly unprepossessing area but then again, it always has been; never more so than at half-past two in the afternoon of 18 March 1946. A chill wind blew down the bomb-damaged thoroughfare; it symbolised the austerity of post-war Britain.

One month earlier, it had been announced that there was just one week's coal left in London; now, the Bank of England had been nationalised and the iron and steel industries would follow suit. Meat was harder to get than during the war and the rationing of bacon and fat had increased. Not only was food rationed; every saleable commodity required ration coupons. And therefore coupons – stolen, recycled or forged – were in enormous demand.

So despite the cheerless surroundings of Percy Street, it was there that a criminal coup was planned during that afternoon; 250,000 forged industrial clothing coupons, worth two shillings each, were due to change hands. So perfectly forged were these coupons that their falsity could only be detected by the Board of Trade, by whom the genuine articles were issued. The plan was the culmination of months of work. Assistant Commissioner (Crime), Ronald Howe CVO MC had sent Detective Inspector Henry Clark and Detective Constable George Price to make enquiries in Nottingham, because it was believed that that northern city was the source of the forgeries; but Howe was wrong.

It was Detective Sergeant John Gosling who secured the information as to the perpetrators of the conspiracy, plus the name of the ringleader in charge of the printing, a man who was the son of the (then) Sheriff of London and who was highly placed in London society. As a front, he carried on a small hairdresser's business in Hampstead Road, on the other side of Regents Park from his home in Maida Vale, and was known to police and criminals alike as 'Benny the Barber'.

Gosling's break came when he arrested a man known as 'Hymie the Gambler', who had been active during the war years dealing in forged and stolen coupons. Hymie was described by Gosling as 'the best informed man in London'; he always dealt with top-class jobs; he knew every receiver of note; and his intelligence was so good that he was one of Gosling's top ten informants, so much so that upon receipt of his information, Gosling stated, "you could go in with your head down". Now, Gosling applied a little pressure to Hymie who, as a result, had infiltrated the circle of forgers; a warrant was granted by the Home Office to intercept Benny's telephone calls, and in this fashion the identities of the co-conspirators were confirmed, their telephones were also tapped, observations were carried out and arrangements had been made by Hymie which resulted in the agreement to meet in Percy Street for the selling of the forged coupons.

The thoroughfare was more or less deserted – ideal for an illegal transaction because if anybody approached the criminals they could immediately scatter. In fact, only one man was in the street; a tall, well-built individual who was deeply involved in repairing the engine of a broken-down furniture lorry. He certainly appeared to know what he was doing, as he selected first one tool then another from an impressive display; in fact, it was natural that he should, because before he joined the Metropolitan Police John Gosling had been a motor mechanic. As he fiddled with an engine which had absolutely nothing wrong with it, Gosling (plus two colleagues who were secreted in a nearby factory) and a number of other police officers waited for the arrival of the gang.

Twenty-five minutes later, Gosling's informant arrived in Percy Street; Hymie was in possession of what appeared to be an impressive wad of currency with which to pay for the forged coupons. In fact, the wad, supplied by Gosling, was nothing more than 'Tops and Bottoms' – newspaper cut to the size of banknotes, then topped and tailed by genuine notes.

Just then, the four-man gang – Eddie Cantor, Harry Fizzon (both of whom Gosling later described as being 'of uncertain nationality and occupation'), Ben Distleman (whose brother Harry had been murdered in a gangland feud five years previously) and Herbert Hare – arrived. One of the gang cast a wary eye in Gosling's direction. He saw only a bulky man, dressed in stained dungarees, repairing the engine of a broken-down van – a common enough sight in post-war England. Anyway, the mechanic had his back to him, and the hidden police officers saw the gangster shrug dismissively and turn back to his associates. He was, of course, unaware that Gosling had balanced a small mirror on the engine and was able to see everything that was going on.

The negotiations got underway, the gang and the informant chatting animatedly, and as one of the gang produced a large bag, so a tubby man, who looked like a gentleman farmer but who was actually Divisional Detective Inspector Jack Capstick, parked his family saloon so that it effectively blocked off one end of Percy Street. At the other end of the street, a tall, thin man, Detective Sergeant Mathew Brinnand, was doing exactly the same.

When a job involving a participating informant goes down, the police officer and the informant have an agreed signal – the rubbing of the ear, a finger inside the collar – by the informant to signify to the police officer that everything is as it should be; the offence has been committed and the arrest can safely be made. It is unwise to deviate from this procedure, and Gosling, as an experienced informant handler, knew this. But when Hymie pulled the 'Tops and Bottoms' from his pocket and offered the wad to the gang, Gosling obviously thought "Why wait any longer?" and gave the signal to his fellow officers. Detective Inspector Clark and Detective Constable Price dashed out of their hiding place, Capstick, Brinnand and Gosling closed in, and, with the assistance of 'C' Division's Detective Inspector Fred Hodge and Detective Sergeant Law, the gang were rushed and, together with the incriminating bag, were bundled into the furniture van and driven the short distance to Tottenham Court Road police station.

Catching the gang red-handed had been a tremendous coup. And now, thanks to Gosling's informant who had successfully infiltrated the gang, they were all lined up in the charge room, with the exception of the leader of the gang who, the officers felt, could be tied into the rest of his associates with the minimum of fuss. There was one problem, however. To be on the safe side, the gang had decided on a dummy run – just in case. As Gosling opened their bag, he discovered to his horror that it contained nothing more than old newspapers. The four gang members smirked amongst themselves, Hymie was justifiably concerned, and the other police officers looked furiously at Gosling, mutely condemning him for his impetuosity. Gosling was mortified and feared that his colleagues would call him a "clever boy", which was exactly how his contemporaries in the CID office at City Road police station had referred to him, when he had presented himself there as a brand-new detective constable, thirteen years previously. It looked as though all was lost: after the infiltration of the gang, the hours of observations and the months of work, the gang leader had not even been arrested. And then, this happened.

It was at that moment that an elderly lady walked into the police station, struggling with a heavy bag identical in every respect to the one in the gang's possession, which, she informed the desk sergeant, she had seen flung from a taxi in Percy Street. It transpired that this taxi contained Benny the Barber who, having witnessed the round-up of his gang and fearing he was next, swiftly jettisoned the bag which the officers quickly discovered contained 250,000 perfectly forged clothing coupons with a street value of £25,000. Moreover, the lady had also made a note of the registration number of the taxi; the driver was traced and took the officers to an address which revealed the gang leader. They found no further forged coupons there; they did, however, discover an incriminating address book containing details of a factory at Shepperton. A search of these premises revealed a printing press capable of printing five-unit industrial coupons, together with a perforating machine, camera, photographic plates, inks and paper.

The maximum sentence for coupon forging was fourteen years' imprisonment; quite understandable when one considers the disastrous consequences that this offence had already had on a staggering economy and would have continued to have, had it not been nipped in the bud. But because the defendants were all dealt with under the Common Law offence of conspiracy at the Old Bailey, Benny the Barber – Wilfred Sidney Halse, to give him his true identity – was sentenced to just two years' imprisonment, the maximum penalty for this charge. When one considers that Halse was clearly the ringleader of this far-reaching scheme, Gosling thought, perhaps with considerable justification, that the framing of the indictment was 'by special arrangement', due to Halse's family connections.

As to Halse's associates, the criminal career of Eddie Cantor (also known as Eli Marks) had commenced twenty-one years previously; he was sentenced to twenty-one months' imprisonment. Harry Fizzon (also known as Harry Martin) had begun his career of crime in 1931; he was sentenced to eighteen months' imprisonment. Ben Distleman (who also liked to be known as Bertram Desmond) had been known to the Criminal Records Office at New Scotland Yard since 1937 and received fifteen months' imprisonment. Herbert Hare, an engineer from Kilburn who was quite content with his baptismal name and whose criminal record commenced that day at the Old Bailey, was sentenced to twelve months' imprisonment. Two ladies, the wives of two of the defendants were acquitted.

And the informant, who was pulled in with the rest of the gang? In the charge room Capstick, flourished the 'Tops and Bottoms' which he had 'discovered' in his possession, in full view of the rest of the gang and demanded to know its provenance. Right on cue, Hymie saucily replied, "Won it at the dogs," and duly received a punch in the face from Capstick. "Leave 'im alone!" muttered the gang members, completely taken in by this bit of inspired stage-management; later, to cement Capstick's duplicity, Hymie was marched out of the cell block after the station sergeant loudly informed the gaoler (well within the hearing of the gang) that the Military Police had arrived "for the army deserter".

* * *

Perhaps unsurprisingly, Capstick's nickname was 'Charley Artful', and he was the leader of an élite group of four Scotland Yard detectives – the others were Clark, Gosling and Brinnand – which had been formed just two months previously. Their brief was to infiltrate the organised gangs of coupon forgers, lorry hi-jackers, warehousebreakers, as well as the thieves and receivers of every resaleable commodity in post-war London, and to smash them. The scheme had the backing of the Home Secretary and the Commissioner of the Metropolitan Police. How the detectives achieved their aim was their business; it was left to their own discretion and capabilities.

The unit was known as 'The Special Duty Squad' and it was shrouded in secrecy; in fact the Home Office papers pertaining to the unit were considered so restricted that originally they were ordered to remain closed for seventy-five years, until 2025.

This is the story of how and why the unit came into existence.

It is also the stories of the men who staffed it, the way in which their prisoners were caught and the tremendous results which were obtained. And when, after almost four years, the unit was disbanded and the detectives were posted elsewhere, the papers were dutifully filed away and the informants disappeared, rather like wraiths. It was almost as if the group had never existed.

It was little wonder that 'The Special Duty Squad' was better known as 'The Ghost Squad'.

CHAPTER 1

The War Years

When the Prime Minister, the Right Honourable Arthur Neville Chamberlain MP, arrived at Heston Aerodrome on the morning of 30 September 1938, he had returned from Munich where he had been involved in negotiations with the German *Führer*, Adolf Hitler, regarding the worsening political situation. As he stepped from the aeroplane, he triumphantly waved a piece of paper, headed 'The Anglo-German Agreement', which had been signed by both leaders. It represented a treaty agreement that Britain and Germany should never go to war again. Upon receipt of this news, the vast majority of the British people went wild with excitement, including (to a more dignified degree) the King and Queen; in fact, the Dowager Queen Mary expressed her anger at those who were not grateful to Chamberlain because, after all, the signing of the agreement meant 'peace in our time'.

Winston Churchill was one of those who could see that this was appeasement pure and simple of a power-mad dictator bent on world domination and considered Chamberlain, who before he had become Prime Minister had been regarded as a brilliant Chancellor of the Exchequer, to be a vacillating weakling. This was an opinion shared by Hitler; after an exhilarated Chamberlain had left to return to London, the German Foreign Minister, Joachim von Ribbentrop, questioned whether it had been wise to sign the agreement. "Oh, don't take it so seriously," replied Hitler. "That piece of paper is of no further significance, whatsoever."

With Germany re-arming at an alarming rate, Chamberlain nervously increased the size of the Territorial Army. The following March, Hitler's troops marched into Czechoslovakia. However, Britain had agreed to stand by Poland in the event of invasion, and when Germany invaded on 1 September 1939, two days later, Britain and Germany – for the second time in twenty-one years – were once again at war.

★ ★ ★

At least the Metropolitan Police were quick to react, under the leadership of the popular Commissioner, Sir Philip Woolcott Game, GCB, GCVO, GBE, KCMG, DSO. Sir Philip was in poor health and at sixty-four he had been considering retirement, but he patriotically decided to remain in office until the end of the war. *Police Orders* dated 31 August 1939 provided details of 1,764 police pensioners and Special Constables recruited to form a War Reserve for the duration, and soon they would number almost 27,000. Many of the War Reserve officers were commended by the commissioner for smart police work during the hostilities and some of them would feature amongst the 308 Metropolitan Police wartime awards for gallantry. Not all of them, though.

John Reginald Christie had been brought up in Halifax and at the age of fifteen he secured a job with the Halifax police. He was sacked for theft, as he was from his next employment, and after marrying in 1920 he obtained a job as a postman; the following year he was jailed for three months for stealing postal orders. This was followed by receiving a bind-over for obtaining money by false pretences and then probation, for assault. Christie moved to London, where in 1924 he was sentenced to nine months' hard labour for larceny and five years later, six months' hard labour for assaulting a woman. In 1933, he was sentenced to three months' imprisonment for stealing a car.

Therefore, Scotland Yard must have been in desperate straits indeed to have accepted Christie as a War Reserve constable. It is possible that his lacklustre sex life – a former girl-friend had referred to him as 'Reggie-no-dick' – was a contributory factor to his strangling Ruth Fuerst whilst having sexual intercourse with her while on duty in 1943. This was followed by six more murders (including that of his wife), and when some of the bodies were later discovered, Christie managed to pin the blame on Timothy Evans, an innocent man, who was hanged. It took another ten years after the initial murder for a similar (and quite justifiable) fate to be meted out to Christie. It was not thought to have been the Metropolitan Police recruitment section's finest hour.

To start with, police work was considered to be a reserved occupation, although many officers wanted to join the armed services. By the end of 1939, reservists were permitted to join their units, and in 1941 officers were allowed to join the Royal Air Force, and those who had been members of the Territorial Army or the Royal Naval Volunteer Reserve were called up. The following year, police officers were permitted to join the Army and the Royal Navy. The Metropolitan Police had been up to strength – 19,000 men at the commencement of hostilities – but now 4,000 officers had joined the armed services. Detective Chief Inspector George Hatherill CBE, at six foot six was a chain-smoking colossus of a man and a talented individual who could speak French, German, Polish, Swedish and Danish. A First World War veteran, Hatherill was back in France in 1939, dealing with the looting of British Army stores, and his recommendations resulted in the formation of the army's Special Investigation Branch (SIB). Detective Superintendent Clarence Campion may well have tired of his posting at the Yard's Criminal Record Office; he was appointed Major, his faithful aide, Detective Sergeant Harold Dibbens, was commissioned as a Second Lieutenant, and the two men set off for France to become part of SIB. Leonard Burt CBE, CVO was an astute murder investigator who was seconded to MI5 in 1940 and promoted to detective superintendent; then almost immediately, his rank was replaced with that of Lieutenant-Colonel, and together with Reggie Spooner, then a detective inspector (and later to become head of the Flying Squad), he set about tracing and arresting spies.

In September 1939 the Emergency Powers Bill was passed, and within a week, in the belief that air attacks from Germany were imminent, evacuation of schoolchildren and 'priority classes' commenced and Identity Cards were introduced. The average weekly wage was £4 9s 0d, and income tax was raised to 37½% in the pound one month after war commenced, later increased to 50%. Those who were considered high earners had to pay 'Super Tax' – or 95% in the pound. A blackout speed limit of 20mph was introduced in November, and in December Ration Cards were issued, the price of petrol rose (until in the summer of 1942, the petrol allowance was abolished) and during the following month, sugar, bacon and butter were rationed. Two months later, meat was also rationed and the following year, margarine, jam, syrup and treacle were put on ration, followed by cheese, two months after that. In 1942 sweets were rationed, and two months later the production of ice-cream was declared illegal. It was the beginning of years of austerity. Traders passed on to the Food Office a list of supplies that they expected to sell, based on the regulations, and these lists were passed on to the Ministry of Supply.

A chill wind heralded the arrival of 1940, and for the first time in fifty years the Thames froze over. On 1 January, two million men and women were called up to join the armed forces and another 1,700,000 men and women joined the Home Guard. Londoners carried their gas masks everywhere and, providentially, Neville Chamberlain resigned; he died six months later from cancer, aged seventy-one. On 10 May 1940, Winston Churchill formed a coalition government and Hitler's push against the west commenced.

The German armed services had developed a strategy known as *blitzkrieg*; it meant, literally, 'lightning war', and Londoners abbreviated it to 'The Blitz' – which commenced on 7 September 1940. The *Luftwaffe* rained bombs down on London; the Blitz would not abate until July the following year, and the police and the other emergency services acted with great bravery, rescuing Londoners trapped in bombed buildings. West End Central and Tottenham Court Road police stations were severely damaged, with loss of life, by the bombing raids; the commissioner was fortunately absent from his office at Scotland Yard when a bomb hit the office above his and tons of rubble crashed down on his desk.

With practically every saleable commodity on ration, the organised gangs of criminals got to work; coupons were stolen, recycled and forged, warehouses were broken into, lorries were hi-jacked, railway depots were raided – the losses in the depots in 1943 alone amounted to £1 million – and even rolling stock was stopped in transit and relieved of its contents. The merchandise at the docks was looted, and 'jump-ups' – where a gang followed a van or lorry, and when it stopped, even momentarily, a gang member jumped up into the back of the vehicle and threw down the packing cases to his associates – substantially increased; the gangs were now prepared to steal anything of any value. In 1941, Billy Hill, the self-proclaimed 'Boss of Britain's Underworld' was released from a two-year sentence for a smash and grab; he and his gang industriously got to work, feeding what had become known as the black market.

Normally law-abiding men and women, who hitherto would never have dreamt of breaking the law, now took a different view; they stole goods from work, obtained ration coupons using false names and purchased stolen or forged ration coupons. Swingeing sentences were introduced and many Londoners received draconian fines and prison sentences of hard labour and penal servitude. Companies overcharged on Government contracts, accounts were falsified and Civil Servants were bribed to secure contracts. Army desertions were frequent – between D-Day and the end of the war 10,000 men deserted from the armed services – and ration coupon and black market offences became so prevalent that by March 1942, the maximum sentence for black marketeering was increased to fourteen years' penal servitude. Much of this work fell to the Flying Squad to deal with, causing an exasperated Hugh Young, CBE, KPM, the Chief Constable of the CID to report to Sir Norman Kendall CBE, the Assistant Commissioner (Crime) in a fiercely patriotic report:

> Black market offences have been the main cause of the extra work and it is pleasing to see that the <u>sewer rats and traitors</u> who impede the war effort by committing this class of offence are being brought to justice.

Being a member of the favoured classes was no protection from prosecution, as Noël Coward discovered when he was served with three summonses for failing to declare money he had earned in America, in contravention of a law which had been passed two years previously. Coward declared he was completely unaware that he had breached these regulations, but on his appearance at Bow Street Police Court, the prosecutor gleefully informed the magistrate that Coward was liable to a £61,000 fine. In the event, he was fined just £200, possibly because the magistrate had been tipped off that during his stay in America Coward had been carrying out work on behalf of British Intelligence. The actor George Arliss did not possess that dispensation – for a similar offence he was fined £4,500 – and the judiciary had no time at all for Ivor Novello who, after being convicted of misusing petrol to power his Rolls-Royce, was sent to prison for two months, later reduced on appeal to just one month.

Crime, in particular sexual and violent offences, increased dramatically. Following several very successful tours on the Flying Squad, Ted Greeno, the two-fisted terror of the racetracks, had been promoted to detective chief inspector and now joined the murder squad. His expertise took him all over the country, successfully solving one murder after another. He conducted the search for a group of tearaways who had committed a murder and robbery whilst an air raid was in progress. Greeno also led the hunt for 'The Wartime Ripper', Gordon Frederick Cummins, who savagely murdered four women and attacked another. Cummins was hanged, as was August Sangret who murdered the victim of what became known as 'The Wigwam Murder Case'. Peter Beveridge was the head of the Flying Squad all through the war years; nevertheless, he too was called upon to carry out murder investigations nationwide, including a triple murder where the culprit had not been seen carrying out the murders, nor did she confess, but was convicted as a result of Beveridge's detective ability to present a case which was as circumstantial as it was watertight.

The Metropolitan Police were all but submerged by the amount of crime they had to investigate; three detective superintendents – Sands, Yandell and Barker – from the Yard were detached from their duties to carry out investigations with the Board of Trade, and a team of Flying Squad officers was sent to the West End of London to assist investigations into 4,584 cases of looting which occurred during the Blitz.

Some of the Army personnel who had been brought in to help clear the debris from bomb-damaged buildings were arrested for looting, as were a selection of the air-raid wardens and members of the Auxiliary Fire Service, some of whom received sentences of five years' penal servitude. By 1942, looting had become so prevalent that many MPs were calling for those responsible to receive the death penalty. This sentence had already been implemented on the German statute books; in fact, just prior to the war, the German representative for the International Criminal Police Commission (Interpol), one Heinrich Himmler, had informed his British counterpart that he had discussed the problem of housebreakers with the *Führer*. Hitler's advice was to behead the next half-dozen housebreakers who were caught. "I followed his command," smugly replied Himmler, "and housebreaking ceased."

Many people would have thought that beheading was too merciful a fate for the gangs of robbers, pilferers and pickpockets who infested the public air-raid shelters, reaping rich rewards; in addition, as a result of the lack of sanitation, there were outbreaks of diphtheria, and 178 people were killed when a stampede occurred at Bethnal Green Underground Station.

Foreign nationals, mainly Germans and Italians, were interned. The Government saw this as a perfect opportunity to get rid of gangsters who had been a thorn in their sides during the 1920s and '30s, but who were now a spent force: men like Papa Pasquale (who had boxed under the ring name of Bert Marsh) and 'Darby' Sabini (whose son was later killed whilst on active service with the RAF), who was interned with his brother Harryboy, the latter two volubly protesting that they had never been to Italy and that their mother had been English; but their pleas fell upon deaf ears. And when Harry 'Little Hubby' Distleman lay dying in Soho's Wardour Street, telling passers-by, "I am terribly hurt. He has stabbed me in the heart. Babe's done it," there was little public sympathy for his attacker, one Antonio 'Babe' Mancini, who was executed. Italian citizens were not highly regarded in wartime London, especially Mancini who, whilst previously serving a sentence of twelve months' hard labour, had been prone to spit in the food of Jewish prisoners.

Just prior to Christmas 1944, a smash and grab was carried out in the City of London, where jewellery valued at £3,800 was stolen. The three-man gang got into their stolen Vauxhall saloon and roared away; a Royal Navy officer, Captain Ralph Binney, attempted to stop them and was run down. The driver of the car, Ronald Hedley, stopped, reversed, then ran over Binney again, dragging his body along the road; although he was taken to hospital, he later died of his injuries. Hedley was convicted of murder, sentenced to death but reprieved, his sentence being commuted to penal servitude for life. His accomplice, Thomas James Jenkins, was convicted of manslaughter and sentenced to eight years' penal servitude. The third man, Thomas Jenkins' brother, Charles Henry Jenkins, was not charged; however, almost three years later he would be hanged for the murder of Alec D'Antiquis, following a botched armed robbery. The Binney Medal was struck, to be awarded annually to a civilian who had exhibited bravery in assisting police.

As the war neared its end, Karl Hulton, a deserter from the US army, re-named himself Ricky Allen and met Elizabeth Maud Jones, a night club striptease dancer who introduced herself as Georgina Grayson; the two of them set off on a sickening six-day orgy of violence and robbery, which culminated in the murder of a hire-car driver. At their trial at the Old Bailey, each of this charmless pair blamed the other and both were convicted and sentenced to death. Jones had her sentence commuted to penal servitude for life, but not so Hulton; he was hanged on 8 March 1945. Nineteen days later, the last V2 rocket fell on London, and six weeks after that, on 7 May 1945, Germany formally surrendered, followed three months later by Japan.

★   ★   ★

With total victory in sight, the country went to the polls, and with almost indecent haste Churchill was kicked out of office and Labour, with 393 seats, was in. Londoners sat back and licked their wounds; 29,890 of them had been killed and 50,000 injured. The fatalities included 2,511 Londoners who had been killed by 1,054 V2 Rockets, which injured almost 6,000. It had been decided that half a million prefabricated dwellings would be built, to accommodate the people whose homes had been reduced to rubble; but with 116,000 homes destroyed, 288,000 needing major repairs and another million needing smaller repairs, the actual number of prefabs that were constructed still fell far short of the amount of housing required.

Fatalities among the Metropolitan police officers during the hostilities numbered 206, with 1,942 injured. After VE (Victory in Europe) Day, the war reserves stood down and only 12,231 regular police officers remained. In December 1945, the commissioner appealed for more special constables to enlist, so that the regular police could get out and fight crime. Police officers returning from the armed services numbered 1,413; 409 had been killed in action and a total of 253 had been decorated. Extra personnel and recruiting, which included many ex-servicemen, from January 1946 added another 1,775, but with other resignations the strength of the Metropolitan Police stood at 14,500 – some 4,000 men short.

The situation was tailor-made for an inevitable explosion in crime, and it duly occurred; indictable offences for 1945 reached a record level of 128,954. The time was also ripe for a revolutionary concept to be implemented in order to deal with this predicament, and the chief constable of the CID provided the answer.

CHAPTER 2

The Plan

With his bow tie and winged collar, his bald head and studious mien, Percy Edgar Worth MBE looked every inch a stockbroker, and a successful one at that. But appearances can be deceptive; born in 1888, he had joined the Metropolitan Police in 1910 and had risen through the ranks as a career CID officer. A cunning and well informed detective, Worth's contribution to criminal investigation had been recognised both by the commissioner, who had commended him on fifty occasions, and by the King, who had awarded him the MBE in the 1942 New Year's Honours list.

In 1932 Worth was the divisional detective inspector of 'X' Division. There had been an enormous upsurge of house-breakings all over the division: Harlesden, Willesden Green and Wembley. Worth gathered ten CID officers, provided them with a rather clapped-out Morris Cowley tourer and told them that their duties would consist of patrolling the area and obtaining intelligence from their informants in order to curtail this localised criminality. The officers were under the direct control of another innovative officer, Detective Inspector Hugh Young, and they were told that once they had carried out the arrests they were not to be encumbered with entries in the crime book or typing and submitting crime reports; these mundane matters were to be left with the ordinary rank and file at the respective police stations on 'X' Division. These specially selected officers were to get out on the streets as soon as possible and continue making arrests. Officially designated 'The 'X' Division Patrolling Group', the officers were highly successful; in their first year, they made over 250 arrests and the housebreaking problem was halved. But the Commissioner, Marshall of the RAF, Lord Trenchard, GCB, OM, GCVO, DSO, looked upon the group – or indeed any section of the CID – with distrustful, envious eyes. He had been promulgating his 'Officer Class scheme' which had been fulsomely praised by the uniform branch but derided by the CID, and it is highly likely that Trenchard thought that axeing this very successful unit would represent 'pay-back' time. After twenty-one months, the Assistant Commissioner (Crime), Sir Norman Kendall CBE, decided – on Trenchard's orders – that if this scheme were to be extended to the other divisions, the cost could not possibly be justified, and the group was disbanded.

But Worth had seen what a small, tightly-knit group could do, and as he rose through the ranks he refused to jettison the idea. Worth had succeeded Hugh Young as the chief constable of the CID in January 1945. Realising that the end of hostilities would mean an upsurge in crime, he submitted a carefully worded and compelling report to the Assistant Commissioner (Crime) just eleven days after Germany's surrender. Then, given the shortage of manpower, the scheme had seemed too controversial. Now, seven months later, manpower shortages or not, it was essential that it be implemented.

Under the heading, 'Suggestion to create a squad of selected officers to be employed solely for acquiring information concerning the activities of criminals', Worth's report is reproduced here, word for word.

18th May, 1945.

A.C.C. (thro' D.A.C.C.)

I wish to bring to notice for consideration, the suggestion of creating a small squad of selected C.I.D. officers for the sole purpose of acquiring information, concerning the activities of criminals.

Every Divisional C.I.D. officer has his local informants, but I have in mind the more valuable information concerning persistent and dangerous criminals about whom, past experience has taught us, knowledge almost invariably emanates from contacts of C.I.D. officers employed on the Flying Squad under the direct control of the Chief Inspector and supervised by Superintendent Central.

These officers have the whole of the Metropolis as their playground and they are chosen for duty on the Squad chiefly by their flair for the work and their ability to contact and control informants.

We have been reminded from time to time how necessary it is for the officer to "run" the informant and not for the informant to "run" the officer. The type of informant contacted by the Squad is well-controlled generally and is the more productive. He is more frequently sure of his ground, will communicate only with one officer, and is opposed to any other officer participating in the transaction. It is true to say that it pays this class of informant to make the first approach to police because he is more often than not remunerated for his services, but, on the other hand, there are some known over the years to well-informed officers who do not expect or accept such payment and would probably furnish more information if they were contacted more often by police. (I feel sure the latter part of this statement applies even to paid informants.)

Squad officers in particular are so busily engaged in dealing with their cases, in the building up thereof, preparing same for presentation at court, and attending remand hearings and at Assizes and Sessions, that they have little time to seek information and rely almost invariably on its being communicated to them.

It is apparent that much valuable information is lost to us through our inability to seek it as even good informants might not bother to pass it on through misjudging its importance and value. Again, generally speaking, the information is useless unless quick action is taken and the informants know this fact as well as we do. We ought to be more active in gaining knowledge in the plotting of crime.

In connection therewith the selected officers would have better facilities of keeping contact with reliable informants if they were relieved of their ordinary duties, in addition to which the chances of securing the aid of fresh ones would be greater.

As police officers are reticent as to the identity of their informants, so are the latter in respect to the police and the public, although some informants are known by many police officers for what they are. The best and most reliable of them, however, are secretive in all their dealings and they are mainly the individuals we should keep in touch with. Our policy for years past has been to pay on results – the safest of all ways – but we should not make this a wooden rule. There may be a few cases in which we ought to pay on failure, such as where a "job" has not matured through no fault of the informant. We should encourage the securing of reliable information and be prepared to pay – win or lose. This course has its dangers and is not one to be encouraged generally. Each case must be judged on its merits, but the one I have in mind is where the informant is reliable, his information valuable, and his circumstances are such as to merit financial support.

We all know that many informants are helped financially by C.I.D. officers without the knowledge of their superior officers, but our fund should be used in a deserving case when a fairly substantial amount is required. I want to emphasise my appreciation of the danger here unless both officer and informant can be trusted, but the application of the wooden rule also has its disadvantages.

It must be admitted that we do not spend enough money on acquiring information; that there is scope to do so, and that it would be wisely spent, I feel confident. Herewith are the annual amounts spent for the past five years from the Information Fund which is maintained at the authorised Home Office grant of £1,000 a year. With the exception of a small amount for applications for Central officers, the amount shown underneath each annual total has been granted on applications from Squad officers; thus the remaining amount has been given to informants on applications from Divisions on the four Districts.

	1940	1941	1942	1943	1944
Total	£825	£540	£892	£649	£789
Squad	£501	£292	£578	£431	£450

These figures speak for themselves. We know the number of Squad arrests and the quality thereof are high. We cannot expect such results from Division – the work differs so immeasurably – but when one considers there are but fifty officers on the Squad, it is apparent they have reliable informants and know how to use them.

It is from the Squad, I suggest, the selected officers should be chosen. There may well be one or two in Divisions for consideration who have already been booked for Squad work.

To commence with, I suggest six, including a 1st. Class Inspector in charge who will be responsible to A.C.C., all of whom are acknowledged to know sound and reliable informants. They must, of course, be loyal, trustworthy and honourable in all their dealings both with the Commissioner and the informant, and for our part, we must trust them. What would it be but of great advantage to spend another £1,000 a year on acquiring information?

I am not apprehensive of the quality of our men to react to the demands of the service in this respect, for we know by long experience that some excellent cases have been attained without a call on the Information Fund when one would have been readily responded to. It is simply a matter of choosing the right officer.

The idea is not only to secure information but to disseminate it. The Squad would not be able to cope with all the information obtained and it would become necessary for the officer securing it to co-operate with the Divisional C.I.D. concerned – this would be necessary in most cases – until the "job" matured.

I do not advocate that selected officers should form a squad to be generally known to all and sundry – that would have its disadvantages. It would appear advisable to augment the C.1 Establishment and to all intents and purposes for them to perform duties as Squad officers. Each member of the Squad proper would carry on in the normal way, and in the dissemination of the information, discretion would be exercised as to the most convenient means for acting upon it.

We shall soon be returning to pre-war strength in the C.I.D. establishment, with augmentation in some ranks. Coinciding with this, crime will doubtless increase for a time – it is unquestionably far from being in a satisfactory state now – and in making my suggestion I do so feeling confident that the experiment would be worthwhile and prove to be a progressive step in combating crime.

It would not, of course, be expedient always to employ the same officer on this work as changes would be necessary with experience. This is but a general outline of the scheme, and no doubt it can be improved upon by due consideration and deliberation.

I would like to see it given a fair trial, say, of 12 months after which period the position could be reviewed.

P. Worth C.C. (CID)

⋆　⋆　⋆

Of course, Worth was quite right in suggesting that officers from the Flying Squad should be selected for this ground-breaking work. Formed in 1919 to combat the sudden outbreak of lawlessness following the end of the First World War, the unit, which had initially been known as 'The Mobile Patrol Experiment', caused shockwaves in the underworld. The originator of the Squad was Frederick Porter Wensley (who had joined the Metropolitan Police in the year in which Worth had been born), and he had considered it essential that coordinated groups of detectives, known for their thief-taking abilities, their physical toughness and their ability to procure and run informants, should be turned into a top crime-busting squad, ready to go anywhere in London where their talents were needed. The 'mobility' in the unit's name initially came from the fact that the detectives travelled to areas where there had been concentrated outbreaks of crime, using two horse-drawn wagons leased from the Great Western Railway. The sides of the wagons had interchangeable boards fitted into slots, giving the names and addresses of businesses suitable for the location which they were visiting, and as the detectives peered from spy-holes under cover of the wagon's canvas hoods, the criminals were astonished to be plucked, literally out of thin air, as they were in the act of picking a pocket, stealing a car or carrying out a smash and grab. Later, the wagons were replaced with sleek, fast cars, and within ten short years what had become known as the Flying Squad had captured the public's attention.

As the years went by, the Squad broke up the racetrack gangs who infested race courses nationwide; smash-and-grab gangs soon found that when they set off on one of their larcenous expeditions, it was they who were smashed and grabbed; and the emergence of just one Flying Squad officer at a racetrack or football stadium would be sufficient for the pickpockets to shout, "Heads up – it's the Squad!"

The Flying Squad developed a reputation for being very well informed regarding the activities of criminals, for speed as they tore across the capital in their fast cars to carry out arrests as a result of the information acquired and also for a certain unorthodoxy in achieving their results, particularly regarding the recruitment and payment of informants.

The ways in which snouts were enlisted varied considerably. One method of acquiring information was through arrest. Charges might be diluted or dropped altogether. A suspect might be bailed from the police station in order to obtain the requisite information, with the suggestion of freedom if he obtained the right result by the time he returned and the promise of charges, together with the hint of incarceration, if he did not. If a suspect was charged to appear at court, the emergence of pertinent information between being bailed and arrival at court for sentence was a deciding factor in what might or might not be said to the magistrate or judge.

Another method of recruitment was through gratitude. If a favour had been bestowed by the detective, by getting the informant a lesser sentence – or indeed, no sentence at all – information could be forthcoming out of a sense of indebtedness. Another reason for informing was the money involved; and as will be seen, the rewards could, on occasion, be enormous. Many of the criminal classes would have been horrified to discover the amount of grassing which their revered and feared leaders participated in. A common motive behind gang leaders' informing was turf wars: where one criminal wanted a rival out of the way, so that he might take over the running of his operation. Another motive was revenge: where one criminal felt he had been wronged by another and wanted him to get his just desserts. And yet another was where the criminal wanted a cloak for his own activities: a highly tricky situation for the detective running him.

Information often came from a woman locked into a brutal, loveless marriage with a man steeped in criminality; it was a comparatively easy operation for her to discover when and where his next big job was going to be and make a phone call to ensure that there would be a reception committee of the boys in blue. The resultant long sentence for her husband, plus an impressive reward from the loss adjusters, meant freedom and a whole new life for the informing spouse. Then there were the personalities of the detectives which prompted information being imparted; as will be seen, many criminals provided information to Gosling because they genuinely liked him; in Brinnand's case, it was because they were terrified of him.

As Worth had mentioned in his report, it was commonplace for detectives to advance informants money from their own pockets to get them working; although what he did not mention was that when a reward was officially paid to the informant, the detective expected reimbursement for his initial expenditure – a disciplinary offence if he was caught, with a possibility of fines, demotion or dismissal. This amount paid could vary quite considerably; during the recession-ridden 1930s, a CID officer might slip a ten shilling note to an informant to motivate him, although Ted Greeno obtained an enormous amount of accurate, up-to-date information at the racetracks and being a committed betting man, following a big win, his informants could expect to have £25 or £50 lavished on them.

So informing and the extraction of pertinent information was not an attractive business. It was risk-filled, with the constant threat of exposure, together with all of the attendant dangers which disclosure entailed. Informing often involved treachery and double-dealing. It meant detectives meeting their snouts in lonely places, often during the most inhospitable weather and at the most inappropriate hours, in circumstances which could involve mortal danger. But for all the risks involved, informants were the life-blood of detectives who relied upon them to provide the best jobs, which could lead to recognition, the best postings within the police and promotion. On the other side of the coin, the detectives running the informants had to keep their foot on the metaphorical accelerator, to know when to slam their foot down to the floor and when to brake; to remain in the driving seat at all times. Men such as those who had served on the Flying Squad took to informant-running as a duck takes to water.

Yes, if anyone could get the required result from Worth's insightful plan, it would come from officers with proven Flying Squad experience.

★   ★   ★

Worth's plan was certainly a shrewd innovation. The Assistant Commissioner (Crime), Ronald Martin Howe CVO, MC, re-read the report on 7 December 1945. "Yes," he mused. "It could work." And then, more decisively, "It *must* work!"

It was an intuitive decision, but then Howe was a perceptive man. Born in 1896, Howe had been educated at Westminster School and at Christ Church, Oxford. Commissioned into the 3rd Battalion, Royal Sussex Regiment in 1915, he was wounded in 1917 and, the same year, promoted to Acting Captain. The following year, whilst a company commander with the 7th Battalion, Howe was awarded the Military Cross; the citation read:

> For conspicuous gallantry and initiative. When the situation was obscure after an enemy attack, he made a reconnaissance towards the enemy's lines under heavy shell fire and skilfully assembled the leading companies in their positions ready for attacking next morning. The following evening, he made another daring reconnaissance, after which he personally led his company into their position in the line. Although he lost all his officers within ten minutes of the attack commencing, he kept his own company and another company organised and ready to move at a moment's notice. He showed marked disregard of personal danger throughout.

He resigned his commission with the substantive rank of Captain in April 1920 and four years later was called to the Bar by the Inner Temple. In 1926, he joined the staff of the Director of Public Prosecutions as a Professional Clerk. He was appointed Chief Constable of the CID in the Metropolitan Police in February 1932, but just twenty-one months later he succeeded Henry Archer as Deputy Assistant Commissioner of the CID and there he remained for the next twelve years. Howe soaked up criminal investigation like a sponge and he became one of the greatest administrators of the CID.

As Hugh Young took over the reins of DAC in 1945, so Howe succeeded Sir Norman Kendall CBE as Assistant Commissioner (Crime). This was a move in the right direction; Kendall had been a fussy, a schoolmasterish and, as has been seen, a sometimes obstructive AC(C) and one who was not really in tune with CID work.

But Howe was in tune with the CID; and now, in 1945, as assistant commissioner, having accepted Worth's idea, Howe put his own stamp on it. "We have wanted a small special squad for a long time but owing to the shortage of men we have not found it possible to go ahead," he told the Commissioner, Sir Harold Richard Scott GCVO, KCB, KBE. "We are now getting some of our men back and in view of the increase in serious crime, I think we should start straightaway. I suggest we pick four men," he continued, "strike them off all ordinary duty, attach them to the Flying Squad and give them a taxi cab for getting around. They are merely to seek information and not get involved in any case. If they do, they must hand it over either to the Flying Squad or to the division concerned. We have never been able to get sufficient information about the big thefts and I think it is partly because, as Mr. Worth says, the men get too involved in cases and have no time to go out looking for information but have to take it when it is brought to their notice."

★   ★   ★

Sir Harold had taken up the appointment of commissioner just six months previously. Born in 1887, Sir Harold had been educated at Sexey's School and Jesus College, Cambridge. He looked exactly like the bespectacled, pin-stripe suited, pasty-faced Civil Servant he had been since 1911. He had been asked by the Home Secretary, Herbert Morrison, if he could ride a horse and, that being the case, if he would wish to be appointed commissioner of the Metropolitan Police. The offer from Morrison was disingenuous. The vast majority of Sir Harold's predecessors had been military men, and the post-war Labour Government wished to do away with what they saw as 'police militarisation'; in this case, Sir Harold looked a safe bet, but not because he was the best man for the job, which he quite conspicuously was not. The affirmative reply which Sir Harold gave to the Home Secretary was also less than frank; his equestrian skills were none too satisfactory and it took no time at all to for him to fall off Norton, his appointed police-trained horse. That Sir Harold had to be encased in plaster underneath his uniform for some time thereafter became the subject of malicious police humour. So the post of commissioner was his first introduction to the Metropolitan Police, and Worth's report must therefore have come as a considerable shock to him. But Sir Harold, albeit nervously, screwed his courage to the sticking place. "This scheme is worth a trial," he replied, apprehensively, "but its value should be kept under close review."

★   ★   ★

A letter was sent to the Undersecretary of State at the Home Office, requesting an augmentation to the establishment of the CID, namely one first class inspector, one second class inspector, one first class sergeant and one second class sergeant, to head this unit 'charged with the duty of obtaining information as to the activities of the more expert and dangerous criminals'.

Two weeks later, Mr. K. P. Whiting of the Home Office agreed – it appeared somewhat grudgingly – but stipulated that the authority for the increase in manpower was 'provisional only and will be subject to review at the end of next year when a further report should be submitted'.

When Howe had decisively told the commissioner, "The man I want in charge is Inspector Capstick, the present divisional detective inspector of 'W' Division," Sir Harold had no idea whatsoever that Capstick was one of the Metropolitan Police's finest detectives and informant handlers. However, if Howe said Capstick was the right man for the job, then he was probably right, Sir Harold thought. It was a prudent move.

Given the commissioner's shaky approval, and the authority of the Home Office, within a month from Howe's re-reading Worth's report the initiative for this new type of war against crime was up and running.

CHAPTER 3

The Gathering of the Squad

On New Year's Eve 1945, Capstick sat back in one of the dark, heavy leather armchairs in Howe's office and as he puffed contentedly at his pipe he looked idly at his surroundings. The room was not especially large; it would seat fifteen or sixteen people at the most around the assistant commissioner's desk, nor, with the walls painted green and mustard yellow, was the decor especially tasteful. But the windows overlooked the Thames and, with a touch of Howe's macabre humour, the chimney breast was decorated with a pair of opium pipes and three death's head masks, which had been filched from the Yard's Black Museum.

Many detectives had joined the Metropolitan Police to improve their lives, and some came from underprivileged beginnings, but not John Richard Capstick; his father was an affluent dairy farmer in Aintree near Liverpool, but Capstick possessed a rather wild and rebellious streak. Stealing a suit from his brother, he escaped the family milk round and ran away to sea; in the Argentine port of Rosario he caught his first pickpocket trying to steal his cigarettes. What was more, before he returned home, the few presents he had managed to purchase for his parents had been stolen by his messmate, while other crew members who had stolen cloth from the ship's cargo threatened to throw Capstick overboard if he informed the captain. Capstick was beginning to get sick and tired of criminals.

Travelling to London to find a better job, Capstick saw an advertisement for careers in the Metropolitan Police; he applied, was successful, and on his twenty-second birthday, 24 August 1925, Police Constable 402 'E' Capstick commenced duty at Bow Street police station. It was a tough apprenticeship; his brand new boots were stolen from the locker room, he had tomatoes thrown at him by the Covent Garden porters and he was lured into an ambush by a feared gang of pickpockets, the Titanic Mob, from whom he received a sound thrashing. But

Capstick was learning, and learning fast; he had a number of private fights with the market porters, who soon stopped calling him by the derisive nickname of 'Baby-face'; they came to admire him and in the years which followed they became valuable sources of information. Likewise, the pickpockets – Capstick learnt quickly from detectives like 'Chesty' Corbett, 'Squibs' Dance and Jerry Johnston how to deal with the 'dips' – became terrified of the short, slim young copper. Capstick was commended by the commissioner twice in two months and during the wild fights he encountered in the pubs of Covent Garden, he used his truncheon quite liberally. He became an aid to CID after just twelve months in uniform and, in less than three years from joining the police, Capstick was appointed detective constable.

Whilst still officially attached to 'E' Division, Capstick came under the guidance of Detective Chief Inspector Walter Hambrook, now heading the Flying Squad, whose unofficial assistant he became. He saw how major enquiries were conducted, he met a number of influential senior officers and, unfettered with paperwork, spent every waking hour identifying then arresting the dips and shoplifters who infested central London. Every prisoner became a potential informant, and Capstick became adept in instinctively knowing the best time to 'put the squeeze' on an informant, in order to produce results. With just eight years' service, Capstick was promoted to detective sergeant (second class); by this time, he had also been awarded twenty-one commissioner's commendations. When the first 'Q' Car was introduced to the Metropolitan Police in 1934 it was crewed by Capstick, and his arrest rate soared; with less than eighteen months' service in the rank, he was promoted to first-class sergeant and posted to the Flying Squad.

Capstick was in his element; Hambrook had moved on from the Squad, and Dan Gooch, a former gamekeeper who would retire from the police with an astonishing 109 commissioner's commendations, was in charge. There were many fine officers there but the one detective who more than any other made an indelible impression on Capstick was Alf Dance, one of the cleverest detectives of all time. At the time of Capstick's arrival, Dance was a detective inspector; he had arrived on the Squad as a detective constable shortly after the Squad was born and had stayed through sucessive promotions. In fact, he never would leave the Squad; after his subsequent promotion to divisional detective inspector, Dance would retire, having spent twenty-three years' unbroken service on the Flying Squad and having collected ninety-two commissioner's commendations.

Alf Dance became Capstick's mentor; he was an expert at disguise, would follow criminals for hours, watch them break into premises and then follow them again until they led him to a receiver's establishment, then arrest the lot. More than anything else, he knew criminals inside out. He knew their haunts, their associates, their wives, their girl-friends. He and his brother Frank (always referred to as 'Squibs') used to attend thieves' weddings and christenings, and Dance introduced Capstick to the practice of attending villains' funerals; it was Dance's reasoning that when the relatives saw him at the graveside of someone he'd sent away in the past, they would realise that Dance bore no malice to the departed, and the relatives (usually criminals themselves) would hold him in greater esteem. In addition, it provided an opportunity to discover amongst the mourners who the deceased's real friends had been, and he had toyed with the idea of taking a miniature camera along, to record who was who, but quickly vetoed the idea. "That wouldn't be playing the game," he ruefully told Capstick. "No, I could never do that."

Capstick adopted many of his mentor's ruses; to carry out observations, he donned a chauffeur's cap and tunic and pretended to be repairing a car; on another occasion, he and his officers 'borrowed' some theodolites and passed themselves off as surveyors. He would wear a gasman's uniform (also on loan) to gain entry to properties to determine whether or not stolen property had been stashed there and used a huge bunch of skeleton keys to enter garages in the middle of the night for the same purpose. Other officers procured spectacles with lenses made of plain glass, as well as coats which had tweed raglan on one side and when reversed became fawn raincoats. Although the officers traditionally wore trilby hats, they also kept berets and caps in their pockets. Bus driver's coats and caps were utilised, and one inventive officer fitted a thick sole to one of his shoes, thus producing a convincing limp. If a member of the public's car was found to be unlocked, it would be used to keep observation on a suspect, although this often led to misunderstandings if the car's owner suddenly turned up. Because courting couples in the back of a car were never suspected (and because of the noticeable lack of women officers), cross-dressing became a popular method of conducting clandestine surveillance.

Capstick stayed on the Squad for three years, scoring one success after another; promotion to detective inspector took him back to Bow Street where he stayed for two and a half years. With the war raging, Capstick received a telephone call from Alf Dance; the Flying Squad had been told to crack down on the profiteers, the thieves and black-marketeers who were playing havoc with the economy, so when Dance requested his help in returning to the Squad, Capstick needed no further urging.

Now he worked round the clock, meeting informants, carrying out observations, following suspects and making arrests. Capstick was usually referred to by his contemporaries as 'Jack' or 'Cappy', but it was Alf Dance who provided him with the nickname which would stay with him, used by colleagues and the underworld alike, for the rest of his service. Capstick had spent days tracking down a gang of silk thieves and their receiver. Now, having finally locked them up, he sat down in the canteen at Old Street police station, unshaven and looking like death, sipping a mug of tea. The head of the Squad, Peter Beveridge, having heard of Capstick's success, walked into the canteen accompanied by Alf Dance, and both men heartily congratulated Capstick. Dance then asked how he had done it. "Alf, it's as simple as this," replied Capstick. "You keep your blokes on duty only fourteen hours a day. We do eighteen – on early closing days."

"Hark at him," laughed Dance. "Old Charlie Artful, himself!"

Capstick received a very well merited commendation for this case, both by the Recorder of London at the Old Bailey and the commissioner, but he had had some help. It was the latest commendation in a string of five with Capstick for Detective Sergeant William Lionel MacDonald. Born in 1906, MacDonald had served with the Royal Army Medical Corps for three years before joining the police in 1929. Walter James 'Pedlar' Palmer had also served in the army, with the Somerset Light Infantry, for seven years before joining the police in 1927. Standing a quarter of an inch over six foot, Palmer had been posted to the Flying Squad as soon as he had been appointed detective constable. It was the first of three such postings; he would spend thirteen years with the Squad, and this was his latest commendation with Capstick. Charles Henry Hackworthy Freeman stood just seven-eighths of an inch over the Metropolitan Police minimum regulation height of five feet eight, so it was inescapable that he would be known as 'Titch'. It was a nickname that would only be used by his friends; a former wheelwright, his physique was impressively muscled, and he accompanied Capstick on some of his most daunting cases. He was midway through his second posting on the Flying Squad, but like Capstick, MacDonald and Palmer, he would leave the Flying Squad, and all of them would later return to make an impressive contribution to the work of the Ghost Squad.

So 'Charlie Artful' continued to make inroads into the underworld, using informants as 'buyers' to mop up the burglars and receivers; during the four wartime years he spent with the Squad, he was promoted to divisional detective inspector and notched up a total of forty commissioner's commendations. The posting to 'W' Division – a home posting – on 8 January 1945 must have seemed like a welcome respite after the long period of unrelenting Squad work, but the posting would last one day less than a year; AC(C) Howe needed him.

★   ★   ★

Capstick's contemporaries often said that he looked like a gentleman farmer who had strayed up to London; and the comparison was not ridiculous. His girth had expanded from that of a young constable who had weighed just ten stone, to a rather portly divisional detective inspector weighing fifteen stone. With his wavy hair, his ruddy cheeks, his large-bowled pipe and the rose in the buttonhole of his immaculate tweed suit, he did have the look of a man with agricultural connections.

If Capstick resembled a farmer, his choice of detective inspector (second class) for the team bore a strong similarity to a bank manager. Henry Clark had been born at Mulberry Cottage, Upney Lane, Barking, Essex. His parents, Charles William and Isabel Elizabeth Clark, had married in 1900 (aged twenty-five and twenty, respectively) and set about producing a large family – five boys and six girls (one of the girls, Daisy May died in infancy) – although for those times a family of that size was not much above the norm. Henry (the second eldest) was born on 14 February 1902, and therefore his parents thought it fitting to give him the middle name 'Valentine'. Clark kept quiet about that one – he was always known as Henry or 'Nobby'. He attended Castle School, Barking, but he always had a desire to go to sea and spent many hours at Barking Creek, watching the boats. Perhaps this longing stemmed from the memories of his maternal grandfather who was a waterman and who shipped timber in his barge down the Thames. But whatever the reason, Clark joined the Merchant Marine at the age of fourteen and served as a ship's steward as well as seeing wartime service. Precisely why he then decided to join the Metropolitan Police is not clear. One reason may have been that his mother worried continually when he was at sea; another, that he enjoyed the camaraderie of his shipmates and wanted to join a profession where this companionship was also available. But whatever the reason, after seven years' service with the Merchant Marine he joined the Metropolitan Police on 26 November 1923, and having been issued with his blue uniform as well as lamp No. 2525, was posted to 'B' Division in London's Kensington area. As Police Constable 476 'B', Clark initially lived at Beak Street Section House and as an aid to CID he worked with Bert 'Iron Man' Sparks, a very tough customer as his nickname implied, who would later head the Flying Squad. Appointed detective constable, Clark was still retained on 'B' Division and was awarded nine commissioner's commendations for catching criminals, including a large number of housebreakers, for which the commissioner also awarded him monetary awards, before he was posted to the Flying Squad on 2 December 1932.

It was the first of three postings to the Squad, which would total seven years. Clark worked with Tommy Symes, another respected thief-taker, and at one time they were pursuing a notorious woman pickpocket, who had jumped bail. At that time, Bob Higgins (who would later be deputy head of the Flying Squad) joined the Squad and he later described how he and his partner, Duncan 'Jock' Crerar, were seeking the same woman. "If you catch her before us," scoffed Clark, "I'm a boy scout!" Unfortunately for Clark, Higgins was on Detective Inspector 'Chesty' Corbett's team and he leant heavily on his senior officer's encyclopaedic knowledge of 'dips' and made the arrest, leaving the crestfallen Clark to be as quiet about his conspicuous lack of success, as he had been about his middle name.

In 1935, Clark was promoted to detective sergeant (second class) and was posted to 'D' Division, and there he stayed for the next five years, almost to the day. "I got twenty commissioner's commendations while I was on 'D'", he later recollected. "Four for every bloody year I was there!" In addition to the commendations, Clark was also married in 1936 to Ivy May Ridgwell, who was ten years his junior, at St Margaret's Church, Barking; the marriage would last for over sixty years.

But in 1940, with promotion to first class detective sergeant, Clark was posted back to the Squad where, once again, he came to the notice of Capstick. In fact, Clark was one of the officers that Capstick called out one wartime Christmas Day when an informant telephoned to say that a warehouse full of spirits in Clerkenwell was about to be broken into. The Squadmen crept into the warehouse and in the gloom, the first of the thieves mistook Capstick for an associate. The 'crack!' from Capstick's truncheon was so loud that it alerted the other five members of the gang, who rushed towards him, brandishing jemmies. Capstick hit the next gang member so hard in the face with his truncheon that it knocked him straight into a lorry, parked outside; grabbing hold of the next, Capstick enthusiastically wielded his truncheon until his opponent's knees gave way. Clark and the other officers tackled the remaining gang members who were pounded into submission. The van took the prisoners to Clerkenwell police station, with Capstick and the others following on. In the charge room, Capstick was perturbed to find only three prisoners; it was explained to him that the others were in hospital, having their injuries stitched up. Some considerable time later, Capstick deposited Clark at his home – a privately rented flat – at 9 Conal Court, Mitcham Lane, Streatham, SW16. Since they had been enjoying the grateful hospitality of the warehouse owners, both were somewhat the worse for wear. Mrs. Ivy Clark gave full vent to her dismay; her husband was mortified. Putting an unsteady finger to his lips, he tried to silence her. "S-s-h!" he whispered, with the sort of earnestness which drunks possess. "He's my guv'nor!" It had little effect. "I don't care who he is!" screamed his wife. "Just look at the state of you!" It was one of the times when Clark did not receive a commendation; but in his three years service with the Squad, he collected fourteen others.

One such was when Clark arrested a man in 1941 for receiving 1,250,000 stolen cigarettes, valued at £4,450, the day after they had been stolen in Peckham; another was awarded the following year, in respect of Seymour Sidney. Clark had utilised his surveillance abilities to follow Sidney, who, it was suspected, was masterminding the supply of an enormous amount of rationed foodstuffs to grocers and restaurateurs, and so it proved. Sentencing Sidney to four years' penal servitude, plus a fine of £2,000, and his assistant, Jean Alphonse Pages, to eighteen months' imprisonment and a fine of £2,000, Lord Caldercote, the Lord Chief Justice, was fulsome in his commendation of Clark.

"He did not talk a lot," recalled his younger sister, Mrs. Mavis Bidmead, "but listened, and when he said something, it had depth and always received a lot of respect. He had twinkling eyes, and a wicked sense of humour."

Clark was going to need that sense of humour. In October 1942, he was selected for the rank of detective inspector, and the following June he was transferred to 'Z' Division, prior to being promoted. In September 1943, an allegation of bribery was made against him and Detective Constable Leslie Roy Stapeley, and before the year was out both officers were transferred to 'W' Division. This was (and is) a common practice, once it is felt that an officer is 'tainted' – it is humiliating for the officer and delights the local criminals (especially those making the accusation) who feel that the officer has been too close to arresting them. Moreover, it provides kudos for the criminal who has accused the officer of malpractice, because he has displayed to his associates the power to get the officer transferred.

Even with this allegation hanging over his head, Clark was still irrepressibly carrying out his duty. In May 1944, an extremely violent criminal named Arthur Frederick Parkyn had stolen cigarettes worth £5,000 from the Arcadia Works, Hampstead Road and had also been concerned in the theft of a Carter Patterson van carrying cigarettes valued at £2,000. When Parkyn discovered a female guard still in the van, he shoved her out of it. Clark saw him driving a Bedford van (stolen in 1943 from Holloway and fitted with false plates) on the day of the theft; later the van was found abandoned with some of the stolen tobacco still in it. Ten days later, Clark spotted Parkyn in Tooting High Street, recognised him as the man driving the stolen van and single-handedly arrested him. Parkyn was sentenced to two years' imprisonment, and Clark received his fifty-first commendation from the commissioner. (Five years later, Parkyn, wanted for inflicting grievous bodily harm on a police constable, was again arrested, this time by quite a lot of Flying Squad officers. He made a very violent – and unsuccessful – effort to escape, and this time the Lord Chief Justice sentenced him to twelve years' penal servitude for attempted murder.)

The bribery allegation was hotly denied by both Clark and Stapeley but in November 1944 they appeared at Croydon Magistrates' Court at the behest of the Director of Public Prosecutions. After two days of committal proceedings the case was thrown out. Four days later, Clark, with the backing of his detective superintendent and the DAC of 4 Area, attended a fresh selection board at the Yard, to determine his suitability for the rank of detective inspector. He failed. Incensed, Clark sent a report direct to the commissioner, seeking an interview to ascertain why he had been rejected for promotion. It was fortunate that the report landed on the desk of Scott's predecessor, Sir Philip Woolcott Game. Sir Philip had served in the Boer War and as a Lieutenant-Colonel in 1915 had been awarded the Distinguished Service Order; appointed commissioner in 1935, he was almost sixty-five when the Second World War commenced and because of his age and ill-health he was ready to retire, but decided to stay on until the war's conclusion, which was Clark's good fortune. Greatly admired by the rank and file for accompanying them on their dangerous patrols during bombing raids, Sir Philip was known as a 'listening' commissioner. He certainly listened to Clark, who also had the backing of Capstick who had arrived on 'W' Division in January 1945; by the following July, Clark, having successfully passed a course at the Detective Training School, was promoted to detective inspector (second class) and was posted back to the Flying Squad.

Like Capstick, Clark was short – five feet ten – but his mild-mannered looks were deceptive. He was tremendously strong, had a punch that was described as being like the kick of a mule and was a terror in a rough-house. Clark also had a thorough knowledge of the thieves and receivers of south London which few other detectives possessed.

Six months after his posting back to the Flying Squad, Clark was the next of the team to join Capstick in Howe's office.

★   ★   ★

Matthew Brinnand was long, lean and wiry, with immense reserves of energy; it was said that he would rather sleep in an office chair than risk being late for a job in the morning. A native of Holme in Westmorland, Brinnand was born on 19 September 1909. He was the second child of George Brinnand and Sarah Ann Towers, who had married in 1905, aged twenty-three and twenty-one respectively. Matthew Brinnand's elder brother Thomas (described as 'the black sheep of the family') had been born two years previously, his younger brother Edward was born two years later and their sister Elsie was born in 1916. Brinnand was raised at 1-2 Primrose Bank, Holme in Cumbria and after attending the village school he went on to complete his education at Heversham Grammar School. There, he was a member of the Officers' Training Corps and was active in the cricket and rugby teams. Upon leaving school, he was apprenticed to Boots the Chemists in Kendal before coming down to London.

Joining the Metropolitan Police on 16 March 1931, where his height was given as five feet eleven and three-eighths of an inch, Brinnand was posted to 'C' Division, right in the heart of London's West End. He would spend the next seven years of his service there, as Police Constable 464 'C', an aid to CID and (after just three years service) a detective constable, getting to know the crooks and racketeers of Soho. Sixty years later, George Price, who knew him well, described him as being "quiet, a loner and able to pluck a result out of the air." Brinnand looked taller than he actually was, because he was so thin. He was known as 'The Ferret' and as Bob Higgins said, "he was excellent at tailing suspects, because of his down-trodden appearance". But in his dealings with criminals there was no middle way with Brinnand – he loathed them, especially pimps, and they in turn were terrified of him. Just the sight of him was enough for gangsters in the night clubs to gulp down their drinks and disappear out through the back entrance. The criminal classes queued up to give him information; they provided it because they were too frightened of Brinnand to do anything else.

During the early 1930s, Brinnand and some fellow officers visited Lyons Corner House in the Strand; it was there that he met twenty-year-old Daisy Adeline Harrison who was working as a 'nippie' or waitress. In 1935 they married and in October of that year they had a son, John George. The family took up residence in Elm Road, Brixton, later in Voltaire Road, Clapham and finally at 58 Tremadoc Road, Clapham.

Among the nine commissioner's commendations he was awarded during his time on 'C' Division, one was for arresting a persistent thief in possession of a firearm, another for the (then) relatively rare crime of robbery with violence. He was posted to the Flying Squad on 2 May 1938; it would be his home for the next eight and a half years.

Brinnand was tough, tenacious and dedicated. The story that follows shows his resolve in stunning style. In 1940, a notorious criminal named Charles 'Ruby' Sparks escaped from Dartmoor Prison, where he had been serving a five-year sentence of penal servitude for burglary. Sparks was intercepted in Neasden in a classic Flying Squad ambush, but the entire scenario threatened to topple into farce. A rubber-faced master of disguise, Sparks was wearing dark sunglasses, was in possession of a forged identity card, denied his identity and called on a passing police constable to arrest the men who were bent on kidnapping him. Just about every police officer present claimed to know Sparks, yet none of them could agree as to his identity and they fell to arguing amongst themselves in Sparks' presence, which must have been sweet music to his ears.

As probably one of the most junior officers present, Brinnand took control of the situation and told his colleagues in typically blunt Northern fashion that if they wished to release Sparks they could do so, but in that eventuality he would arrest him on the pavement outside because, as he fiercely informed them, "I'm telling you, that man is Sparks!"

Sparks, realising the game was up, tore off his sunglasses and grudgingly admitted his identity; yet Brinnand had not been one of the officers who claimed to know Sparks, because he did not. He had seen him fleetingly just once before – at Kingston Assizes on 10 February 1939 when he had received his five-year sentence. Out of all the officers who were commended by the commissioner for Sparks' recapture, perhaps only Brinnand really deserved the award, his eleventh. It could well have been a contributory factor in his promotion to detective sergeant, second class, one month later.

Capstick thought that Brinnand was so unobtrusive that he had frequently passed him in the street without noticing him. He was the third member of the team, in Howe's office.

★ ★ ★

The men in the assistant commissioner's office looked round as the last member of the team walked through the door – then they looked up. John Neville Gosling was six foot one tall, and his large frame filled the doorway.

Gosling was born on 13 August 1905 in Manningtree, Essex. His was a prosperous family which, after successfully running a number of pubs, turned their hand to road haulage and a farm. Gosling had a somewhat difficult childhood – his mother already had two sons and twin daughters from a previous marriage. Widowed at the age of twenty-four, she had later married Walter Gosling, and a daughter, Joan, was born, followed two years later by the birth of John Gosling. The youngest of the Goslings had an exceptional singing voice and as a boy soprano he was encouraged by his father who was the organist at St. Mary's church, Mistley for twenty-five years. John Gosling attended Colchester Royal Grammar School, where he was judged to be 'difficult' – stories abounded of extreme practical jokes played on unsuspecting schoolmasters.

He worked as a clerk at Brooks, a large company of corn merchants and maltsters, and by now his size and strength were becoming noticed. On one occasion, in a burst of youthful impetuosity, he put a sack of wheat on his back, prompted his best friend to climb on top of the sack and proceeded to run up Brook Street, Manningtree, carrying a combined weight of over 400lbs. His pugnacity was never in any doubt; a letter exists from a Major King, congratulating him having 'tanned' a fellow schoolboy in a fight. And later, in Dunkirk, where he had gone for a trip with a friend on board the Thames sailing barge *Vigilant*, a couple of Norwegian seamen made an unwise comment to Gosling's companion. Gosling, who had taken no part in the conversation but had been directing his attention to the Norwegians' girl-friends, turned and knocked out both of the seamen. The girls' screaming attracted the attention of a passing *gendarme*, and all of them were hauled off to the local gaol. After a highly unofficial excise of fifty francs, Gosling and friend were permitted to leave the following morning. Prudently, no mention of this little misadventure was included in his job application to the Metropolitan Police.

He worked for a short while at the family firm, but the relationship with his father was becoming strained, and, unlike his half-brother, Gosling decided that the family business was not for him; aged twenty-four, he decided it was time to move on. He had considered the Army and joining the Brigade of Guards; either that, or the Metropolitan Police. Since the pay was marginally better, the police won, and he joined on 15 April 1929. As Police Constable 950 'N' (and later as an aid to CID) he was posted to the King's Cross and Islington districts of London – very tough areas indeed.

Right from the start, he was a success. In September 1929, at two o'clock in the morning, in a turning just off Essex Road, Islington, PC Gosling was chatting to an elderly constable from an adjoining beat when an off-duty bus driver walking his dog approached them and said, "Guv, there's four right geezers breaking into the pawnbrokers on the corner of Essex Road and Rotherfield Street; they'd got the street door half open when I passed."

For one so young and inexperienced, Gosling displayed considerable acumen; seeing a look-out man outside the shop in a thoroughfare which was well lit by the streetlamps, he removed his helmet and tunic, borrowed the bus driver's dog and strolled towards the pawnbrokers shop, trying, as he put it, "to look as small as possible". It was to no avail; when he was fifty yards away, the look-out shouted a warning and the four men dashed off down Rotherfield Street; Gosling took up the pursuit, together with the dog who entered into the spirit of the chase. One of the men, William Byrne, stopped and flung a jemmy at Gosling, who actually heard it whistle past his head before it landed in a front garden.

The chase continued for over a mile, and during the course of it Gosling actually overtook the other three miscreants but ignored them; he was utterly committed to capturing, as he later put it, 'the marksman'. Byrne disappeared around a corner, which led to a canal, and vanished; while Gosling was getting his breath back, he heard a noise and discovered his quarry attempting to climb over a wall. Byrne's legs straddled the wall but he was so exhausted, he had not the strength to lift his trailing leg over. Gosling grasped hold of the hanging ankle and the two men stayed in that position, both gasping for breath, for five minutes until with a tug Gosling landed the prisoner on his side of the wall.

Both returned to Essex Road, where they were reacquainted with the flung jemmy and the bus driver's dog, who had abandoned the chase long before. In addition, Gosling was reunited with his uniform tunic and helmet, which were being guarded by his uniform colleague who suffered from gout and, as Gosling later put it with masterly understatement, "was not fired with ambition." Nevertheless, he brightened up at Gosling's reappearance; apparently, he had just lost his second wage increment – 2s 6d – for being drunk on duty. "Well done, boy, I'll have him," he exclaimed, adding, "This'll do me the world of good!"

Gosling was not that green; as he put on his tunic, he remarked, firmly, "You can have the next one!" Byrne was sentenced to nine months' imprisonment at the County of London Sessions and on 17 June 1930, Gosling received the first of his thirty-three commissioner's commendations.

"A couple of years after I joined the police, I applied for a transfer to the plain-clothes section but was turned down as having too much of 'a policeman-like appearance'", recalled Gosling after his retirement, adding (no doubt with tongue firmly in cheek), "They let me into the plain clothes section for one reason only – I was the only officer who could start the old twin-cylinder police cars we had then, on a frosty morning."

This was a piece of self-deprecation; Gosling had already proved that he was a natural thief-taker. In those days, an officer who wished to be considered for permanent inclusion in the CID had to have been commended by the commissioner on at least three occasions before he could go on to what was known as 'The AC(C)'s List'; by the time he was appointed detective constable, Gosling had been commended by the commissioner on five occasions. "When I came out as a plain clothes policeman I was fabulously lucky," he remembered. "If I walked round a corner, there was somebody pinching a car or doing something wrong. I had twelve commendations from judges and magistrates in less than a year – it was always my luck to be in the right place at the right time."

One of those occasions arose when Gosling drove his boss, Divisional Detective Inspector Charles Wesley, to Woodford, where there had been a spate of housebreakings. Upon discovering that six more offences had been reported, Gosling was dispatched to round up the ten aids to CID who had been carrying out observations of the housebreakers and return them to the police station for a 'pep-talk' from Wesley. En route to gather in the recalcitrant aids, Gosling stopped to admire a Bentley Coupé parked by some houses. As he did so, he also spotted a suspect individual in some bushes and instinctively punched him on the chin, knocking him out. A few moments later, the unconscious suspect's associate climbed over the balcony of an adjoining house, dropped two suitcases into the garden and climbed down to the ground, whereupon he received the same treatment as his partner. An enormous amount of property was recovered, and the two men, Frett and Richardson, were sent to penal servitude. The Bentley? It belonged to a local resident; nothing to do with the two housebreakers. As Gosling remarked, "Anyone could have done it". But the fact is, none of the ten aids to CID did – it was Gosling.

As well as being enormously strong and fearless in a fight, Gosling was a naturally kind, good-natured man. His good nature was put to the test early in his career at Islington when he was attacked by a gang of local hooligans and quite badly injured, to such an extent that he was given extended sick leave, returning home to his parents at Manningtree to recuperate. His injuries included the loss of a top front tooth, and the gap was plugged with a single false tooth on a dental plate which reposed nightly in a glass of water on his bedside table. Returning to duty, Gosling made it his personal mission to hound his attackers right out of the district. But he also realised the value of a kind word to a criminal at court and discovered when to turn a blind eye to the transgressions of his more wayward parishioners. In return, they queued up to give him information. In retirement, Gosling recalled that an old CID officer had once told him, "A detective is only as good as his information. Like any other citizen he has only one pair of eyes, one pair of ears and can only be in one place at a time. Without help, he can't win."

Gosling started early, recruiting his first informant when he was still a uniformed constable. 'Harry the Cabby' used to chat to Gosling at the cab rank in Islington High Street. Harry taught Gosling the mental processes of the Cockney, his reaction to questioning, a glossary of cockney rhyming slang and how to tail a suspect vehicle. Aged about sixty, he possessed a ragged moustache, wore a thick overcoat summer or winter and was addicted to roll-ups made of strong shag tobacco. And although Harry provided Gosling with some excellent information, every job would be arranged so that there was absolutely no come-back on him. He would never accept money in return; in fact, he was quite comfortably off. Harry had no known relatives and when he died it was rumoured that he left a fortune.

On the day following his twenty-eighth birthday, Gosling was appointed detective constable and posted to 'G' Division. He joined the staff at City Road police station, whom he described as "six middle-aged and boozy second-class detective sergeants and three detective constables who were afraid to speak". None would communicate with him or offer any advice. After a week, Gosling got on the trail of a thief who had stolen a lorry load of cigarettes and arrested him. By means of some clever detective work, Gosling discovered the identity of the receiver and after getting assistance recovered the stolen cigarettes. But he received no praise for his actions; indeed, he was admonished for not seeking assistance sooner. For the next six months his colleagues referred to him as "clever boy", but it was not too long before he was widely addressed as 'Johnno', 'Johnnie' or 'Jack'. The locals referred to him as 'Mr. Magawslin', this being the Islingtonian interpretation of his name. He was also rather dismissively referred to as 'The Yokel' due to his Suffolk accent which was more pronounced at the beginning of his career; but any criminal who believed that Gosling really was the country bumpkin that nickname implied was in for a very rude awakening indeed. Gosling was certainly a country boy; stupid, he was not.

Gosling met an attractive divorcée, Marjorie Charlotte Pritchard Fell, née Field, who was two years younger than him, and they married at Shoreditch Registry Office on 21 February 1934. He moved out of the Shepherdess Walk Section House and the couple set up home in Highbury New Park. There a baby daughter was born; later the family was increased by two sons and they moved to New Malden. Bombed out during the war, the family then moved to Hilbury Road, Warlingham, Surrey.

Another of Gosling's early informants was Bob Francis, a shocking character with many convictions for violence, whom Gosling arrested one evening for shopbreaking. The following day, Gosling and Marjorie were due to go on holiday; instead, he had to drive to court. With Marjorie waiting in the car, which he had borrowed from a friend, Gosling – who in view of Francis' previous convictions, should have had him committed to the Old Bailey to stand his trial – accepted a plea of guilty at the lower court. Gosling put in a good word for Francis, who was sentenced to four months' imprisonment, and Gosling also gave him some cigarettes; then he noticed Francis' wife and their four skinny children outside the court. He gave Mrs. Francis (pregnant with their fifth child) a few shillings for groceries, which left him completely out of pocket. Then he resumed his holiday, which of necessity was a cheap one, staying with his in-laws; he recollected that the car ran out of petrol on the way to the coast.

But several months later he started receiving a series of mysterious telephone calls from an unknown source, who provided him with one piece of excellent information after another – the whereabouts of suspects who were circulated as being wanted, stolen cars, men breaking into shops – and the resultant arrests caused profound jealousy amongst the other CID officers at Islington. Eventually, he discovered from Francis' wife that it was her husband who was the informant; nobody else even remotely suspected him because of his record of extreme violence against everyone in authority. Francis refused payment from the informants' fund, muttering with acute embarrassment, "One good turn deserves another," and adding, "they're a no good lot of bastards, anyway". With the help of a probation officer Gosling got him a job digging trenches for a building contractor at Hammersmith, working on the assumption that it would be impossible for him to steal anything and therefore he would keep out of trouble. Unfortunately, this employment came to an end after Francis' temper flared up and he almost brained the site foreman with a pickaxe handle. Gosling later arrested Francis, again for a shopbreaking, and this time he received a substantial prison sentence. Not one to profit from life's experiences, Francis attacked warders in Pentonville Prison using a broken glass wrapped in his handkerchief as a knuckleduster; he died in Highgate Infirmary as a result of serious internal injuries sustained in the fight which ensued.

Dick was a bookies' runner, a big, powerful man who was a terror in a fight; in turn, he was scared stiff of his wife who was just four feet three and a consummate nagger. Gosling thought that the reason why Dick furnished him with information was because he trusted him; "In those days, I did not mix with the (criminal) fraternity any more than necessary," said Gosling, "and he knew that I would not let slip the unguarded word." Through him, Gosling got to know all the fiddles going on in the district, although Dick despised the professional informer and was another who refused payment. "Want to see you get on, Johnnie," was the way he accepted Gosling's thanks.

Laurie was a half-Jewish fishmonger who exuded a permanent smell of cod. Aged about fifty, he was five feet six tall and moved with quick, bird-like movements. His language was appalling, and he boasted that he could "spot the law half a mile away, in either direction". His fishmonger's premises were a front for his more lucrative activities which involved receiving stolen jewellery, and he had duped a rather unintelligent employee named Steve to carry the swag for him, with Laurie himself bringing up the rear in case "trouble reared its ugly head". Precisely what Laurie would have done had that eventuality arisen is debateable. He made no secret of being terrified of getting caught, and as far as he was concerned anybody but he could go to prison – including his wife. In fact, it was after Gosling just missed arresting Laurie but was able to send his brother away for a considerable period that Laurie decided it would be prudent to become one of Gosling's informants; an informant with a hidden agenda, of course.

Gosling described 'Peter the Pawnbroker' as "a dried-up little man, aged anything between fifty and seventy". His premises were in a back street in Islington and he knew all the local thieves; he preferred reward money to the attendant risks which receiving stolen property entailed. Peter had the ability to tell instantly from a customer's attitude and reaction to just one question if the goods he was offering were stolen. "I got his confidence soon after starting as a CID officer," recalled Gosling. "I am very sure that he did not tell me everything, but he was a very good connection."

If Gosling had understandable doubts regarding 'Peter the Pawnbroker's' dependability, he had none in the case of Johnnie the lorry thief who, if a prospective customer asked him for goods which were not immediately available, would reply, "If it's foggy tonight, I shall have some tomorrow". Completely unscrupulous, Johnnie, referring to a fellow thief, told Gosling, "He's my best friend," adding, with a satanic laugh, "but you can have him!" Known as 'Tommy the Talker' in Gosling's memoirs, during two years' concentrated snouting, Johnnie stated that he had earned £2,000 per year – £50,000 by today's standards – tax free from the insurance assessors; these payments were probably a drop in the ocean compared to his income from his more clandestine activities.

Then there was the lady street trader, who took a maternal interest in Gosling. She was married to a thief who on one occasion let her 'carry the baby' for a load of stolen goods. For this she was sentenced to six months' imprisonment; she never forgave him and hated everything that he stood for. In the years which followed she provided Gosling with a great deal of help and advice; she also put away her husband and his brother.

Gosling's energy was inexhaustible. Having just finished a very strenuous twelve-hour night duty at six o'clock in the morning, Gosling was about to walk home to Highbury for the joint purposes of getting some exercise and saving the 3d bus fare – as he put it, "Times were bad" – when in Pitfield Street, Hoxton he saw a Bentley turn the corner and four very scruffy characters emerge from it. It was later established that the Bentley had been stolen from Berkeley Square. All four men took to their heels at Gosling's approach and during the ensuing chase they turned the corner into Hoxton Street; by the time Gosling arrived, they had vanished. Reasoning that they must have entered the main entrance of a block of tenements, Gosling ran up the stairs and arrived on the fourth floor very much out of breath. There, a man clad only in a vest and trousers who was leaning over the banister rail, pointed upwards, saying, "That way, Guv". Gosling then realised that his informant was in a worse state of exhaustion than he was and after a quick look round discovered the man's coat, waistcoat, hat, tie and shirt in an adjacent dustbin. "It was quite original," later observed Gosling, "and he deserved to get away with it, but didn't."

Having left an informant in a pub at ten o'clock at night, Gosling was driving along Baring Street, Islington when a car cut across him on New North Road, travelling towards Hoxton with a uniformed police constable clinging on to the running board. Gosling gave chase, the car swerved into Poole Street, which runs alongside the Regent's Canal, mounted the pavement and crushed the constable against the canal wall, knocking him off. The car's two occupants leapt out whilst it was still moving and as it crashed into a brick wall the men ran off into an alley which led to the canal tow path and thence into Bridport Place. Gosling saw the constable get up, assumed, correctly, that he was not badly hurt and drove on into Bridport Place. Only one shop had a light on, an Italian café which had just one customer – a tall youth aged about twenty-five who was attempting to persuade the proprietor to serve him.

Gosling entered the café, went over to the solitary customer's table and simply stared at him. Eventually, the youth, whose name was George Matthews, grinned and said, "No tea, tonight," to which Gosling grimly replied, "No – but I'll guarantee plenty of porridge later on." With that, Gosling and prisoner left the premises, picked up the very shaken constable and drove to Shepherdess Walk police station.

"Friend Matthews had no guts," noted Gosling in his retirement. "I took my overcoat off preparatory to interrogating him, and with that the last show of resistance vanished."

"None of that, Guv'nor," said Matthews hastily, "I wasn't the driver and I didn't pinch the car." Demanding the driver's name, Gosling received the reply, "Len Dutton – he lives at 14 Bridport Place."

As Gosling approached the address, he saw a light go out in the basement and, discovering a key hanging on a string inside the letter-box, he let himself in. There, in the passageway, Gosling saw two enormous, malevolent green eyes staring at him and, lighting a match, saw that they belonged to an aggressive and very large German Shepherd dog. Ignoring the dog, Gosling continued into the basement, lit the gas lamp and discovered Len Dutton in bed, the bedclothes up to his chin and snoring gently. Pulling back the bed sheets revealed that Dutton was fully dressed and that his trousers were saturated, the result of a partial immersion in Regent's Canal.

Both men were charged with stealing the car. Despite the fact that both Matthews and Dutton profusely apologised to the injured officer and later pleaded guilty to the charges, the uniformed officer (who, Gosling later stated, "was a Salvationist") would not take any part in charging the men, as he virtuously said he could not identify them. The dripping Dutton had remarked when Gosling led him from the house, "I wish that bastard dog had killed you". This gave a good indication of his character. He was later sentenced to fourteen years' imprisonment for robbery with violence.

Gosling had a fund of stories, and many of these tales would later be inserted into his memoirs, including an amusing anecdote from his early days at Islington which involved two committed thieves who specialised in stealing from unattended vehicles. The first was 'Tiddler' Aiken, who stood no more than five feet four and weighed twenty stone; his counterpart was 'The

Reverend' Liddle who was six feet three and weighed only nine stone. It was inevitable that this unlikely (and instantly recognisable) pair could not avoid capture for very long, and at North London court Liddle begged the magistrate, Basil Watson Esq., to "give them a chance". To this, the magistrate replied, "Certainly," adding, "a chance to do twelve months!", and he was as good as his word.

There is little doubt that Gosling was assisted in his career by the immaculately dressed Divisional Detective Inspector Bill Salisbury whom he met at City Road. It is clear that Gosling had unbounded admiration for him, describing him as being (after Wensley) "the greatest of them all". Salisbury had joined the police in 1920 after seeing four years' wartime service as a second lieutenant with the Royal Field Artillery. He had spent five years with the Flying Squad, where he worked with Ted Greeno; on one occasion they followed a gang of housebreakers into a burgled house, who then attempted to escape through a bathroom window. The officers dragged them back inside, and, because they had left their truncheons in the Squad car, Greeno crowned his prisoner with a lavatory brush, while Salisbury felled his man with a sink plunger. Nothing would faze Salisbury, who was a shrewd and immensely successful investigator, and Gosling learnt an enormous amount from him. Sadly, Salisbury was medically discharged suffering from bronchitis after just over twenty-three years' service, having collected sixty-five commissioner's commendations, several of them rare 'high' commendations for excellent police work.

Gosling worked on 'G' Division for almost five years, building up a further stock of informants and earning another nine commendations from the commissioner, before being promoted to detective sergeant (second class) and being posted to the Flying Squad.

Brinnand had already been a Flying Squad officer for the best part of a year before Gosling's arrival. They soon teamed up and in the following five years Gosling was awarded an astonishing fourteen commissioner's commendations; six of them were with Brinnand. Gosling always described Brinnand as being his antithesis (he also, rather unkindly, referred to him as "the tape-worm" due to his height and sparse physique) because of their dissimilar ways of dealing with informants; Gosling liked many of his snouts and inspired confidence in them whereas Brinnand's informants provided equally accurate information but did so quaking with fear.

A prostitute, one of Brinnand's informants, received the staggering payment of £1,000 in 1939; she had shopped the whereabouts of a group of IRA men who planned to deposit and detonate bombs simultaneously at New Scotland Yard, Westminster Abbey and the Bank of England. Brinnand and Gosling raided 32 Leinster Gardens, Bayswater on 25 August 1939 and arrested four men in possession of explosives and timers, which were primed to explode at 2.30 that afternoon. As the men were being locked up, at 2.30 precisely a bomb (of exactly the same type as had been found in London) was detonated in Coventry. Five passers-by were killed and fifty were injured; Brinnand's informant contacted him again and gave the names of the persons responsible. That evening, Brinnand and Gosling arrested one of the suspects at 176 Westbourne Terrace, Paddington and recovered more explosives. The arrests led to the ringleaders being hanged and four others each being sentenced to terms of twenty years' penal servitude.

The two Squad officers then turned their attention to a notorious family named Fishberg, receivers of stolen property at their shop off Black Lion Yard, Whitechapel, the father having convictions going back to 1921. Gosling was informed about the theft of a jewellery box, taken from a Rolls-Royce in Manchester Square whilst the chauffeur had been distracted, the previous day. The owners of the property were the Honourable Charles and Lady Wynn. Wynn, a cousin to the Queen, had listed the property stolen as being valued at £2,500; in fact, he had been mistaken, having reported just half of the items. The stolen property was worth double that sum. Gosling had been told the jewellery would be disposed of at the Fishbergs', and because it was almost impossible to keep observation on Fishberg's premises Gosling used his informant, who knew every car thief in the district, to keep an eye on the shop. Suddenly the informant gave Gosling the signal; a known thief had entered the premises carrying a parcel, then left. Gosling rushed to the shop and loudly demanded admission, but the door had been locked as soon as the thief departed. Running round to a side entrance, Gosling was in time to see Fishberg's son leave the premises – his suspicions were aroused because although it was bitterly cold and snow was falling heavily, Fishberg junior was not wearing a coat or hat.

Gosling escorted him back to the shop and as he searched the premises he saw the son slip a parcel into a drawer which Gosling had already searched; it contained the stolen jewellery. Meanwhile, Brinnand had collared the thief, who was in the act of getting into a car in Watney Street, which adjoins Black Lion Yard. At their trial, Fishberg senior and junior made every allegation of misconduct possible against Gosling and Brinnand but eventually both were found guilty, with Fishberg senior receiving three years' imprisonment and ordered to pay £500 costs and his son receiving eighteen months' imprisonment. Both of the officers were commended; and Wynn told the court that because of the allegations which had been levelled against the officers he felt compelled to inform the court that Gosling and Brinnand had recovered twice as much property as he had originally reported stolen. Both of the officers received an engraved Dunhill silver cigarette case from a grateful victim; Gosling's was inscribed, 'From C.W. in appreciation. March 1941.'

Gosling was also involved in a case of a conspiracy to dope greyhounds, in which the Squad's chief, Peter Beveridge, also participated. Before the fraud could be put into effect, Leonard Jones and Monty Kosky were arrested at a flat at Bryanston Square, where boxes of Corytone, a drug which acts on the nervous systems of dogs, were found. In his official pocket book Gosling recorded that when arrested, Kosky replied, "Conspiracy? When nothing happens?" and Jones replied, "What's it all about? It didn't happen". En route to Marylebone Lane police station, Kosky rather cockily suggested, "You want to be a psychologist," while Jones commented, "I can't understand it; it's all like the Wizard of Oz". Matters became marginally less amusing for them when both men were sentenced to two years' imprisonment.

Having been promoted to detective sergeant (first class), Gosling was posted to 'C' Division in the heart of London's wartorn West End in July 1944. He was affectionately remembered by George Price (later one of the participants in the Percy Street venture) who described him as a charismatic character, a typical man of Essex who had an agile brain and a ready wit. At about eight o'clock in the evening, they would retire to the Camden Arms for a beer until an hour later when Gosling would leave for Charing Cross Station to catch his train home to Whyteleafe Station with the words, "Don't forget to book me off duty!"

Capstick described Gosling as "a slow-speaking Suffolk giant who could lift a couple of hundredweights with one hand. He could put away a pint as quickly as most men would drink a whisky. With his trilby over one eye, a cigarette dangling from his lips, he looked almost sleepy; it was then that he was at his most dangerous". With that, and Gosling's tremendous success as an investigator and an informant-runner, it is little wonder that Capstick had invited him to be the fourth member of the Ghost Squad.

★   ★   ★

Capstick glanced at his companions – Clark, Gosling and Brinnand – the three officers he had personally chosen, and in turn Ronald Howe surveyed the four men, glanced at Percy Worth and nodded briefly. If anybody could crack the present crime wave, he thought, these four could. All of these officers had the attributes which a special duties squad needed. They knew the underworld of the Metropolis – and beyond – as very few other detectives did. They had enjoyed the toughest slice of police work and they had all been on the receiving end of the most damaging phoney allegations by criminals who knew they had everything to gain and little to lose by making them, yet walked away unscathed. They were physically very tough, they ran informants and they were willing to take a chance. Fixing them with his striking grey eyes, Howe leant his slight frame across the desk and, although he could not possibly be overheard, he addressed them in almost conspiratorial tones, telling them why they were there and what he wanted them to do. They would infiltrate the underworld, he told them, run informants and gather as much information as possible, in order to pass it on either to the Flying Squad or divisional CID officers to act upon; they would not, he added, get involved themselves.

They would be released from their Flying Squad duties and be given an office of their own with a key – an unprecedented move. A car would be provided for them (the original taxi-cab idea had been vetoed, since a driver would have to have been provided) and they would be empowered to go anywhere, anytime; they would not be required to book on and off duty and never – and this was most important – *never* would they be required to reveal the names of their sources.

Howe believed in sending his troops out on to the field of battle with their heads held high. "This Special Duty Squad has got to succeed," he said forcefully, and as he shook hands with all of them he added, "I know you won't let me down."

As news of this secret Special Duty Squad leaked out to the newspapers, they were given a new title. The press christened them 'The Ghost Squad'.

The four men repaired to the Red Lion pub in Derby Gate, situated right next door to the Yard. "Tomorrow, we'll get cracking," said Capstick, following a short briefing of his own. "We've got a lot of work ahead of us." They downed their drinks and emerged into the street, eager to get home to celebrate the New Year with their families, yet each of them occupied with their own racing thoughts.

A chill wind blew down Whitehall as the men went their separate ways; its coldness reflected the austere times in which they lived. Further down Whitehall, a cabinet meeting was in progress and it was nothing like as convivial as the Squad men's conference had been. The worried ministers were agreed that Britain had run out of money. There was now the very realistic prospect of famine.

CHAPTER 4

The Squad Goes to Work

T he year 1946 had a dismal start for the British people; the cheery optimism of the wartime 'Britain can take it' spirit had receded in the face of the Labour party's grim austerity. It was little comfort that William Joyce, 'Lord Haw-haw' whose radio broadcasts from wartime Germany had attempted to demoralise Britain, had been hanged for treason. It was of far more concern to Londoners that by February the capital had just one week's supply of coal left. There was a shortage of wheat for bread, which became darker and coarser; the weight of loaves was cut and when by July the country had only enough grain left for eight weeks' supply, bread was rationed to just nine ounces per day. The beer supply had been halved, the cheese ration had been cut to two ounces per week and queues formed before dawn at shops to buy food; usually, whatever food there was had been sold out by eight o'clock the same morning. Nor was it just food and clothing which were rationed; just three-quarters of a ton of coal or coke was permitted to each household for three months. When the television licence was introduced on 1 June, nobody really cared; and there was no rush to switch on televisions a week later when television broadcasting resumed for the first time since the war, because only a minuscule proportion of the population possessed a set.

★　★　★

The Ghost Squad's unmarked office was on the third floor of Scotland Yard, near the lift and overlooking the Thames; there was a huge plane tree between the window and the road. The office was as austere as the rest of England; the walls were decorated in grey distemper and it was furnished with two tables, four straight-backed chairs, some filing cabinets and a telephone – as well as a key for the door, a first for the Yard. There was an electric socket, used for powering an illicit kettle, a modest luxury which was frowned upon by senior officers. In addition, there was a small locker which, if the senior officers had known of its contents, would have upset them even more; this, said Gosling, was to house skeleton keys, coshes and other relics of the past.

The four officers would meet in the office, usually at 10.30 in the morning; they would telephone Capstick at six o'clock in the evening to let him know what they were doing. In their absence, messages were received by a discreet police constable known as 'Archie' who, Gosling said, would have made a good butler. Any messages for the officers when their office was unmanned – and this was often the case – were telephoned through to the world-famous WHItehall 1212 number and then transferred to C1 Reserve on Extension 106, to be passed in turn to the duty inspector – and thence to 'Archie'.

The promised car was a matter beset with difficulties. An Austin 16 saloon from the fleet at C1 had been allocated to the officers and a Wolseley had been assigned to the superintendent in its place. However, the Assistant Commissioner (B) (in charge of traffic) was as obstructive as possible; it was only when Howe tersely demanded to know, "Is the point that you want me to obtain Home Office authority?" that the AC(B) capitulated; but as a matter of principle the transport department dutifully dragged its heels and the Receiver – the man in charge of the expenditure of the Metropolitan Police and, naturally, a civilian – sulkily noted that "the Austin will be re-issued as soon as the repairs now in progress have been completed". Since six weeks had passed since Home Office approval had been received, Howe was prompted to expostulate, "I spoke to you. If the Austin will take some time, we should like any car, temporarily. The matter is urgent". The rather pompous reply two days later was, "Barring accidents on a service which we must maintain (e.g. prison van, dispatch) the Austin should be ready by 13 February" – and the day following that date it was.

However, Howe had made the right choice of resourceful officers for the Special Duties Squad; car or no car, by the time the Austin arrived they had already netted twenty-two prisoners.

Following the initial meeting with Howe, the four officers met their snouts and pressed them into action. Capstick was the first to get a result; it was his information which led Detective Sergeant Coles of 'W' Division to visit 8 Oak Avenue, Shirley,

Surrey, where he arrested John James Lane, who had been a very busy housebreaker in and around that area. The property, valued at £3,000, which he had amassed was discovered at 56a Bickersteth Road, Tooting and it was sufficient to charge him with seven cases of housebreaking. After he appeared at the Old Bailey three months later, Lane asked for ninety-seven other cases to be taken into consideration; he was sentenced to eight years' penal servitude. Fired with this success, Capstick's snout provided details of a receiver who had taken the part-proceeds of Lane's larcenous endeavours, and once again Sergeant Coles made the arrest, as he did six days later, when he arrested another habitué of 'W' Division for the larceny of a motor van stolen from Orsman Road, N1.

Nor was Brinnand idling; one of his snouts tremblingly offered up John Caffney, and Detective Sergeant Carter of 'C' Division arrested him for stealing cash and insurance stamps in Sheffield. Blucher Willmott, a Borstal escapee, refused details of his address and occupation when he was arrested by the crew of the 'W' Division 'Q' Car; however, he was persuaded to admit one case of burglary and another of housebreaking and asked for sixty-four other offences to be taken into consideration when he was sentenced to three years' Borstal detention.

On 2 January 1946, a north London shop was broken into and a number of dresses were stolen; this was followed by a break-in at a similar premises in Mayfair, but the perpetrators fled after they set off the alarm. There was nothing to connect the two offences until a week later, when one of the occupants of a stolen Humber saloon fired shots at a pursuing police car; when the Humber was traced (minus the occupants) it was found to contain the dresses stolen from the north London shop. Another week went by; early one morning, there was a smash and grab at a Mayfair furriers and, alerted by the noise, a nearby resident looked out of her window but was warned that if she interfered she would be shot. A Free Norwegian Army lorry arrived, the gang loaded furs worth £3,000 into it and as they drove off and a patrolling police officer tried to stop the lorry the gang demonstrated that shooting at busybodies was no idle threat, by firing a shot at him.

On 7 February, Detective Inspector William Judge and his Flying Squad team searched a number of premises and took possession of two pistols, four revolvers, a quantity of ammunition, a selection of other weaponry and housebreaking tools and the part-proceeds of the smash and grab at the furriers. They also made a number of arrests, including George Albert King, a highly dangerous young gangster with a drugs dependency who admitted shooting at the police officers. There was one of the gang outstanding; and it was here that the Ghost Squad snouts came into play, who knew just where and when to find him. The following day, William Vigars, a coalman who had been known to the police since the age of thirteen, was enjoying a quiet drink at the Royal Exchange Public House, Kentish Town, when he was rudely disturbed by Detective Sergeant Bradford, who issued him with a no-nonsense invitation to join the other prisoners.

Thomas Leslie Bradford had joined the police eighteen years previously; within three months of joining he had been awarded his first commissioner's commendation for his ability in a case of car stealing and had received a monetary award of 10s 0d. He had served four years with the Flying Squad; now on 'D' Division, he was utilised to draw attention away from the Ghost Squad involvement, but within eighteen months he would be back again with the Flying Squad and would be making an impressive number of arrests, on behalf of the Ghost Squad.

At the Old Bailey King naturally received the heaviest sentence, that of seven years' penal servitude, but the offences were considered so serious that Vigars, unusual for a nineteen-year-old, received the severe sentence of four years' penal servitude.

Possibly because of this case – but certainly because of the proliferation of firearms which had found their way into the country and were being used in crime – the commissioner decided to announce an amnesty. It proved a success; within three months 75,996 firearms were surrendered, together with 5,873 bombs and 2,207,751 rounds of ammunition. However, this huge amount of ordnance was not handed in by hardened criminals; whatever firearms they had, they kept.

The arrest of Vigars was not the only case to be dealt with by the Ghost Squad informants on 8 February; three more arrests which produced a total of nine prisoners were carried out on the same day.

After a quantity of furs valued at £1,000 was stolen by means of a shopbreaking from Curzon Street, Mayfair, a Ghost Squad snout was responsible for Detective Inspector Little of 'X' Division hurrying to 36 Pevensey Court Buildings, Harlesden. Frederick Smith liked to be known as Thomas Bardsley or 'Manchester Freddie', but no matter how he was addressed his file had graced the Criminal Records Office at the Yard since 1926; now he, together with Michael Kiley, William George Doraile, Cecilia Murphy and Alfred Richards, was caught with the stolen swag.

The same day, William Weinberg and Julius Solamovitch – both aged nineteen and both Canadian airmen – were arrested at Shirland Road, London W9, by Detective Constable Glisby of 'X' Division, they being in questionable possession of an electric razor, three bottles of brandy and 152 pairs of ladies' silk stockings. Shirland Road was a popular venue for arrests on 'X' Division; eleven days later, it was there that Detective Sergeant Holcombe arrested Glen Sitwell, a soldier and Phillip Groves, a mechanic, for a robbery at a jeweller's at 157 King's Road, Chelsea, the previous day. The stolen property valued at £800 was recovered intact; both men were sentenced to three years' penal servitude.

Then Jack Novitsky, a furrier, and Joseph Wagenfeld, a leather worker, were interrupted during their visit to the Alexander Social Club, Stoke Newington by Detective Constable Bland of 'N' Division, who arrested both of them for receiving a quantity of army clothing; three days later, it was the same officer at the same venue who arrested Laurie Schear for receiving foodstuffs.

Detective Sergeant Stapeley (who like his colleague Henry Clark had been promoted since the bribery allegations) had a profitable run on the 'M' Division 'Q' Car, courtesy of the Ghost Squad informants. During a three-week period he made five arrests: two greengrocers for receiving 300 lbs of pork, two for larceny of toilet requisites and toothpaste and one industrious young absconder from an approved school who was arrested as a suspected person, loitering with intent to break into a shop whilst being in possession of housebreaking implements by night and stealing identity documents. Exactly two months after his last arrest for the Ghost Squad, Stapeley was transferred back to 'W' Division and there he stayed, without further promotion until his resignation, eleven years later.

Waddon Lodge, Cockfosters Road, was the scene of an officebreaking on 6 March, where four typewriters valued at

£162 2s 6d were stolen. Within twenty-four hours, Detective Sergeant Murray of Leyton police station had arrested Henry Morris, a thirty-three year old printer from Hackney, for the offence.

When a shop at 367 Wrythe Lane, Carshalton, was broken into on 11 March 1946 it did not take the Ghost Squad snouts too long to finger Stanley James and Kenneth Fordham for the offence; they were picked up the same day by the 'D' Division 'Q' Car.

Joseph Kazinnery Lewkowicz, a fifty-two-year-old Polish journalist from Gloucester Terrace, W2, was arrested by Detective Sergeant Hare from 'D' Division for receiving a quantity of cloth, hosiery and clothing coupons; the following day, 14 March, at Marylebone Magistrates' Court, he was sentenced to three and three months' imprisonment, to run consecutively.

Kate Smith, a dealer with premises at both Lea Bridge Road, E10 and Green Lanes, N1, was arrested by Detective Sergeant Cooke of 'N' Division after she was found to be in possession of six fur coats, twenty-four dresses and a quantity of jewellery, valued together at £1,400. The property was found to have been the proceeds of warehousebreakings in Manchester and Newcastle, and Mrs. Smith was sentenced to a total of twelve months' imprisonment.

Michael Goldstein, Gertie Joseph and Samuel Cooperman were all arrested for receiving two rolls of cloth (as was Morris Stock, three weeks later); the arresting officer was Detective Sergeant Jim Moyle, who was nearing the end of his six-and-a-half year posting with the Flying Squad. This was the first occasion on which he had been involved in arrests courtesy of the Ghost Squad informants, but it would not be the last. Although within two months he would be posted to 'L' Division, where he would remain for two and a half years, his following posting would be back to the Flying Squad, when he would immediately be snapped up by the Ghost Squad.

It is a common fault of many thieves that they simply do not know when to keep their mouths shut regarding their larcenous intentions. It was not known upon whom to lay the blame – whether it was Thomas Francis Ramsey, William George Walker or John Arthur Dipple, because they all possessed impressive criminal records and therefore should have known better. But after they stole a lorry containing five tons of plywood valued at

£1,500 from Usher Road, Bow, a Flying Squad Railton containing Detective Inspector Crawford was fortuitously waiting for them. Each of the gang had twenty-one months' imprisonment in which to attempt to work out who had grassed them.

Leonard William Crawford requires an introduction at this juncture, because he features time and again in the pages which follow. An exceedingly tough former Royal Naval telegraphist, Crawford had joined the police in 1927, and as soon as he was appointed detective constable he was posted to the Flying Squad. It was the first of three postings, which would total nine years. He had a rather Semitic appearance and he was used for undercover purposes and effected the arrest of a large number of fraudsters. In 1935 he was commended by the commissioner for the arrest of a violent criminal for pavilionbreaking and in 1940 was highly commended by the commissioner after arresting a struggling member of the IRA on a roof top fifty feet above the ground, then rendering abortive four time-bombs which were 'live' – he was also awarded £10 from the Bow Street Police Court Reward Fund. With his courage and ingenuity, Crawford was tailor-made to assist the Ghost Squad.

Mary Theresa King and Maurice Dean were arrested for receiving £1,000 worth of lipsticks; the arresting officer was Detective Constable Tommy Butler of the Flying Squad. It was the first (but not his last) work with the Ghost Squad; he would arrest Richard Edward Dalton for stealing a car, Lloyd Evans for receiving forty clothing coupons which he had hidden at his address at Phoenix Mansions, Charing Cross Road and Henri Ordioni, Henri Lefevre, and Marcel Grimaldi at Sloane Square, where they were found to be in possession of three false French passports. Butler had spent an action-packed five years on the Squad and had collected thirteen commissioner's commendations during that time; within three months he would be promoted to detective sergeant second class, but would return to the Squad time and again. The pinnacle of his career would come seventeen years later when, as detective chief superintendent of the Flying Squad, he would lead the hunt for the Great Train Robbers.

When the Ghost Squad officers apportioned information from their snouts to officers to carry out observations and arrests, they had to be sure that these officers were reliable. No such doubt existed about the capabilities of Detective Sergeant George

Burton of 'S' Division; he and Gosling had known each other since they were detective constables on 'G' Division, and four months after Gosling's promotion to detective sergeant second class and a posting to the Flying Squad, so Burton followed him to the Squad, having similarly been promoted. Now Gosling passed Burton information from one of his snouts which led him to arrive at 33 Perrin's Lane, Hampstead, where he discovered a number of Remington typewriters worth £400 and arrested Cyril Alexander Bourne and Joseph Francis Walters for receiving them; initially, at least. Burton probed a little further and was able to charge the men with breaking and entering the Army Education Offices, Palace Court, W2, three days previously and stealing a total of fourteen typewriters valued at £700. Burton would not remain on 'S' Division for very much longer; within six months he would be back on the Flying Squad and straight into an empty slot on the Ghost Squad.

It was part of the Ghost Squad's brief that they were not to get involved in the arrests which their snouts had put up to them. This was not always possible, as has already been recounted in the case of the Percy Street arrests. In company with Flying Squad officers they took part in a four-day observation on a garage in the Barking Road, Plaistow, which was used as a run-in by a gang of criminals. The Ghost Squad had received information that part of a consignment of carpets valued at £6,000, stolen by means of a factorybreaking on 'G' Division, was on its way there at a time unknown; hence the prolonged observation. In the event, carpets valued at £3,000 were recovered and Arthur William Stowe, William Robbins, Harry Carvalho and Nathan Shannon were arrested by Detective Sergeants Walter 'Pedlar' Palmer and Allan 'Jock' Brodie (who had been decorated with the Distinguished Flying Cross during his wartime service with the Royal Air Force) of the Flying Squad; the first three men were each sentenced to twenty-one months' imprisonment, the fourth was bound over and the wives of two of the men were acquitted. So whilst the Ghost Squad officers might have escaped actual involvement in the arrests, they nevertheless had to give evidence during the trial; this was also inescapable in the arrests which took place eleven days later.

John Gosling decided to pay a visit to Albert Goodman, a fifty-six-year-old garage proprietor whom Gosling strongly suspected of permitting teams of warehousebreakers to use his garage in

Belvedere Road, Leyton, as a run-in. As Gosling entered the garage, so Goodman emerged from his office and after his initial shock of seeing Gosling, whom he knew well, insincerely congratulated him for a smart piece of detective work. That was enough for Gosling, who immediately searched the garage and discovered seventeen chests of tea valued at £500 which had been stolen by means of a warehousebreaking at Bethnal Green the previous day; also present were the three men responsible. Gosling induced Goodman to telephone the local police station, and the arrests were carried out by Detective Sergeant Richards from Leyton police station. However, Gosling had to give evidence at the trial, which contributed to Goodman (whose criminal career had commenced eleven years previously) receiving two years' imprisonment, Charles Bonner (whose introduction to the law had started five years before Goodman's) being sentenced to twenty-one months' imprisonment, James Price (a comparative newcomer to the world of crime, whose first conviction only dated back to 1940) to eighteen months' imprisonment and Richard Roberts, a first-timer, receiving twelve months.

Giuseppe and Antonio Romano, aged fifty-nine and thirty-eight and domiciled in Muswell Hill and King's Cross respectively, were arrested by officers from Kentish Town police station for receiving half a ton of dried eggs. Perhaps this was a necessary ingredient in ice cream, of which both were manufacturers.

Just after the war, 'G' Division had acquired a bad reputation for corruption; Detective Inspector Bert 'The Iron Man' Sparks was one of the officers posted there to eradicate these questionable practices. Therefore, it made sense for Sparks to be the officer to respond to a Ghost Squad snout's information that one Dkarampel Nayyar was up to no good – and so it appeared. Sparks arrested him at 7 Artillery Passage, Stepney where he was found to be in possession of over 1,600 men's undergarments, plus £400 in cash, all of which merited further investigation and explanation.

A warehouse at Riverton Place, Riverton Street, Shoreditch was broken into and tapestry valued at £250 was stolen; Detective Sergeants Marr and Bowery of the Flying Squad arrested two army deserters for both carrying out the break-in and receiving the loot. Another deserter, James Carroll, and

Thomas Edward Bishop, a dealer, were arrested by Detective Inspector Robinson from 'G' Division for stealing £400 cash from a van belonging to Barclays Bank, at Upper Street, Islington. Deserters, this time of a naval variety, featured a few days later. Walter Sharp and James Henry Trigg, both of no fixed abode, were unable to find a suitable buyer for the 714 pairs of shoes and the sixteen bales of leather, valued at £1,021 6s 8d, which had been obtained by means of a warehousebreaking in Holloway a week previously. It was sufficient time for a nark to pinpoint the whereabouts of the deserters and their swag to Detective Sergeant Miller of 'N' Division. Two days later, the energetic Sergeant Miller also arrested Eva Elizabeth Clayton and Sarah Nelly Nelson for factorybreaking at 432 Seven Sisters Road, N7, the previous night and stealing cloth to the value of £150. Since the two ladies were aged forty-seven and forty-six respectively, this athletic venture did sound somewhat unlikely, but they were also charged with receiving dresses, suits and blankets, which appeared to be a more suitable charge.

The Greeks have a saying, 'Don't shit where you eat', and John James Gadstin and John Joseph Gadstin should have taken this particular homily to heart. Both lived in Shoreditch, and the three premises which they broke into and stole carpets and leather from were also situated there. This was an area much favoured by some of Gosling's best informants; it also led to Detective Sergeant Hope and Detective Constable Jones of 'G' Division arresting both men; it also caused the prisoners to miss the Victory Parade to celebrate the end of the war, which was held in London the following day. Carrying out these arrests often led to a knock-on effect, with the officers concerned receiving more and more information from the Ghost Squad office, as it did in this case; it led Detective Constable Jones to arrest William Powell for stealing motorcycle parts and four days later to the arrest of Sidney Sherman, William Taylor, John Spirali and William Zammit whilst they were in the act of breaking into 8 Rhoda Street, Bethnal Green and stealing electrical machinery valued in total at £67 12s 0d.

It seemed the height of foolishness to leave a suitcase on an unattended motorcycle in Lower Regent Street. When Detective Sergeant Green from 'C' Division arrested George William Benstead for stealing the said suitcase, it appeared equally irrational for him to refuse his address; it led to Bow Street Magistrates' Court remanding Benstead in custody.

The Flying Squad arrested Richard Henry Hilditch, Gladys Elsie Ford and Ethel Rose Hawkins, all of Clifton Street, EC2; it may be assumed that Peter Edward Holloway Stanley was also residing in that thoroughfare but he was simply listed as being a deserter from the Royal Ulster Rifles. All were charged with two cases of workshopbreaking, the first involving the theft of cigarette cases valued at £450, where property valued at £110 was recovered, and the second where handbags (which were recovered intact) valued at £200 were stolen. As a bonus, Stanley's fingerprints were found at the scenes of three shopbreakings on 'X' Division; he and Hilditch were both sentenced to twelve months' imprisonment and the two ladies received two months each. Deserters were commonplace at this time; Francis Patrick James O'Reilly had deserted from the navy and was caught by Detective Sergeant Law of 'C' Division in Margaret Street, W1, on 2 July in possession of 4,500 clothing coupons.

There was no hiding place for Joseph Goorewitch, a forty-seven-year-old furrier; his name had been circulated as being wanted for receiving by police on the Channel Island of Jersey for almost three months. As a result of a tip-off by a Ghost Squad snout, Goorewitch, who had been known to the police since 1917, was arrested by Torquay police officers. It seemed that distance was not respected by the Ghost Squad informants; after the arrest in Torquay, a few days later Benjamin Ernest Folds, a thirty-six-year-old cafe proprietor from Hemel Hampstead, was arrested by Detective Sergeants Trebess and Rawlins of the Flying Squad for receiving 10,000 Players and 3,000 Players Weights cigarettes; he was dealt with at the local Magistrates' Court.

Brinnand had an informant named Harry, a thoroughly nasty piece of work whom Brinnand had arrested in 1937. Harry had been running a café in Lisle Street, off Leicester Square, and he had three young, good-looking, homosexual Irishmen living with him in a flat above the café. These young men would befriend young, obviously moneyed men of a similar persuasion, and once they were ensconced in a hotel in a suitably compromising position, into the room would burst Harry in the guise of a detective sergeant. To the victims this meant nothing less than complete disaster, since many of them were well-known political, social and legal personalities, and they were willing to pay

'Detective Sergeant Harry' considerable sums of money for the whole business to be hushed up. In this fashion, it was believed that over the years he had managed to extort over £100,000 from his victims. In the subsequent press reports, Harry, with considerable justification, was dubbed 'The King of the Blackmailers'. He was sentenced to seven years' penal servitude and his young chums were each sentenced to three years' Borstal detention, the trial judge recommending that each should be housed in separate Borstal institutions.

Harry was also a receiver of stolen goods, and following his release from prison Brinnand and Gosling had met him and – Brinnand especially – had promised Harry that unless he started naming names and providing substantial information, ill would befall him. Harry knew Brinnand only too well to realise that this was no idle threat and consequently made himself busy.

On 6 July 1946 Brinnand and Gosling were just about to leave the Ghost Squad office when there was a telephone call from Harry, who asked them to meet him as a matter of urgency in a café in Bishopsgate. They duly met Harry, who told them that within half an hour a group of very tough housebreakers whose names he professed not to know would be arriving at his house in Gourlston Street, Aldgate, in possession of a large amount of jewellery, the provenance of which was unknown to him. However, so unnerved was Harry that he pleaded with the officers to arrest the housebreakers before they could arrive at his address.

Having contacted the Flying Squad, Gosling and Brinnand then kept observation close to Harry's home. Within half an hour a car arrived containing five men; two of the men got out – Richard Adrian Graydon, an actor, and Thomas Henry Carman, a driver – and walked towards Gourlston Street. As soon as they were out of sight of the other occupants of the car, Gosling and Brinnand arrested them, put them into the back of the Ghost Squad Austin 16 and, with Brinnand sitting between them, Gosling drove off to Commercial Street police station. However, Gosling had taken the precaution of adjusting the car's rear view mirror; and as they drove along, he could see that Graydon was busy, furiously pushing property down the back of his seat. The two men were lodged at the police station; then the officers returned to the car and lifted the back seat. There were a number of diamond brooches, rings and bracelets – and also a hole in the bodywork which had not been repaired and had been left to permit the differential to move up and down without hitting the body of the car. It appears that the rather dismissive note from the Yard's Receiver, dated 5 February, that the car would be available as soon as the repairs had been completed, suggested that the restoration had not been carried out as assiduously as one would have wished.

Gosling and Brinnand carefully retraced the route they had taken, but as Gosling later wryly pointed out it was not entirely surprising that no trace of the missing jewellery was found, as this was the East End of London. Back they went to the three other men waiting patiently in their car for the return of Graydon and Carman and, with the assistance of Detective Sergeant Trebess and Detective Constable Gloyne of the Flying Squad, arrested William George King, a driver, Bryan Mooney, a musician and Harry Mann – who would later figure in another celebrated Ghost Squad case. The men insisted that they knew nothing about the housebreaking; in fact, they stated they were doing a favour for Peter Tilley-Bailey, an ex-public schoolboy of independent means. Pressed as to where they intended to meet him, the officers were told he would be at Broadly Street, off the Edgware Road. In fact, this proved to be the case; Tilley-Bailey was found in his sports car, carrying on a languid conversation with an attractive blonde. Rather unkindly, perhaps, Gosling later noted that, "In keeping with his kind, he put up no resistance, mental or otherwise and he was promptly arrested".

The property was identified as the proceeds of a housebreaking the previous day at Thorney Court, Kensington; the niece of the householder had left a fanlight open and insisted that the reason for this was to permit Tilley-Bailey to pay her a nocturnal visit. "Although I had grave doubts as to the validity of this explanation, she was not arrested," Gosling drily remarked later. The men arrested were regarded as an active gang of West End housebreakers and they were charged with the housebreaking and receiving the recovered amount of jewellery. All of them had criminal records: William King, who had been first convicted in 1929, Richard Graydon in 1945, Thomas Carmen in 1932, Harry Mann in 1931 and Peter Tilley-Bailey in 1936, were all sentenced to two years' imprisonment. Bryan Mooney, first convicted in 1938, received eighteen months.

Of the jewellery stolen, which was valued at £3,147, just £632 worth was recovered; this undoubtedly led to some red faces at the trial, at which Gosling and Brinnand had to give evidence, although both of them were subsequently commended by the commissioner.

* * *

This case represented the end of the Ghost Squad's first six months of work. Capstick was required to submit a report to the commissioner to show how the unit had fared. The results were impressive: 106 arrests had been made and property valued at £16,829 14s 6½d had been recovered. In part, Capstick's report reads as follows:

Since we commenced this work on 8th January 1946, I have had every opportunity of studying the modern thief and his methods whilst engaged in crime. I compare him with my dealings with thieves during the past ten years and find that the thief of today is a cunning and most difficult man to catch and a more difficult man to convict.

These days, thieves take every precaution against detection and arrest and are most careful who they confide in regarding an offence they have committed or contemplate committing. Such cunningness makes work more difficult for our informers.

Thieves are now most secretive as regards the actual place or 'run in' as referred to by thieves, where they conceal stolen property prior to it being disposed of.

In most gangs there are only two persons in the gang who are actually aware of the place in question. Such places in former days were mostly the dwelling houses of thieves or a garage, shed or stable adjoining same.

Today, stolen property is seldom found in a thief's house or the immediate vicinity, thereof. It is more often than not found in a garage or similar premises, whereupon enquiries being made to trace the person who rents the premises, we find it has been rented by an unknown person who has tendered a false name and address, thus thwarting police being able to prove control of the property.

The majority of informers agree that in practically every heavy case of theft, whether it be a lorry load of goods or high class housebreaking, there is invariably collusion either with a lorry driver, caretaker or such like.

Our informers realise we reimburse them for their services as well as we can from the Information Fund. They appear to be satisfied with our financial efforts, especially when assessors of property invariably pay the informers personally 10% cash valued of the stolen property recovered from a prisoner.

Superintendent Thompson felt that the results obtained by the 'freelance' CID squad fully justified the experiment and added that consideration should be given to 'suitable appreciation' of the officers' good work. Hugh Young acknowledged that the work of the unit was much appreciated and that C5 Department should make a note on the officers' records, there being no need for a commendation in *Police Orders*. The papers were passed to C5 but although that unit's chief inspector stated that this note had been made – and despite the fact that C5 had never been the most over-worked department at the Yard – it had not. ACC Howe forwarded the papers to the commissioner who noted, "Excellent. A most promising start".

⋆   ⋆   ⋆

It was indeed a promising start, but the arrests in the case involving stolen jewellery was the last job in which Brinnand participated; he resigned from the police on 6 October 1946, after fifteen years' and 205 days' service with an 'Exemplary' character reference. He had been commended by the commissioner on twenty-two occasions and to all intents and purposes had a glittering career in front of him; in the next ten to fifteen years he could easily have risen to the highest ranks on ability alone. In his book, *The Ghost Squad*, Gosling's explanation was that Brinnand felt that he had been passed over by lesser men in the struggle for promotion and that he felt badly about it. That was a lie – a white lie and perhaps a rather necessary one, but nevertheless very far from the truth. Brinnand had been appointed detective constable within three years of joining the police. Three and a half years later, he was posted to the Flying Squad where after two years he was promoted to detective sergeant (second class) and, unusually, remained on the Squad. Within three months of his Ghost Squad posting he was promoted to detective sergeant (first class). Ordinarily, anybody in Brinnand's position with two consecutive promotions would have been posted off the Flying Squad (and therefore, off the Ghost Squad), but prior to his promotion, Ronald Howe thought so highly of Brinnand that he sent a minute to the Assistant Commissioner 'D' Department, (which dealt with personnel) in the following terms:

> Within the next week, P.S. (2nd. Class, CID) Brinnand will be advanced to Sergeant (1st Class).
>
> This Sergeant is attached to the Special Squad of C.I.D. officers responsible for obtaining information of the activities of expert and dangerous criminals authorised on these papers, and it is essential that he should be retained on this very important duty. Will you please send a suitable letter to H.O. asked for the authorised establishment to be adjusted to cover P.S. Brinnand's advancement.

In a hand-written note inscribed on the back of Howe's minute the AC(D) wrote:

> ACC. As a temporary measure, you can promote the 2nd. Class Sergeant to 1st. Class, without HO authority. The establishment permits this, at present.

The note was dated 29 March, and three days later Brinnand was promoted – yet six months later he resigned. Whoever was passed over for promotion, it certainly was not Brinnand. The truth of the matter was far different and is dealt with later.

★   ★   ★

On the day Brinnand left, so Detective Sergeant George Burton (who had already carried out sterling work for the Ghost Squad as an 'S' Division officer) was transferred back to the Flying Squad and slotted neatly into the vacancy left by Brinnand. Burton, born in Stepney in 1909 and formerly a labourer, was a big, well-built, ruddy-faced man, just one-quarter of an inch shorter than Gosling and, like him, fond of a drink and liable to burst into song at the slightest opportunity. He had joined the Metropolitan Police on 6 January 1930 and was posted to 'X' Division; within three months he was commended by the commissioner for his actions in a case of attempted shopbreaking. As an aid to CID and then as a detective constable on 'F' Division, Burton was a committed thief-taker and informant-runner and was commended by the justices at Ealing Petty Sessions and the commissioner on four further occasions for arrests involving housebreakers, suspected persons and "two persistent thieves, whilst off duty". Teaming up with Gosling on 'G' Division, Burton had been commended with him on three occasions and later on four more occasions with him on the Flying Squad.

★　★　★

Donald Bertie Walters had been an industrious seventeen-year-old in the time since his escape from Approved School. After Detective Inspector Len Crawford of the Flying Squad arrested him in Edmonton for two cases of housebreaking and larceny, young Donald asked for three housebreakings on 'M' Division, two provincial cases and two larcenies on 'N' Division to be taken into consideration when he appeared at court; he was probably lucky to be returned to Approved School to complete his education.

Sam Brochofsky, a fifty-three-year-old boot repairer from Limehouse, was arrested by Detective Sergeant Bowery for receiving ladies' costumes valued at £350; he was sentenced to six months.

Directed by the Ghost Squad snouts, arrest after arrest was made of men in possession of stolen or forged coupons. Aaron Friedlander, a forty-four-year-old bookkeeper from Shoreditch, was arrested by Detective Sergeant Gerrard of 'G' Division in Commercial Street in possession of 644 clothing coupons, and although a builder and a clerk were arrested by aids to CID, Police Constables Sullivan and Colyer of 'G' Division, in possession of 3,877 clothing coupons, they were discharged at court. However, six weeks later, Maxwell Goldstein, a thirty-six-year-old job buyer from Electric Avenue, Brixton, was fined £50 with ten guineas costs for the same offence. Samuel Nicholls, aged forty-one who described himself as 'a hawker' from Manor Park, was stopped at Ridgmount Gardens, WC1 by Detective Sergeant Law and Detective Constable Baldwin of 'C' Division, being in possession of 1,925 clothing coupons; he was sentenced to three months' imprisonment.

Rather harsher was the penalty meted out to Edward Malcolm Saunders, a thirty-eight-year-old general dealer, after Detective

Sergeants Mackay and Deans of the Flying Squad arrested him for stealing 4,850 clothing coupons. His co-accused, a thirty-five-year-old barman walked free from court but Saunders was sentenced to twenty-one months' imprisonment. Just six months later, one of the arresting officers – Detective Sergeant William Hosie Deans – would be propelled into the limelight. He took part in an operation to foil a robbery where he masqueraded as a bank manager, whom the gang planned to attack and kidnap in order to seize the keys to his bank. Deans was savagely beaten, the keys were taken from him and he was dumped in a deserted spot, where for the previous twenty-four hours it had been snowing heavily. It was more than an hour before he was found and a doctor who examined him stated that it was "a miracle" that he had not died, both from the attack and exposure to the elements. The gang were sentenced to a total of twenty-nine years' penal servitude and Deans was awarded the King's Police Medal. Detective Inspector Len Crawford was in charge of the operation; when the first suspect was caught, Crawford carried out a speedy and impromptu interview with him in a police van. He was commended by the commissioner for "ability and enterprise".

Gosling met an informant one evening who admitted that he had transported what was obviously a printing press for an unknown man to an address "somewhere in Finchley", and having done so discovered a forged five-unit clothing coupon in his vehicle, obviously left by his passenger. Gosling and his snout spent the next few days touring the Finchley area, visiting cafes and pubs in the hope of seeing the forger, but without success – until Gosling ventured into Wealdstone where his snout spotted Edward Cato, whose criminal record stretched back to 1932. He was followed home by Gosling, who then ensured that Detective Sergeants Brodie and Cox from the Flying Squad paid him a visit. A search of his premises revealed 442 industrial clothing coupons, the printing press and paper were traced to his possession, "and" noted Capstick, "will be the subject of further charges". But whether further charges were proffered or not, the fact remains that Cato was sentenced to a very modest two months' imprisonment.

Courts could show often bewildering compassion; when Kenneth Sidney Weiber was arrested by Detective Sergeant Mozelle of 'G' Division for shopbreaking, he was returned to Borstal; but when in the same case Detective Constable Johnson arrested three teenagers, David Charles Gilbanks, Thomas Joseph Quirke and Stanley Pritchard, for three incidents of shopbreaking, North London Magistrates' Court simply bound them over to be of good behaviour. Edward Charles John Shirley, a thirty-three-year-old labourer from Walthamstow, was arrested by the Flying Squad's Detective Inspector Jackson for receiving a quantity of shoes and slippers valued at £60; two weeks later, he was joined in the dock by Herbert Arthur Darke, an eighteen-year-old garage hand who had been arrested by Detective Sergeant Bowery on the same charge. Shirley was fined £10 or two months' imprisonment in default, Darke was bound over in the sum of £5 for twelve months. And when Hubert Wheeler, a sixty-three-year-old dentist from Walthamstow, was arrested by Detective Constable Pilbeam of the Flying Squad for feloniously receiving 149 pencils, an electric motor and four books of clothing coupons, he was fined just £5.

On the other side of the coin, however, when a handbag and cash valued together at £45 were stolen from 14 Swanfield Street, Bethnal Green and Alexander Milowsky, a thirty-one-year-old labourer who lived a short walk away in Cheshire Street was arrested for it by Detective Inspector Bayfield, he was sentenced to twenty-one months' hard labour.

Twenty-nine-year-old Ada Wiseman, first convicted in 1938 and described as 'an expert housebreaker', failed to surrender to her bail at the September Sessions at the Old Bailey and a warrant was issued for her arrest. One of Capstick's snouts pointed Detective Inspector Oliver of 'W' Division in the direction of the Eagle Public House, Clifton Road, W9, and it was there, at nine o'clock in the evening of 15 October 1946, that he arrested her; the fact that she had attempted to disguise herself by dyeing her hair making not the slightest bit of difference. She later admitted three cases of housebreaking and asked for twenty-nine other offences of housebreaking and larceny to be taken into consideration when she appeared at the Old Bailey; she was sentenced to twenty-one months' hard labour.

The following day, 16 October, saw Capstick fleetingly detached from his Ghost Squad duties. A thief had broken into Ednam Lodge, Sunningdale, the country estate of the Earl and Countess of Dudley. The owners were absent at the time; instead, the Duke and Duchess of Windsor were in residence, and jewellery valued at £20,000, the property of the duchess, had been stolen. Capstick whipped his informants into action, commenced his own painstaking enquiries and then set his sights on one particular prime suspect. In fact, he spent years endeavouring to prove the guilt of this suspect, but for once Capstick was wrong. What was more, his informants were unable to put up any information at all as to the identity of the guilty party. The prime suspect was arrested three years later and not by Capstick, either. His name was Barry Fieldsen, a gentleman 'cracksman' who was suspected of a string of high-value jewellery burglaries from the homes of the great and the good. Before he could be questioned regarding the duchess' missing jewels, he booked into a hotel and blew his brains out.

The case of William Thompson and Sydney Graham, of Kentish Town and Holloway respectively, appeared to be a fairly unremarkable Ghost Squad case when they were arrested on 17 October; they had committed an offence of larceny in a dwelling house at the prosperous 40 Agincourt Road, Hampstead and were dealt with on the day of their arrest at Clerkenwell Magistrates' Court. Both were sentenced to hard labour; six months for Thompson and four months for Graham. What was of interest was the identity of the arresting officers: Detective Inspector John Jamieson and Detective Sergeant Sid Ray, both from 'D' Division. Within three months Jamieson would be promoted to divisional detective inspector, transferred, and would head the Ghost Squad. Ray, however, later resigned and became managing clerk for Sampson & Co, a firm of solicitors famed for defence work and later to defend the Kray brothers. A week later Jamieson struck again, this time arresting George David Lee, a seventeen-year-old labourer from Somers Town, for stealing cigarette cases and clocks; he was bound over in the sum of £5 for a period of twelve months.

Nathan Donert, a tailor aged forty-six, was arrested by Detective Sergeant Wynn of 'C' Division for receiving a parcel containing eighteen boys' shirts; this was the result of an operation involving observations being kept on him by Ghost Squad officers. As a result of a search at his premises at Howland Street, W1, a great deal more property was found. The following day, Clement Stanley Eden, a twenty-six-year-old bookmaker's clerk and Henry William Bessell, a nineteen-year-old motor dealer, both from Holloway, were stopped in Howland Street in possession of a parcel containing eighteen rolls of fabric. Eden and Bessall, both active railway thieves, admitted stealing the items from the LMS Railway at Euston Station and selling them to Donert, who had long been suspected of being an active receiver of property stolen in transit from various railway systems. In addition, labels from many other railway parcels were found at Donert's premises, the contents being valued at more than £1,000, so with that, plus the property recovered amounting to £600, ten charges of receiving and larceny were preferred against Donert; the three men were dealt with at the Old Bailey the following year.

One of Burton's snouts put up George Foster Nicholson from Paddington, who was arrested by Detective Sergeant Driscoll of the Flying Squad for a housebreaking at 401 Great West Road, Hounslow and stealing a fur coat valued at £150. Nicholson also admitted three schoolbreakings on 'T' Division and two larcenies in dwelling houses on 'X' Division.

A type of case which more than any other in the 1940s was guaranteed to raise the blood pressure of any jingoistic magistrate was the involvement of those whom they referred to as 'filthy foreigners', particularly when having arrived from exotic locations they committed offences which tended to deprave the morals of British subjects. Only two decades previously, high society's favourite drug dealer, Chan Nan, otherwise known as 'Brilliant' Chang, had been sentenced to fourteen months' imprisonment, and Eddie Manning, a Jamaican import described as 'the worst man in London', had been sentenced to three years' penal servitude for drug dealing.

Therefore, when Amil Hussain appeared at Old Street Magistrates' Court after Detective Sergeant Marr of the Flying Squad had arrested him for being in possession of three packages of herbs, ("which I believe to be Indian Hemp," said Sergeant Marr, ominously) he was tailor-made to receive the wrath of the magistrate. For the possession of an amount of cannabis so small that nowadays any enterprising copper would tip it down a drain rather than fill out the necessary time-consuming paperwork, Mr. Hussain was sentenced to six months.

In the run-up to Christmas, wood, always in short supply during the post-war period, suddenly emerged as a stolen item on 'G' Division; Joseph Tice, aged thirty-six, and Edward Henry Naylor, aged thirty-two, both furniture manufacturers, were arrested in George's Square, Hoxton by Detective Constable Chester for receiving 156 sheets of plywood. Six days later, Alec

Shapiro, a thirty-eight-year-old cabinet maker from Chingford and Nathan Grossman, a forty-four-year-old furniture dealer from Romford, were arrested by Detective Sergeants Brodie and Marr of the Flying Squad at Shepperton Mews, Islington for receiving sixty-two sheets of plywood.

Michael O'Mahoney, a thirty-seven-year-old cattle dealer of the Metropole Hotel, Cork, was stopped in the Edgware Road by Detective Constable Baird from Paddington police station. O'Mahoney was in possession of 1,810 Punch Corona cigars valued at £800 for which he gave an explanation that the bench at Marylebone Magistrates' Court thought so unsatisfactory that he was remanded in custody.

Whatever the circumstances of their attempt to obtain the sum of £5 by means of false pretences, Harry Adcock and George W. Harris, both waiters, cannot have been too duplicitous in their *modus operandi* when they were arrested by Detective Inspector 'Nobby' Clark and Detective Sergeant Burton, because the magistrate at Bow Street fined each of them just forty shillings. A few weeks later, Clark was busying himself again, this time at the Strand Palace Hotel, arresting Phillip and Frances Barr of Glasgow, for being in possession of 8,936 five-unit petrol coupons – sufficient to obtain 44,680 gallons of petrol. Both were handed to an escort from Glasgow, which was where the coupons had originated, by means of a storebreaking – or, under Scottish law, 'opening lockfast places'.

James Gerald Murphy and William John Bradley were both arrested by Detective Sergeants Gerrard and Marchant – the latter would later become a much admired CID commander of 3 Area – after a period of observation, for attempting to break into a flat at 17 Heyworth Road, Stratford, being found in a dwelling house for an unlawful purpose and being in possession of a loaded firearm. Also traced to their possession was a quantity of jewellery, and they were further charged with larceny in a dwelling house at Paddington two days earlier. And three days after that arrest, the same officers arrested Stephen Owen and Claude Henry Forward who were in possession of razor blades valued at £400 from warehousebreaking on 'G' Division; also in their possession were goods valued at £1,100, the proceeds of other warehouse-breakings and larcenies from heavy goods vehicles.

Frederick Harris, a thirty-two-year-old soldier of no fixed abode, and Terrance Arthur Anthony Fitzsimmonds, a twenty-two-year-old labourer, were arrested by Detective Sergeant Fisher and Detective Constable Vibart of the Flying Squad. The officers recovered property valued at £1,050 arising from the theft of two Austin motor cars, one on 'C' Division, the other on 'K' Division, as well as the theft of sables from an unattended car, also on 'C' Division. Jasper Peter Vibart, a former soldier, would rise up the ranks of the CID; working with Tommy Butler, he would become known as being one half of 'The Terrible Twins', specialising in arresting armed, dangerous criminals. Retiring with the rank of detective superintendent after thirty-three years' service, Vibart was commended by the commissioner on thirty-nine occasions, awarded the Queen's Commendation for Brave Conduct and decorated with the Queen's Police Medal for distinguished service.

Richard John Crawford was serving a sentence of three years' penal servitude when he escaped from Wandsworth Prison. After six weeks of freedom he was recaptured on 18 December 1946, following a tip-off from a Ghost Squad snout. Traced to his possession were the part-proceeds of a housebreaking which had occurred at 'Taygate', South Godstone, Surrey, where property valued at £292 11s 3d had been stolen. The property recovered amounted to £280, so it was a smart piece of police work by Detective Constable Robert Robertson of 'X' Division. It was the first of fourteen such arrests by Robertson whilst he was attached to 'X' Division; later, as a member of the Flying Squad (and as an unaccredited member of the Ghost Squad), he would carry out another thirty arrests. What would happen thereafter – and it is detailed later – did the reputation of the Metropolitan Police no good at all.

Phillip Raymond Soloman, of no fixed abode, described his occupation as being that of 'a traveller'. He failed to travel very far; for two weeks prior to his arrest he had been circulated as being wanted on 'D' Division for the larceny of jewellery valued at £1,100. It was on 'D' Division that he was arrested by Detective Sergeant Hare of that Division, and it was to 'D' Division's Paddington Green police station that he was taken.

The year finished with Inspector 'Nobby' Clark making the final arrest for the Ghost Squad. On 28 December he arrested John William Kemp for being in possession of paint and carpets valued at £200, all stolen from Weybridge, Surrey. It would be Clark's swansong.

By the end of the year, 171 persons had been arrested, 204 offences had been cleared up and the property recovered was valued at £24,126 14s 6½d. Rewards from the Informants Fund amounted to £558, plus the ten per cent reward which was paid out to the informants – almost £2,500 (or £100,000 by today's standards) – by the loss adjusters for the amount of property recovered. So how had these sensational results been achieved?

As well as the Ghost Squad officers working their informants at full stretch, Capstick had introduced the innovative practice of pairing up two informants to concentrate on infiltrating gangs of thieves. The practice of using the same two informants in two different gangs in the same police division was to be avoided whenever possible, although when this could not be averted, detectives from different divisions were used to carry out the arrests. When a pair of informants had produced the arrest of a gang of thieves, they were usually split up thereafter and were introduced to other informants, in different districts in the Metropolitan Police Area. Capstick felt that this dual informant system gave them more confidence and courage in gleaning the required information. He accepted that there would always be those informants who preferred to work alone but felt, nevertheless, that if an informant accepted Capstick's introduction to a second informant, twice as much work would be obtained.

Many ruses were adopted to confuse the criminals as to the sources who had betrayed them. One has already been mentioned: if the same officers in the same district continually made arrests, it might lead to the thieves pinpointing the informant, therefore officers from different divisions (or the Flying Squad) would be brought in to make the arrests.

Another example of subterfuge would be used when, for example, a van-load of stolen property had been delivered to a house in a certain street. It might well be that the informant had been seen in the vicinity, either by the thieves or the receiver. Therefore, when the police arrived in a car, the officer in charge would be briefed to go to a house opposite to the one where the stolen property had been stashed and ask the householder which way the numbers of the street ran. Inevitably, the occupier, in an effort to be helpful, would point in the direction of the receiver's house; hopefully, anyone watching would be convinced that the householder had pointed the way to the receiver's address. At other times a slight collision might be staged with a lorry carrying stolen property; when police were called to the scene, the arrest of the occupants of the lorry would be viewed as 'just one of those things'.

Both Worth and Howe had stipulated that the arrests should be shared between divisional CID officers and the Flying Squad, without the Ghost Squad operatives getting involved, and during the first year of operations this principle was generally adhered to: 105 arrests were made by divisional officers and sixty-three by the Flying Squad, and although some of the Ghost Squad officers inescapably had to give evidence in court as a result of a few of those cases, just three independent arrests were carried out by them alone.

Capstick's report was greeted enthusiastically by Detective Superintendent Thompson of C1 Department, who remarked, "There is no doubt that this squad has been a success and that the augmentation which enabled us to make the experiment is justified". He recommended that application should be made to the Home Office to permanently employ four officers on this work, and in support of this request stated that the facts showed it was worthwhile. The average Flying Squad officer, pointed out Thompson, made fifteen arrests per year, at a cost to the informant's fund, plus incidental expenses, of just over £3 per prisoner. The Special Duties Squad averaged nearly forty prisoners per officer at a cost of £6 10s 0d per prisoner; however, those officers were exempt from all other duties. As a word of caution, Thompson noted that sometimes the Flying Squad and the Special Duties Squad used the same informants which meant, as he perhaps wryly noted, "that a friendly rivalry has developed". To ease this situation, he suggested that the Squad should be attached to and work under the direction of the Flying Squad's chief inspector.

The report was forwarded to the Deputy Commander (Crime) William Rawlings OBE, MC. Rawlings had joined the Metropolitan Police in 1919 following active service in France as a Company Sergeant-Major with the Welch Fusiliers; he was appointed to the CID with less than eight months' service and now, in his present rank, was a highly experienced career detective. He largely backed Thompson's minute, noting, "One thing emerges with perfect clearness, this Special Squad is able to and has in fact obtained excellent information." Rawlings played down the issue of overlapping informants, believing that this happened only in very isolated cases, but although he agreed that the squad should be under the direct supervision of the officer in charge of the Flying Squad he should not have absolute discretion in all matters. He was against the Flying Squad dealing with all of the arrests, and in this matter only would the Flying Squad chief inspector give any direction. Rawlings also felt that there might be a danger of the present officers on the squad becoming a little 'stale', and for that reason he felt that because there were other officers who possessed excellent informants, it might be prudent to introduce fresh officers to the squad.

Howe agreed with Rawlings and suggested to the commissioner that a letter should be sent to the Home Office, asking that the augmentation of the four officers be made permanent. The commissioner, feeling that this was 'a very satisfactory record', directed that a letter be sent, and the Home Office agreed to the request.

Meanwhile, and quite apart from the crime wave, the civilian population of Britain had its own share of problems. Earlier in the year, the Government had announced plans to nationalize the iron and steel industry. Then in November the nationalization of railways, ports, long-distance road transport and inland waterways was announced. The wheat content in bread had been cut to the level used in 1942 and in the summer bread had been rationed – something which had not occurred in wartime. The butter, margarine and cooking fat ration was cut. Meat, poultry and eggs were considered luxury items. Incredible though it seems, the Government actually urged the population to catch squirrels in order to make them into pies.

England was starving.

CHAPTER 5

The Struggle Goes On

January 1947 swept in as one of the coldest winters ever recorded – snow had started falling prior to Christmas – and to make matters worse, a transport strike started in London. After normal running was resumed, it was found that trains were snowed-in and would remain so until February. When they did start moving again, 1,000 trains around London came to a grinding halt one month later due to further atrocious weather conditions. Nationwide, 300 roads were closed and lorries were buried in snow-drifts, some of them twenty feet high. As the temperature fell to minus 16 degrees Fahrenheit, Cable and Wireless and the British coal industry were nationalised. It did little good. Factories shut down because there was insufficient coal to sustain them. The cotton mills closed and the Midlands planned a four-day week. Domestic and industrial power supplies were turned off one day per week, homes and businesses were lit with candles, and gas and coal fires were banned until the autumn. It was so cold that ships could not put to sea – the sea actually froze off Margate and icebergs were seen off the Norfolk coast – and aircraft were unable to take off. When the snow eventually thawed, the countryside flooded and two million sheep were drowned. The thaw was only a temporary respite; the following month, snow and gales returned with a vengeance. Even if you felt minded to venture out, there was little to do: greyhound racing had been banned and cinemas were restricted to one daily performance. Theatre-land in London's West End fared no better; from the warmth of America's Palm Springs Noël Coward received details of faltering ticket sales for his musical *Pacific 1860* and glumly rechristened the theatre at which it was playing 'Dreary Lane'.

In spite of the restrictions already in place, rationing actually increased. The meat ration was cut and in mid-July it was cut again. Troops were drafted in to London to deliver food supplies. Those who could afford a holiday in Britain – there were not many – had to use their ration books at hotels. And the very fortunate few who could actually afford a motoring holiday either in this country or abroad were also doomed to disappointment, after both were banned. To cap it all, silver was no longer to be used in British coins.

So this was the state of London in 1947 – bombed out, starved out and practically bankrupt. The population had dropped to 3,245,000, a decrease of 20% from 1938. In the April budget profits and purchase tax and stamp and tobacco duties were raised. The only people profiting from this lamentable state of affairs were the black-marketeers and the receivers and the other assorted crooks who were their hangers-on.

★   ★   ★

The year got off to a cracking start for the Ghost Squad; Thomas Graham, John Brown and William Peter Heap were all arrested at Chatsworth Road, Willesden by Detective Sergeants Duncan 'Jock' Crerar (who had taken a decisive role in the arrest of prison escapee 'Ruby' Sparks in 1940) and Bill Marchant of the Flying Squad, for factorybreaking and stealing carpets valued at £4,185 – all of which were recovered intact. Less than one month later, the three men appeared at the Old Bailey and were sentenced respectively to two years', fourteen months' and ten months' imprisonment.

Next, it was the turn of Erich Jack Le Baub and Robert John Boyd who were arrested six days later for housebreaking at Esher, Surrey and stealing jewellery, valued at £110 5s 6d – which was recovered. At Kingston Petty Sessions two weeks later (justice was dispensed very speedily in those days), Le Baub was sentenced to five years' penal servitude. Boyd must have had a dock brief with a very nice line in mitigation, because he was fined just £15. And just three days after that arrest, Lewis Barnett (a deserter) and Mark Bass were arrested by Detective Sergeant Gullett from West End Central police station for the larceny of 157 pairs of nylon stockings and were also found to be in possession of five rolls of cloth and 480 handkerchiefs.

The arrests in these three cases were effected as the result of information supplied by Capstick's snouts; they would also serve as his swan song. Both Capstick and Clark were replaced on

27 January 1947, with Capstick being retained on C1 duties and Clark being posted to 'L' Division.

Capstick's successor was John Pretsell Jamieson, who was known as 'Jack, 'JJ' or 'Jock'. Born in 1898 at Corstorphine, Edinburgh, Jamieson served in the British Army as an engineer for eighteen months before joining the Metropolitan Police in 1926; after eleven years' service and acquiring sixteen commissioner's commendations, he was posted to the Flying Squad and during the next six years was promoted to detective sergeant (first class) and retained in post. Amongst the further twelve commissioner's commendations he received, one was with 'Nobby' Clark for a case of receiving stolen goods and another was with Capstick, who had infiltrated a gang of warehouse-breakers with one of his informants. The gang had cleared out a warehouse in Woking, Surrey of its entire stock of suit lengths. Armed with a suitcase full of 'tops and bottoms', the snout had tempted the gang sufficiently to want to do a deal and alerted Capstick as to the location of the stolen gear – a house in Homerton, East London, backing on to some railway lines. Capstick split his team in half – four to go in through the back at precisely the same moment as the others went in through the front. He knew that the gang members were as hard as nails, with shocking records of violence, and he prudently advised his team that they should "hit first and argue afterwards". They did – and the gang fought back so savagely that even when the officers got them into the Flying Squad tender, the walls bulged in and out with the renewed fighting, and at Hackney police station a strong guard of uniformed officers were posted to contain them.

After several postings and promotions, Jamieson returned to the Flying Squad as a divisional detective inspector on 23 December 1946. Six feet tall, hawk-faced, with a military moustache and immaculately attired in a dark suit and a Homburg, he was a complete professional and one month later became a worthy successor to Capstick.

Clark was replaced by Detective Inspector Percy Burgess, and it is difficult to imagine a better all-round police officer: hard-working, well-informed, brave, loyal and a deep-thinking strategist. However – and for a number of reasons which will become apparent – he was not at that time ideal Ghost Squad material.

Percy Herbert Edward Burgess was born in 1905 in Gibraltar. After five years' service with the British Army, Burgess joined the Metropolitan Police in January 1926. As an aid to CID on 'B' Division he teamed up with Bill MacDonald (later to become a leading light in the Ghost Squad arrests) and both were commended on two occasions. On 'X' Division, Burgess, a new detective constable, was part of Worth's 'X' Division Patrolling Group' and was again commended by the commissioner, this time for the arrest of thirteen persons for conspiracy to steal, plus numerous cases of larceny. In addition, he was awarded £1 10s, a welcome bonus to his weekly wage of £4 7s 6d. Promoted detective sergeant (second class), he was posted to 'C' Division in the heart of London's West End. It was the first of three postings there and lasted almost four years. George Price, who remembered him well from two of those tours, recalled that he was quiet, friendly, laid-back and "never afraid to take a chance". His reputation as a thief-taker was growing daily. He was commended for his part in the arrest of the Mayfair Playboys with Bob Fabian ('Fabian of the Yard') and, again with Fabian, for courage in making safe a bomb, an incident for which Fabian was later awarded the King's Police Medal. Burgess later admitted feeling resentment at Fabian's award, adding rather sulkily that he believed that none of the officers present on that occasion merited an award. Another of his contemporaries on 'C' Division was Matt Brinnand; Burgess was awarded two commissioner's commendations with Brinnand, one in a case of larceny and the other in a case of robbery with violence. After Brinnand left the division to join the Flying Squad, his new partner was a detective constable named Tommy Butler who, as a Flying Squad officer, would go on to materially assist the Ghost Squad.

In 1941 Burgess was promoted to detective sergeant (first class) and was posted to the Flying Squad, having been commended on twenty-five occasions. After four years, during which time he had notched up twelve more commendations, Burgess was posted back to 'C' Division, having been promoted to detective inspector (second class).

Whilst he was there, he received word from one of his informants that counterfeit £5 notes were in circulation and that a group of crooked bookmakers intended to form a syndicate to buy up a large consignment of these notes and dispose of them to working class men and women at the race tracks. The notes had a curious provenance: in 1941 Hitler had tasked *SS Reichsführer* Heinrich Himmler with devising a strategy to ruin the British economy. Himmler, in turn, got the experts from the *Sicherheitsdienst* (Security Service) to manufacture forged £5 notes, which were absolutely first-class. This was the verdict delivered by the Bank of England when millions of these forgeries started flooding into Threadneedle Street from all over Europe a couple of years later.

After several weeks, Burgess' informant told him that a large consignment of the notes had been flown in from a captured enemy airfield in Germany to RAF Northolt and gave him their destination; a block of flats near Bedford Square.

Arriving at the venue, Burgess noticed a large saloon car outside the block of flats. Posting a man to keep watch on it, Burgess and his team entered a flat on the first floor and there discovered three men in RAF uniform in possession of a briefcase which was found to contain envelopes filled with hundreds of forged £5 notes. All of the men were arrested and the car outside the block of flats was seized and stripped to its chassis. Further envelopes were discovered, similarly containing wads of forged £5 notes. It transpired that two of the prisoners were members of the Free Norwegian Air Force and that the other, an English Wing Commander, had been posted to an airfield in Holland, which had previously been used by the *Luftwaffe*. Whilst searching the *Kommandant*'s office, they had discovered the forgeries secreted in a false panel behind the wall and had decided to bring them back to England. The men all appeared at the Old Bailey and were each sentenced to three years' imprisonment. The case also provided Burgess with another commissioner's commendation to join the other four he had been awarded on 'C' Division before, on 27 January 1947, he was summoned to the Yard.

Deputy Commander Rawlings told Burgess that not only was he to be transferred back to the Flying Squad, he was also going to be immediately attached to the Ghost Squad. Burgess replied that he was very happy where he was on 'C' Division, and this instantly raised the ire of the former Company Sergeant-Major. Rawlings informed Burgess that he would go to the Ghost Squad whether he liked it or not, he (Rawlings) would not countenance any further discussion on the matter and that if Burgess failed to cooperate fully, his promotional prospects and any possibility of returning to 'C' Division would be seriously jeopardised. As a concession, Rawlings added that provided Burgess did cooperate, he would see that his tenure on the Ghost Squad would last just twelve months and at the end of it he would do his best to return him to 'C' Division. "With that, I was forced to accept the appointment gracefully," Burgess stated, adding, "although filled with deep depression."

The incident raises the question of why Burgess was forced into an élite unit in the face of such opposition, when so many other detective inspectors would have been delighted at such an opportunity. Undoubtedly, the likeliest answer is that Rawlings felt his authority was being challenged, something that no old-time Guv'nor would tolerate.

But in addition, why did Burgess not wish to be part of the Ghost Squad? He had obviously been recommended, probably by Hugh Young, who would have remembered him from his "X' Division Patrolling Group' days. Possibly one reason for Burgess' reticence was because Fabian, whom he obviously did not care for, was now head of the Flying Squad. But Fabian would have had nothing to do with the day-to-day running of the Ghost Squad. Perhaps it was the presence of Gosling; he would have known Gosling from their time on the Flying Squad and also from 'C' Division; but Gosling had been based at Tottenham Court Road and Burgess at West End Central. Possibly there was friction between the two men; even though they were working closely together, Burgess never once mentioned Gosling's name in his memoirs. All very confusing. There were, however, several other pertinent reasons. On the evening of 24 September 1940 a parachute mine landed on the front doorstep of West End Central police station. Detective Sergeant Frank Collins had been speaking to Burgess when the blast blew Collins through two internal walls; he was one of three people killed, and Burgess, one of the thirty officers badly cut and injured, was placed sick for a considerable time. The incident understandably adversely affected Burgess' mental health for some time. In addition, the stress of the war had so profoundly affected his wife – her brother in the RAF had just been killed – that she suffered a severe nervous breakdown and required hospitalisation. But whatever his reason for doing so, it was a bad move on Rawling's part to send Burgess to a sensitive unit which he wanted no part of.

Burgess had heard that the Ghost Squad had the advantage of unlimited expenses, obtainable immediately on request. This was undoubtedly apocryphal, the more so because Burgess never referred to the matter of expenses again. The Ghost Squad officers' expenses were certainly enhanced over the heads of their colleagues but not by much. Capstick welcomed Burgess to the unit and showed him two cars (one was almost certainly 'borrowed') which they had at their disposal; both Capstick and Burgess would say in their respective memoirs that the cars had supercharged engines under their bonnets, but this notion was nonsense. They were simply clapped-out old police cars that nobody wanted. Burgess asked permission to use his own Ford Anglia saloon, since it would not be known to the underworld, and Capstick graciously gave assent, probably because within days he would have left the squad. Capstick told Burgess to keep up his West End contacts to try to stem the flow of watches and rings being smuggled in from Switzerland.

The Ghost Squad had its disruptions because for the first three months of the year Gosling was absent attending a course of instruction at the Detective Training School. Therefore, the unit was down to a staff of three, two complete newcomers and one detective sergeant (second class) who had been with the unit for three months; but nevertheless, the information still came pouring in, as did the arrests.

Albert Blanchett, a twenty-five-year-old labourer, was arrested by Detective Constable Carpenter from 'X' Division for receiving the part-proceeds of a housebreaking at 142 Brondesbury Villas, Kilburn where property valued at £100 had been stolen; he was sentenced to three months' hard labour.

Mary Bennett, a forty-eight-year-old cleaner, Rose May Wheatley, a twenty-six-year-old housewife and Lily Knight, also a housewife aged twenty-nine, all from East London, were arrested by Detective Inspector Pirie and Detective Sergeant Edwards from the Flying Squad after being found in possession of cloth and linings, which the officers reasonably suspected of being stolen. Things, however, are not always as they seem; the ladies were guilty only of acquiring the material without coupons; Mrs. Bennett was fined £5 or twenty-eight days' imprisonment, with her companions each being fined £2, or the option of fourteen days' imprisonment.

Far less fortunate was Jessie Pound, a twenty-six-year-old housewife from Walworth who was arrested by Detective Inspector Crawford from the Flying Squad. For two cases of receiving a number of children's dresses valued at £11 1s 6d, on her first conviction Lambeth Magistrates' Court sentenced her to two concurrent terms of two months' imprisonment.

Robert Lawrence, a car hirer, and George Nicholas, a driver, were driving a Standard saloon along Regent Street, W1 on 10 February when they were stopped by Detective Inspector Judge and his Flying Squad team. Unfortunately for them, the car in which they had been stopped was a stolen one; another Standard stolen from 'E' Division was traced to their possession and so was a third stolen car. The total value of the three recovered cars was £2,000, and at the Old Bailey Lawrence (whose criminal record stretched back to 1930) was sentenced to three years' penal servitude and Nicholas, nine months' imprisonment.

This was the second tour of duty on the Flying Squad for William Cyril Judge; he had already been commended for his work in the case of King and Vigars the previous year and he would work energetically for the Ghost Squad, enjoying a distinguished career.

The disparity between the presentation of cases and the results at court could be astonishing. When George Veasey was arrested by Detective Sergeant Fisher of 'F' Division for housebreaking on the Isle of Wight, Veasey pleaded guilty to four cases of housebreaking where a total amount of property valued at £3,342 16s 3d was stolen – with not one penny of it being recovered – and asked for five other offences to be taken into consideration. He was bound over in the sum of £10 for two years to be of good behaviour and was ordered to pay £20 costs. And when five corking villains with long criminal records – one of them stretching back to 1921 – were arrested by Detective Sergeants Cole, Cox and Acott of the Flying Squad for receiving £215 worth of plastic material, all were acquitted at the County of London Sessions. Much the same happened when Detective Inspector Jackson of the Flying Squad arrested a man in possession of 307 Postal Orders – these were identified as the proceeds of a Post Office breaking at Edgware – and a Post Office date stamp which had come from a Post Office breaking at Iver, Buckinghamshire; he was discharged at Marylebone Magistrates' Court. The same fate at the same court awaited a wireless dealer who was arrested by Detective Sergeant Peter Sinclair of the Flying Squad for storebreaking and stealing five wirelesses, with £112 worth of them being recovered. Surprises were in store for Detective Sergeant Sinclair; within sixteen months he would be promoted to detective inspector and during 'The Battle of Heathrow' (*see* Chapter 6) he would sustain a badly broken arm – although there was an undoubtedly malicious rumour that during the wild mêlée it was another Squad officer who had been responsible for the fracture.

It was at this stage that Burgess was introduced to a young officer. Short, at just over five foot nine, and fit, he nevertheless walked with a slight limp; his name was Detective Constable Reginald George Grose and he was a remarkable man.

⋆   ⋆   ⋆

Grose joined the Metropolitan Police as a nineteen-year-old on 29 November 1937 and after a short spell at Streatham he was posted to 'D' Division; it was there, as Police Constable 418 'D', that he received his first commendation, for his actions in effecting an arrest for larceny from a motor car. It was during the Blitz that, together with William Aubrey Bailey, a Captain in the Church Army, Paddington, Detective Constable Sidney Cyril Coomber and Police Constable Edwin John Pope, Grose was awarded the newly struck George Medal. The citation (in respect of the first three men) read as follows:

> As a result of enemy action, buildings were damaged. Detective Constable Coomber and Police Constable Grose entered one house and found several men lying severely injured and one man trapped. They removed all of them to safety and then climbed to the second floor where they were joined by Captain Bailey. Search was made for two men known to be trapped on the premises. After removing a quantity of debris, one man was released and lowered to the ground. The rescuers then climbed to the third floor and eventually located the other man who had apparently fallen through to the floor below. Coomber, assisted by Bailey, tunnelled under the wreckage while Grose removed rubble passed out to him. In spite of the fact that debris was continually falling around them, and a large slab of stonework was hanging overhead in a dangerous position, they succeeded

in releasing the casualty. The rescues were performed while an air attack was still in progress. Huge pieces of masonry and timber were poised in perilous positions and the danger was further increased by escaping gas and water.

Within four months of receiving this award, Grose, by now an aid to CID, was again commended by the commissioner for acumen and ability in a case of possessing offensive weapons. Matters were now moving very fast; in March 1942 Grose was married, one month later he was appointed detective constable and posted back to Streatham, and three months after that he had joined the army. As a member of No 3 Army Commando, Grose was captured in the ill-fated assault on Dieppe and was appallingly treated by his captors, sustaining injuries to his spinal cord as a result of some brutal kickings. When the war came to a close, Grose was thought to have taken appropriate action against some of the guards who had 'overstepped the mark', action in which a pond figured prominently – the exact details of the retribution are unknown. Demobilised in time for Christmas 1945, Grose rejoined the police and was posted to 'X' Division; just over a year later he was selected for the Flying Squad.

It was not too long before Grose was selected as an undercover officer for the Ghost Squad; he was issued with forged army discharge papers in the name of 'Arthur Silkstone' and was introduced into some of London's toughest gangs. Alternatively, he wore his battledress and infiltrated gangs posing as a deserter. Burgess used Grose to discover how smuggled items were being brought into the United Kingdom from Switzerland.

What Grose uncovered was a sophisticated plot by a number of racing car drivers. Motor racing had re-commenced on the continent, and the watches and rings were being smuggled in concealed in false bottoms fitted to the vehicles' petrol tanks. This was how John MacDonald came to be arrested in Praed Street, Paddington, by Detective Sergeant Gerrard of the Flying Squad for being in possession of 3,120 uncustomed metal bracelets valued at £1,500, for which MacDonald was fined £200 with ten guineas costs. Sergeant Gerrard struck again a few days later when he arrested Chaim Laufer in possession of 283 smuggled gold wristlet watches valued at £6,000. The watches were confiscated by His Majesty's Customs, and Marlborough Street Magistrates' Court fined Laufer £3,000 with thirty guineas costs.

Frank William Cahill was arrested by Detective Sergeant Fisher and Detective Constable Peter Vibart of the Flying Squad for four cases of possessing 172 smuggled bottles of scent with intent to avoid purchase tax and he was sentenced to nine and nine months' imprisonment to be served consecutively and fined £100 with £25 costs.

Grose's undercover career lasted for nine months until the gangs started to smell a rat. He had been arrested on many occasions on suspicion of being a deserter and on each occasion Ghost Squad officers had gone to secure his release; the word inevitably filtered through to the underworld. One of Burgess' top informants told him that Grose's cover had been blown and Grose was brought in and informed of the circumstances; he accepted the situation philosophically and told Burgess how much he had enjoyed himself. Grose, who dressed so scruffily during his undercover work that he was refused entry to Scotland Yard to collect his pay, returned to more conventional Flying Squad duties.

★   ★   ★

The offence of larceny servant – theft from one's employer – has always been frowned upon by the courts, although it could hardly be considered to be Ghost Squad fodder. Nevertheless, stealing is stealing, so when Detective Inspector Jackson of the Flying Squad arrested Joseph Barnett and Leonard Gough on 29 March for stealing and receiving paint to the value of £34, it was quickly discovered that the property had been stolen from Barnett's employer. For two cases of larceny servant (with one case taken into consideration) Barnett was sentenced to three and three months' hard labour, consecutive, and for two cases of receiving the paint Gough received four and four months' hard labour, to be served concurrently. Two days after the initial arrests, Inspector Jackson picked up James Joseph Pearson for stealing paint valued at £120; with no previous convictions, for two cases of larceny servant, Pearson was sentenced to one and one month's imprisonment, to be served consecutively. And if those sentences seem rather harsh, consider the plight of the informant; the Informants Fund did not cater for offences of stealing from one's employer. Perhaps 10% of £34 from the loss adjusters was a small consolation.

The Ghost Squad informants offered up three active villains, plus one outsider. Detective Inspector Len Crawford and Detective Sergeants Gerrard and Dawkins swooped on a gang for housebreaking in London and the Home Counties and stealing a total of £900, of which property valued at £580 was recovered. Forty-five-year-old Thomas Edwards was sentenced to nine months' hard labour. Ethel Rose Ash, aged fifty-three, who described her occupation as that of being a 'window cleaner' and whose criminal career had commenced at the tender age of twelve, received eighteen months' hard labour. William Oswald Featherstone – a general dealer – with a criminal record dating back to 1931 received a hefty five years' penal servitude and five years' preventative detention. The outsider was a twenty-year-old Chinese waiter; it is not known how precisely he fitted into the larcenous equation, but at any event he was acquitted. Nine weeks later, two women from the same area of London as Ash had their premises searched; information had been received that they were in possession of the part-proceeds of the housebreakings committed by Ash and her associates. But nine weeks is far too long for stolen property to remain in a static position, especially when it was known that the housebreakers had been arrested; however, as a small consolation they were arrested for unlawful possession of ration books and irregularities arising therefrom.

There was a short spate of arrests of receivers of stolen furs; Daniel Desmond and Joseph Gibbons were arrested by Detective Sergeant Fisher of the Flying Squad in possession of seven fur coats valued at £140 3s 2d which were the part-proceeds of a shopbreaking four days previously. At Hampshire Assizes, Desmond, who hailed from Shirland Road, W9, was dealt with sympathetically, being bound over in the sum of £5 to be of good behaviour for a period of two years. Gibbons, however, was dealt with rather more severely, after he admitted living on the Isle of Wight, which was where the shopbreaking had taken place, and he received six months' hard labour. And one of Burgess' informants fingered Robert Evelyn Hayley for a larceny dwelling at 9 Brett Street, SW3, where furs valued at £150 were stolen. The property was recovered intact, and Hayley was charged with receiving the goods and sentenced to one months' imprisonment.

Eric John Bailee, a thirty-seven-year-old steel erector, was arrested by Detective Sergeant Wallis of the Flying Squad for receiving a quantity of revenue and postage stamps valued at £400; at the County of London Sessions he was sentenced to eighteen months' imprisonment.

Joseph Janes, a forty-year-old clerk, had received his first criminal conviction in 1931. He was arrested by Detective Sergeant Cornish of 'D' Division in Plymouth for housebreaking and possessing housebreaking implements by day. Janes had had a good run for his money; he had been circulated as being wanted for those offences for twenty-one months, so it was rather fitting that at the County of London Sessions he was sentenced to twenty-one months' imprisonment.

All that was recovered when Alan Murray and Michael Taylor, both aged twenty-eight and both clerks, were arrested was £150; a poor return for the jewellery valued at £3,000 which was the result of a 'snatch' in Watford, together with the housebreakings at Richmond and Esher, where property valued at £1,000 was stolen.

A combined operation by Detective Sergeant Cook of Leyton Police Station and Detective Inspector Jarvis and Detective Sergeant Veasey of the Flying Squad resulted in arrests for two cases of attempted housebreaking on 30 April. Richard Cannadine, John Walker and Jeremiah Patrick Harrigan, dealer, dealer and painter respectively and the proud possessors of substantial criminal records, appeared at the County of London Sessions five months after their arrest and were sentenced to twenty-one months', nine and nine months' imprisonment.

Patrick Joseph and Agnes Swift, aged twenty-nine and twenty-four respectively and both of no fixed abode, were arrested by Detective Inspector Jackson and Detective Sergeant Bowery of the Flying Squad for being in unlawful possession of 168 pairs of nylons, valued at £252. At Clerkenwell Magistrates' Court, both were fined £100 and ten guineas costs or the option of two months' imprisonment in default. Sadly, the fines and costs were not paid. Frank Dominic Phelan did ease the pain by paying his fines after he and Thomas Christopher Michael Eaton-Eland were arrested by Detective Inspector Davis of the Flying Squad who found them in possession of 500 pairs of nylons valued at £750. On two counts of receiving Phelan had been fined £55 13s or the option of two months' imprisonment and £75 or three months' imprisonment. However, with the fines paid, he still had two one-month concurrent sentences to serve, as did his co-accused. A fifty-seven-year-old retired gentleman, known to the police since 1932, had his case discharged. Far more fortunate were Stanley Pickering Lasenby and his brother, Jonathan Pickering Lasenby, aged sixty-one and sixty-eight respectively, after they were arrested by 'X' Division's Detective Constable Robertson for receiving a quantity of gents' suitings worth £100; each were fined £10 by the magistrates at West London Court, and the fines were promptly paid.

★   ★   ★

Crime trends go in patterns; one that the commissioner and the Home Office wanted eradicated sooner rather than later was the impersonation of police officers. The gangs – there were several of them – were highly credible. They dressed like detectives, complete with raincoats and Homburg hats, drove cars similar to those used by the CID, showed convincing-looking warrant cards and used police phraseology.

Their ways of working were diverse; sometimes they would enter a jeweller's shop, ask to see the owner's most recent purchases of second-hand jewellery, declare that some of the items appeared to be stolen and, after providing a receipt, leave with the goods. Other gangs would get one of their group to take stolen goods such as a consignment of cigarettes or a crate of whisky to a shopkeeper for sale; after he left, the bogus detectives would enter the shop. Having discovered the stolen goods, a heavy hint would be dropped to the shopkeeper that for a fee, they could turn a blind eye to his activities and, pocketing the bribe (which was inevitably offered) and taking the stolen merchandise, they would leave the premises. A variation on this theme was for the 'detectives' to enter the shop whilst the illegal deal was being transacted and arrest both the seller and the terrified shopkeeper. Whilst the seller was dragged outside and the commodity was being safely stowed away in the boot of the 'Squad-car', the proprietor of the shop would receive a 'once-in-a-lifetime' offer; when he paid up, as he inevitably did, the whole phony team would vanish.

So convincing were these fraudsters that it was widely thought that the persons responsible for these offences were indeed off-duty police officers; and when the finger of accusation was pointed at the Ghost Squad something had to be done quickly. It seemed not to be a moment too soon, since a scandal of near-catastrophic proportions was just about to hit the Flying Squad.

Two police officers named Albert Edwin Compton and Harry Gordon Cooper had joined the Metropolitan Police on the same day in 1930. After being promoted to detective sergeant (second class) Compton was posted to the Flying Squad in 1939 and there he stayed for over five years. This was followed by a short divisional posting until six months later he was promoted to detective sergeant (first class) and posted back to the Flying Squad in 1945. Cooper was already there; he had arrived on the Flying Squad in 1944 as a detective constable. Three months after Compton's arrival on the Squad, Cooper was promoted to the rank of detective sergeant (second class) and was retained on the Squad; the two men worked together and were commended together by the commissioner on three occasions in 1946 for offences involving forgery, robbery – and bribery. It brought Compton's total number of commendations up to a very creditable fifty-nine.

And then, in March 1947, Cooper was transferred to 'T' Division; there was nothing particularly unusual in that, because he had been serving on the Flying Squad for three years. However, arrest swiftly followed and later that year both men stood trial at the Old Bailey charged with four counts of larceny, with four alternative charges of robbery and one count of conspiracy to steal. What was alleged was that Cooper and Compton had, in the course of their duties, searched premises and, upon finding property reasonably suspected of being unlawfully obtained, had either demanded money from the occupant or had taken the occupant's wallet from his person and helped themselves to cash from it. The jury acquitted them on the substantive counts but found them guilty of conspiracy; "a bad and illogical verdict," remarked the Attorney General, Sir Hartley Shawcross, the following year. On 1 July Compton was sentenced to twelve months' imprisonment and Cooper to nine months. Both men immediately appealed, their convictions were quashed and they were reinstated. Because of their acquittal, no discipline proceedings could be instituted, since this would have placed them in double jeopardy. Nevertheless, on the same day in November 1947 both Cooper and Compton were abruptly returned to uniform and posted, Cooper to 'V' Division and Compton to 'W' Division.

The case caused a great deal of adverse publicity for the police and, indeed, there appeared to be a backlash for the Flying Squad themselves following Compton and Cooper's convictions. Three days after the men were initially convicted, the *Daily Mail* proclaimed, 'CID men seeking decision on suspects' and suggested that Flying Squad officers operating in the West End of London were seeking an audience with both the commissioner and the AC(C). The officers wished for clarification on the handling of enquiries into the black market, stated the newspaper, and were anxious that clear-cut rules should be laid down as to the procedure they should adopt when dealing with intelligence supplied by informants. This probably arose from the rumour which was circulating that the financial status of certain officers might well come under scrutiny. The *Daily Mail* reporter further commented:

> There is no suggestion that the Yard men are relaxing any efforts in the drive against crime, but I understand that no major arrests have been made for ten days. Detectives, it is believed, are carrying out their duties strictly to routine.

The reporter certainly had good sources of information; for fourteen days prior to the publication of that edition of the newspaper, no arrests, major or minor, had been carried out by the Ghost Squad – they would not resume until four days later.

No doubt conciliatory words were spoken to soothe the ruffled Flying Squad feathers, because they now redoubled their efforts to find and arrest the bogus detectives. One obvious customer was Robert William Cole, a forty-year-old carpenter whose criminal record had commenced when he was sixteen. Cole had been working with an accomplice who had offered a quantity of stolen whisky to a shop-owner. The transaction completed, Cole had entered the shop, pretending to be a police officer, seized the £250 which had just been paid over and left with the money, the whisky and the accomplice. He had been arrested for this offence but had failed to surrender to his bail at the Old Bailey on 7 January 1947. Cole was arrested by Detective Sergeant Gerrard of the Flying Squad and was sentenced to eighteen months' imprisonment for two cases of larceny (trick) and conspiracy.

However, during his period of freedom, it was clear that Cole and his associate had been boasting of how easy it had been to commit this type of offence, and this would have been given credence to those criminals who believed Compton and Cooper to be guilty. Two more would-be detectives, Thomas Jones and Ronald Spencer, went a little further by threatening to accuse a shopkeeper of receiving stolen property, adding that they would accept £150 as a suitable recompense for neglecting to carry out their duties. Instead, Jones (who asked for two other offences to be taken into consideration) received five years' penal servitude and Spencer eighteen months' imprisonment. Once again, the arrests were carried out by the Flying Squad: Detective Inspectors Davis and Robinson. Still the lesson had not been learnt by the criminals. It was not until the following year that Ghost Squad informants put up the names of two thieves who had stolen a carpet from Maples Store, Tottenham Court Road and sold it to a shopkeeper; no sooner had they left when Laing Johnstone Ratcliffe and Walter William Thompson appeared as bogus detectives and demanded £250 from the buyer.

One of Gosling's informants heard what had happened, telephoned Gosling and rather recklessly accused Gosling and his officers of being responsible. Using all of his persuasive charm, Gosling induced the snout to tell him all he knew. He did – and with that information, plus intelligence from other snouts, Gosling went into action. The same day, the two men were traced to London's West End and arrested by Detective Inspector Judge of the Flying Squad and John Gosling; the arrests were carried out in a pub, and a fake police warrant card was found in their possession. It was only when the third member of the gang was arrested two weeks later that this type of offence was effectively smashed. Clifford Johnstone was arrested by Inspector Judge and the gang appeared at the Old Bailey, which resulted in Ratcliffe being sentenced to two years' imprisonment, whilst Thompson and Johnstone received three-and-a-half years and three years' penal servitude, respectively.

★   ★   ★

Then something rather curious happened. On 30 May Detective Sergeant Carter of 'D' Division arrested Francis George Farringdon. He was well overdue. He had been charged with housebreaking on 'S' Division and had failed to answer his bail. Carter arrested him for stealing a quantity of dangerous drugs from Messrs John Bell and Croydon of Wigmore Street, W1, and once arrested he was found to be in possession of a further quantity of dangerous drugs; he was further charged with stealing a £500 car. At the County of London Sessions Farringdon was sentenced to three years' penal servitude. Eleven days later – a long gap between Ghost Squad arrests – Richard Worthing Patenson was arrested by Detective Constable Carpenter of 'X' Division for stealing a quantity of dangerous drugs from 222 Kensal Road, North Kensington and was duly sentenced to one month's imprisonment. There may have been a connection between the two men, if only because possession of dangerous drugs was an uncommon offence in 1947 and the disparity between the divisions used for the arrests may have been to cloak the identity of the informant – a common Ghost Squad ploy. After all, Farringdon – who declined to give his address – was arrested by a 'D' Division officer, whilst Patenson – who lived in Paddington which was situated on 'D' Division – was arrested by an 'X' Division officer.

But the strange thing that occurred between those arrests was that on 9 June the officer in charge of the Ghost Squad, Divisional Detective Inspector Jamieson, after just over four months in the post, was abruptly transferred to 'D' Division, which was where he had originally served prior to his transfer to the Flying Squad. Why, it is not known; whether it was at his own request is not recorded. No impropriety should be inferred on Jamieson's part; indeed, he went on to bigger and better things. It is possible that Jamieson felt that with the arrest of Compton and Cooper, followed by the arrest of Cole, the search was on for other bogus police officers, and the Flying Squad in general and the Ghost Squad by imputation was tainted. In fact, it was about the time of Compton and Cooper's arrests that Bob Fabian was transferred to another department at C1 after just two short years as the head of the Flying Squad. John Gosling had returned to the Ghost Squad from the Detective Training School and within six weeks of Jamieson's transfer was promoted to detective inspector, second class, but that can have had no bearing on the matter. In fact, Jamieson had stipulated that he would only take on the job of heading the Ghost Squad, if Gosling remained there. It was simply a curious incident in the history of the unit.

Jamieson was replaced by Claud Reginald Baker. Born in 1904 at Colchester, Essex, Baker had been a salesman prior to joining the Metropolitan Police in 1925 when he was posted to 'C' Division. For the next nine years Baker applied himself to learning his trade as a uniformed police constable, an aid to CID and finally a detective constable. London's West End was a first-class, cosmopolitan area to learn the art of coppering, and having passed all of the necessary examinations and collected sixteen commissioner's commendations for outstanding police work, he was well suited for his promotion to detective sergeant (second class) in April 1934, when he was posted to the Flying Squad. During the next seven and a half years, his hard work continued and he was promoted to detective sergeant (first class) and retained on the Flying Squad. By the time he was promoted to detective inspector (second class) on 27 October 1941 and transferred to 'M' Division, he had been awarded another seventeen commissioner's commendations. He stayed on 'M' Division a bare two and a half years before being posted back to the Yard, this time to C1 Department where he applied himself to the investigation of murder, forgery and offences under the Consumer Rationing Order. Promoted to divisional detective inspector, one year later he headed the Ghost Squad.

★   ★   ★

Detective Sergeants Johnny Franklyn (a useful boxer) and Gullett of the Flying Squad arrested Frederick Andrews, a thirty-two-year-old salesman from Westbourne Terrace, W2 for being in unlawful possession of 7,700 petrol coupons, a rubber stamp and pad and, rather incongruously, two overcoats; he was sentenced to four months' imprisonment. And four days later, Rubin Jesse Benabo, a nineteen-year-old clerk who had been found in Denman Street, W1 in possession of $300, appeared at Bow Street Magistrates' Court and was fined £50 with eight guineas costs.

Probably the most tremendous piece of informing from a Ghost Squad snout came with the arrest of Wilfred Kenneth Laidler. The arrest was carried out not by the Ghost Squad but by Chief Inspector Ames of Wakefield Police, and Laidler, a twenty-eight-year-old lorry driver, decided that for reasons best known to himself it would not be prudent to provide his address. He was arrested for being concerned with others in garagebreaking and stealing a lorry, vacuum cleaners and clocks;

appearing at Wakefield Magistrates' Court, he was remanded on a charge of being concerned in the theft of cigarettes to the value of £27,000. The reward offered of at least £2,700 – well over £100,000 by today's standards –would have been sufficient to have purchased the industrious snout in 1947 three very respectable houses. The arrest by a constabulary officer was part of the Ghost Squad's genius; when suspicion fell on a local villain for being an informant, it was not unknown for associates of the arrested thieves to keep observation on the addresses of loss adjusters in an attempt to identify the grass and his detective handler.

Thomas Albert Lobb was another lorry driver who declined to give his address when he was arrested by Detective Sergeant Brodie from the Flying Squad; all Brodie had to do was to hand Lobb over to the City of London Police at Bishopsgate where he was wanted for larceny of a safe and contents, together with a car. The productive Mr. Lobb was also wanted for larceny at Chelmsford, Essex, North Woolwich and also at Clerkenwell, as well as for failing to surrender his bail at North London Magistrates' Court. The magistrates must have been in a benign mood when sentencing him, because he was fortunate in being sentenced to a total of six months' imprisonment.

Receivers of stolen property continued to be pulled in; Alfred George MacDonald, a thirty-six-year-old window cleaner, was arrested at Hertford Road, Dalston by Detective Inspector Davies and Detective Sergeant Veasey of the Flying Squad after he was found in possession of eight fur coats, three fur coatees and three fur capes, valued together at £1,000. MacDonald was sentenced to two concurrent terms of four months' imprisonment; two ladies from the same address who were also arrested walked free. Alfred Thomas Rouse was arrested by Flying Squad officers, originally for the offence of warehousebreaking and stealing whisky valued at £175; he was convicted of receiving and, due in part to his criminal record which had commenced twelve years previously, was sentenced to three years' penal servitude.

At the other end of the criminal scale, Albert Russers, a twenty-nine-year-old labourer, was arrested in Paddington by an aid to CID, Police Constable 571 'X' Sanderson, who discovered that he was in possession of a quantity of tin foil 'and other metal'. Since the property was valued at £2, Marylebone Magistrates decided that a fine of £3 was a proper punishment. The following day, 17 July, saw a further arrest courtesy of 'X' Division; Detective Constable Robertson arrested Peter Johnson, an eighteen-year-old soldier from the Royal Artillery at Woolwich, whose criminal career had commenced when he was fourteen. Johnson was in possession of two wristlet watches and other property valued at £30, the proceeds of a housebreaking at 218 Randolph Avenue, Paddington, which had occurred the previous day. It was darkly hinted that 'other property' found in Johnson's possession 'will be the subject of further charges'; but whether it was or not, Johnson was bound over in the sum of £5 for a period of twelve months. On the same day as Johnson's arrest, Detective Sergeant Brodie of the Flying Squad was carrying out an arrest of his own in the Brixton Road. Frederick Weiner, a forty-six-year-old advertising contractor, was far from his home in Antrim Road, Belfast when he was stopped in possession of sixty-six pairs of nylons valued at £99. But these were not stolen nylons, they were smuggled ones, and for three Custom and Excise offences Mr. Weiner was fined a total of £150 by Lambeth Magistrates' Court. Smuggling was one offence often encountered by officers, who acting on Ghost Squad information (although not that supplied from Burgess' informants) were in reality looking for thieves and receivers. However, a really unusual case occurred when Detective Sergeants Elliott and Aspinall of the Flying Squad arrested Percy Victor Trinder, a forty-four-year-old pig breeder of Hounslow, for receiving three and a half tons of wheat. The wheat was not stolen, any more than the nylons in Mr. Weiner's possession had been. Instead, Brentford Magistrates' Court fined Trinder £150 with five guineas costs or three months' imprisonment in default for 'obtaining unauthorised feeding stuff'.

Samuel Gerrard, a twenty-year-old labourer of no fixed address, was arrested by Police Constable 118 'C' Ward (an aid to CID) for storebreaking and stealing four adding machines, which were recovered, valued at £270. Within three weeks Gerrard appeared at the County of London Sessions, where he was sentenced to three years' Borstal detention.

Detective Inspector Judge and his Flying Squad team were waiting to arrest Albert James Tidiman, Ernest Page, David Joseph William West and John George Whale, all from East London and the possessors of criminal records, for the theft of electrical equipment valued at £2,200 from a lorry on 22 July. Two days later, the fifth member of the gang, William Kirby★ was arrested by Detective Sergeant Acott and the court decided that although he and West did not possess the longest criminal records, they were the most culpable because they received the longest sentences: twenty-one months' imprisonment, with the other three gang members each receiving eighteen months.

The arresting officer, Detective Sergeant Acott, has already featured in the Ghost Squad return of arrests. Born Basil Montague Acott (but never known as anything other than 'Bob') in 1913 at Ilford, Essex, Acott joined the police in 1933 and after collecting four commissioner's commendations on 'G' Division as a detective constable, he volunteered for wartime service with the Royal Air Force and was awarded a Distinguished Flying Cross. Posted to the Flying Squad as a detective sergeant in 1946, Acott busied himself with Ghost Squad arrests and also participated in what would become known as 'The Battle of Heathrow' the following year.

★   ★   ★

Two stokers, Brian Prestedge aged twenty-four and Edward Edwards, seven years his junior, were arrested by Detective Sergeant Brodie of the Flying Squad for shopbreaking at 39 Old Compton Street, W1 and stealing shirts and ties which, bearing in mind the prestigious location, amounted to the rather paltry value of £11. The case produced one of those strange anomalies of sentencing. Edwards admitted three other offences of shopbreaking plus another of larceny and was bound over in his own recognizance in the sum of £10 to be of good behaviour for two years. Prestedge (who did not admit further offences) received twelve months' hard labour. On the same day, the 'G' Division area car stopped and arrested William Mason, a thirty-six-year-old glassblower from Shadwell, for stealing two tons of sheet lead and a lorry. The total value of £250 seemed inappropriate for such a weighty amount of metal, as did the penalty imposed: a fine of £5 or one month's imprisonment. And

---

★ To his shame, a relative of the author.

later the same day the indefatigable Sergeant Brodie was busy again; this time in Cartwright Gardens, NW1 where he arrested Charles Ashe and Harold Steele who were in possession of eighty-five pairs of nylon stockings. In fact, these were uncustomed goods and for that offence, plus evading purchase tax, Ashe was fined £125 or three months' imprisonment in default and Steele was fined £300 or six months' imprisonment in default. Sadly, neither of the defendants had the means to pay the fines.

Next came a case which caused Gosling considerable concern. At seven o'clock on the morning of 30 July, he and Burton were keeping observation behind a wall at the bottom of a mews off Hackney Road. Gosling had received information that a lorry-load of stolen property would be arriving there, and this indeed proved to be the case. A large lorry arrived at the bottom of the mews and as it came to a halt both doors of the cab were covered by Detective Inspector Judge of the Flying Squad and his men, and the occupants, Edward Simpson, a stallholder and George Skidmore, a driver, were detained. The lorry was found to contain tobacco and a million assorted cigarettes, valued at £7,000, stolen from a warehouse by means of robbery with violence; the night-watchman had been assaulted, tied up and gagged and was currently in hospital suffering from shock and abrasions. So far then, so good.

It was now that doubts started to be raised. The lorry, which belonged to a small firm of contractors, was promptly reported stolen – "Wonderful," noted Gosling, "how news gets about". The owner of the lorry was most irate, notwithstanding that he was Simpson's brother-in-law. Both Simpson and Skidmore insisted that they had taken no part in the theft; Gosling was completely unconvinced because he had no doubt that they were specialists in stealing cigarettes. However, the night-watchman was brought to the police station and Gosling discovered that he was an ex-guardsman, aged about twenty-five, six feet three and extremely muscular. Simpson and Skidmore were both quite short, neither of them weighed much more than eight-and-a-half stone and their physiques could at best be described as 'scrawny'. Gosling was convinced that neither of the two men could have lifted the large cartons of cigarettes without assistance. The night-watchman was given, as Gosling put it, "a going-over" but he stuck to his story and at the Old Bailey he gave evidence of being brutally assaulted. There was nothing that Gosling could do about it. Simpson was sentenced to twenty-one months' imprisonment and Skidmore to three years' penal servitude. As Claud Baker noted in his report to the commissioner, both men were believed to be part of a gang of violent criminals, so perhaps it was other members of the gang who had brutally assaulted the victim and lifted the cartons of cigarettes into the lorry. And perhaps not. The case raised more questions than it answered and although the night-watchman was sacked, it was not, as Gosling put it, "a very satisfactory conclusion".

Detective Sergeant Walsh and his team from West End Central police station had their hands full when they made arrests for a shopbreaking at 2 Coventry Street, W1, where ladies underwear was stolen. One of the prisoners, George Henry Bull, was already circulated as being wanted for a shopbreaking at Luton, Bedfordshire and for escaping from military custody, and charges were preferred against Bull and George William Christie for a shopbreaking in Regent Street.

The way in which the courts dealt with receivers of stolen property still fluctuated; John Fraser Stone and Kenneth William Appleby were arrested by Detective Sergeant Rawlings and other members of the Flying Squad for receiving 16,200 stolen cigarettes valued at £135; both were fined £25 or the option of six weeks' imprisonment in default – they paid. And when Detective Inspector Bradford and Detective Sergeant Gullett of the Flying Squad arrested Alji Seymsiewicz (a Russian of no occupation) for receiving suit lengths and linings valued £1,500, it transpired that, in fact, he had acquired cloth without the benefit of coupons – his subsequent fine of £200 was promptly paid. Inspector Bradford had much more luck the following day when he and his team arrested William Leonard Jones, a clerk, George Edward Potter, a street trader and William Henry Fisher, a driver, for receiving a quantity of ladies' coats valued at £800. It was thought that the men were part of a gang of active shopbreakers; nevertheless, the evidence – or lack of it – proved otherwise and they were dealt with for conspiracy and receiving, with Jones being sentenced to fifteen months' imprisonment and Potter and Fisher two years each. A thirty-five-year-old bill poster with no previous convictions also stood trial with them; he was acquitted.

Just two weeks later, Inspector Bradford and his team struck again; this time at the prestigious Dolphin Square, SW1. This was a case put up to Gosling by 'Harry the Cabbie', and forty-five-year-old Richard Fenton, whose criminal pedigree stretched back to 1918, was arrested for being in possession of three fur coats and a quantity of jewellery, valued together at £2,000, the result of two housebreakings at St. Albans, Hertfordshire. A lady who shared the same address as Fenton was brought in, as well; she was acquitted but Fenton was sentenced to four years' penal servitude.

Another two weeks went by, and once more Inspector Bradford and his Flying Squad team were pointed in the right direction by a Ghost Squad snout. This time Frederick Short, a soldier, Alfred Florey, a labourer and Kathleen Smith, a waitress, were arrested for receiving fur coats and capes valued together at £1,600, the proceeds of a shopbreaking in Portsmouth. Short was sentenced to fifteen months, Florey to twelve months and Smith to six months; sadly, the man thought to be the principal receiver was acquitted.

Some Ghost squad cases were best forgotten. Morris Freeman, a fifty-four-year-old managing director of Harlow, together with Hannah Sumray, a receptionist aged forty-nine, appeared at court for rationing offences – they had unlawfully supplied thirty-six dozen eggs. Freeman was fined £50, Sumray £25, and both were ordered to pay five guineas costs. Little better was the case of Max Wender, a fifty-five-year-old costumier and William Phelan, a forty-year-old general dealer, who appeared in court for possessing and transferring 1,000 forged clothing coupons in Berners Street, W1, six months previously. Wender was fined £40, Phelan was fined £60, and JB Sandbach, the chairman at Marlborough Street Magistrates' Court, ordered both of them to pay ten guineas costs. Surely the bottom of the barrel was scraped with the arrest of Leonard William Debenham, a forty-four-year-old salesman from Maidstone, Kent. He was stopped in Charing Cross Road by an aid to CID, Police Constable 352 'C' Rees, for unlawful possession of a tennis racquet, value £5. It is entirely probable that the Ghost Squad snout who fingered him was dissatisfied with his reward.

Stuart Ellis, a barman, was arrested by Detective Sergeant Anderson of the Flying Squad for receiving eight shirts valued at £11. In fact, the shirts were not stolen; Ellis had acquired them without coupons, an offence for which he was fined £12, a good result for him. Unfortunately, Ellis was also a deserter, so he was handed over to a military escort, which was a less good result.

On 13 August James Noonan was arrested for being in unlawful possession of 380 petrol coupons for which he was fined £5 or the option of one month's imprisonment; three weeks later, three arrests were made for receiving twelve hundredweight of strip copper; the culprits were either bound over to keep the peace or discharged. They were commonplace, unremarkable arrests; but the common denominator was the arresting officer, who was Reggie Grose, now carrying out regular duties.

But other officers were performing more unconventional duties, and strange things were happening in the world of police-work, to those not in the know. Fred Lambert (later to rise to the rank of detective chief superintendent) recalled, as a post-war aid to CID, patrolling with his partner one evening when a van roared past them, closely followed by a marked police car, its bell ringing. The van came to an abrupt halt, the occupants leapt from the vehicle and were jumped upon by the crew of the pursing police car. The driver sprang out of the van and appeared to be completely unnoticed by the uniform officers as he dashed off down the street. "Come on!" cried Lambert, but his partner restrained him. Muttering the name of a certain detective sergeant whose back could be discerned vanishing in the distance, his more worldly-wise companion added, "Ghost Squad business!" Said Lambert, almost sixty years later, "I was learning fast!"

Len Crawford has already been mentioned as another officer who had dabbled in undercover work; having not shaved for a week, he was introduced to a gang of con-men as 'Morrie Freedman'. The meeting took place at the Angel, Islington, and the bearded Crawford arrived in his own Ford 10. After going from one pub to another (with Gosling in hot pursuit in a 'borrowed' taxi) the gang finally accepted that Crawford was indeed Morrie Freedman and tried to sell him a carton supposedly containing cigarettes, but which was in fact full of rubbish. The magistrate, however, dismissed the case, saying that Crawford had been aware of the fraud from its inception. By 17 September, a clean-shaven Crawford was involved in more conventional policing, arresting Alfred Fraser, a deserter, for receiving ration and identity cards and seeing him sentenced to one month's imprisonment; this had a knock-on effect three days later, when Crawford arrested Frederick Joseph Whitney for being a deserter from the Royal Navy.

Thomas Droy, a sixty-two-year-old painter from Islington was arrested by Detective Inspector Bradford of the Flying Squad in possession of handbags, clocks and cigarette cases, valued at £2,000. Although he had no previous convictions, Old Street Magistrates sentenced Droy to three concurrent terms of three months' imprisonment. And Terrence Foy, a twenty-two-year-old street trader foolishly declined to give his address after he was arrested by Detective Sergeant Wallis of the Flying Squad for attempted officebreaking at Leyton High Road. It prompted Stratford Magistrates to remand him in custody for a week, and on his next appearance Foy demonstrated even more obtuseness, because having been fined £5 for the offence he decided not to pay and settled for one month's imprisonment instead.

Thomas Waistle, aged twenty-four from Darlington, and John William Chadwick, aged twenty from Salford, were stopped in possession of jewellery valued at £250 by Detective Sergeant Fisher and Detective Constable Vibart from the Flying Squad; the property was identified as the proceeds from four cases of housebreaking in the Manchester area. Three days later Sergeant Fisher arrested Israel Farra, a fifty-two-year-old jeweller from Tottenham Court Road. The $275 in his possession should have been offered to the Treasury; because it had not been, Bow Street Magistrates fined Farra £204 with twenty guineas costs. Martin Cardash, another jeweller, aged thirty-four, was arrested in possession of twenty-five watches worth £150, which were uncustomed goods, and for harbouring them Cardash was fined £100 with ten guineas costs. It was clear that Burgess' informants had been working at full stretch again in the battle against smuggling. However, the ten furs and the jewellery, valued at £50 and found in possession of Gilbierre Rolande D'Oliverre, a thirty-two-year-old secretary, were certainly stolen; but he was bound over in the sum of £5 for twelve months with forty shillings costs, which were paid.

With some offences it proved hard to convince jurors or magistrates of the guilt of the prisoners in the dock. Among these was the case of the furriers, one male from Ilford, the other female from Dagenham, who were arrested by Detective Inspector Robinson of the Flying Squad in possession of two stolen fur coats valued at £1,400; both of them were acquitted. The same conclusion awaited a husband and wife from Harrow, who were arrested by Detective Inspector Judge of the Flying

Squad in possession of thirty-seven forged Bank of England notes. The following day, the same officer arrested a twenty-year-old salesman from Bethnal Green who was in possession of jewellery valued at £135 and stolen by means of housebreaking on 'V' Division; his case was discharged.

Detective Sergeant Gullett of the Flying Squad has already featured prominently in the catalogue of Ghost Squad arrests; his arrest rate continued, unabated. On 2 October he arrested Johannes Redel for being in possession of two forged $100 bills; he was sentenced to nine months' imprisonment. Three days later he arrested William John Bevan and Raymond Larkin. A ring, vacuum cleaner and items of clothing, the proceeds from a larceny in dwelling, were found in their possession, as was property from a shopbreaking. Both were dealt with for receiving and both were sentenced to concurrent terms of three months' imprisonment. Four days after that, Gullett and his team arrested John Henry Steele, who described his profession as that of "a film artiste", for being in possession of two suits, the proceeds of a housebreaking on 'C' Division. Dealt with for receiving, Steele was sentenced to six months' imprisonment.

Burgess was called out late one evening by an informant whom he met in a pub in Chelsea and who pointed out a man drinking in the saloon bar. The informant told Burgess that the man was in possession of some valuable jewellery and that an associate was en route to purchase it; therefore action had to be taken at once. Burgess struggled with his conscience – it meant breaking the rule that Ghost Squad officers did not get involved in arrests – but nevertheless, the arrest of the housebreaker and his associate were made, ostensibly by Detective Sergeant Goddard and Detective Constable Guiver from 'B' Division's CID. The owners of the property, Sir Laurence Olivier and his wife, Vivien Leigh, were delighted to be reunited with at least some of the jewellery, valued at £250, which had been stolen from their London home in Smith Street, Chelsea, by means of housebreaking a few days previously. It had been a good year for the actor, who had been knighted and had produced, directed and (with his hair dyed blond) starred in the Two Cities film, *Hamlet*. The outlook for 1947 (and much of 1948) was far less rosy for Frederick John Parsons and Ivor Morris, who had been arrested for the Oliviers' housebreaking; Parsons was charged with the housebreaking and both men were also charged with receiving. It was felt that both men had been actively engaged in housebreaking in the West End prior to their arrests, and Parsons went away for twenty-one months, with Morris receiving twelve months' imprisonment.

Even less impressed than Parsons and Morris were the British public. Three weeks after that intrepid duo's arrest, the bacon ration was halved, the King's speech outlined proposals for the nationalisation of the gas industry (this was implemented on 1 May 1949) and a ban was imposed on the importation of tobacco from the United States. A fortnight later, potato rationing was introduced and during an emergency budget the Chancellor announced an increase in Profits and Purchase tax as well as a rise on drinks duty.

★ ★ ★

It was around this time that Detective Constable Robertson of 'X' Division made another excellent pair of arrests. Robert Stocker, a labourer, and Michael John Grogan, a dealer, were arrested for stealing fur coats and other furs valued at £800 by means of housebreaking at Epsom. Stocker was sentenced to twelve months' imprisonment and Grogan to eighteen months; two weeks later, a further arrest in this case was carried out by Robertson – his time to a posting with the Flying Squad was getting closer.

Thomas Gullett (no relation to the enterprising Flying Squad officer of the same name) was arrested by Detective Sergeant Mannings for a burglary at Bow Street, and property was recovered to the value of £41 10s 0d. Gullett was sentenced to fourteen days' imprisonment and his Borstal licence was revoked.

Tommy Butler, now a detective sergeant on 'G' Division, arrested Kathleen Florence Roberts, a forty-six-year-old housewife. The musquash coat valued at £50 found in her possession was the proceeds of a housebreaking at Luton.

Detective Sergeants Marner and McVernon of the Flying Squad now started a good run of arrests. First, over a period of four days they carried out two arrests for an officebreaking at St. James Street where they recovered typewriters valued at £300 which had been stolen. Later the same day, they made three arrests for a shopbreaking at Messrs. Alkits Ltd., Charing Cross Road where clothing valued at £1,070 was stolen. Then the day following their last arrest, they caught Gordon Fitzgerald and

Ernest Perren, both Coldstream Guardsmen, for being found in a building by night for an unlawful purpose; Perren was sentenced to three months' imprisonment, whilst Fitzgerald was fined £5. Two days later the duo arrested Ernest William Juden, a labourer from London's Victoria. He was charged with two cases of larceny dwelling, at 21 Ealing Village, W5 and 22 Elm Crescent, W5, and was sentenced to a total of six months' imprisonment.

Detective Sergeant Fisher made a late-night arrest in the Old Kent Road of a nineteen-year-old labourer for being a suspected person, loitering with intent to commit a felony and possessing housebreaking implements by night. A few days later he arrested forty-four-year-old Abraham Pevovar, who described his occupation as that of a merchant. Fisher, however, preferred to describe him as "a most persistent receiver who has eluded arrest for some years" and after he searched his premises at Noel Street, W1, Fisher recovered a quantity of woollen goods stolen in transit on the railway. Another of the Flying Squad's customers who described himself as a merchant was arrested by Detective Sergeants Driscoll and Acott, together with a forty-one-year-old clerk from Wapping. They were in possession of three bales of cloth, the result of a larceny from a vehicle, together with three bales of blankets, at a total value of £400. Then Detective Constable Vibart arrested Albert Henry Martin for a housebreaking at Eden Grove, Islington, three months previously and for stealing property valued at £350; and a fifty-year-old lady, described as a dealer, was charged with feloniously receiving part of the proceeds, jewellery valued at £200.

Information given to Detective Sergeant Charles of 'W' Division resulted in Brian George Willy, George William Webb, Minnie Elizabeth Webb and Jack Raymond Driscoll – all labourers, with the exception of Mrs. Webb – being arrested after being found in possession of eighteen fur coats and a sable, valued at £800, the result of a shopbreaking at Guildford. Willy was sentenced to two years' imprisonment, Driscoll to fifteen months and forty-six-year-old Webb and his forty-four-year-old wife, considered by the court to be the least culpable of the quartet, were bound over in the sum of £5 to keep the peace for two years; which they undoubtedly did.

Alfred William Sharp, a dealer, was arrested by Detective Sergeant Wallis of the Flying Squad on 19 November for a robbery at Northampton; the same day, Sidney Munn, a clerk, and Millicent Harlick, a saleswoman, were arrested by Detective Sergeants Aspinal and Elliot, part of the same Flying Squad team as Wallis, for housebreaking at Northampton. Although they were handed to an escort, Munn must have been given bail, because on New Year's Day 1948 he was arrested again, this time by Detective Sergeant Gloyne of 'N' Division, for falsely representing himself as someone who could secure accommodation – in this fashion he had obtained the sums of £45 and £30. The outstanding member of the gang, Robert Mantle, was arrested by two 'C' Division aids to CID three weeks later. The total value of the stolen property was £1,600; at Northampton Assizes Mantle was sentenced to seven years' penal servitude, Sharp to five years' penal servitude, Munn to four years' penal servitude and Harlick to eighteen months' imprisonment; a forty-year-old commission agent was acquitted.

Robert H Smith, aged nineteen of no fixed address, was arrested by Detective Constable Grose of the Flying Squad on 20 November for stealing a radio worth £65 from the Regent Palace Hotel. Perhaps to mark the wedding of Princess Elizabeth and Philip of Greece at Westminster Abbey the same day, Bow Street Magistrates' Court exercised a measure of mercy and fined him just £15.

Between 7 and 11 November, a shopbreaking occurred at 44 Charlotte Street, W1 where ladies cloth coats valued at £2,281 were stolen. Two weeks later a twenty-six-year-old labourer, James Shepherd, who declined to give his address, was arrested in possession of part-proceeds of the property, valued at £1,000. "Further arrests," said the arresting officer, Detective Sergeant MacKay, optimistically, "are expected."

When Detective Sergeant Gullett of the Flying Squad arrested the exotically named Pancha Patel Nana, who described himself as an export merchant, he was in possession of 7,842 clothing coupons which Sergeant Gullett believed to be forged. They may not have been; Nana was fined just £50 with £5 5s 0d costs. However, when Detective Sergeant Careless of 'C' Division arrested Kenneth Young, a twenty-three-year-old labourer in possession of 114 ration books, they were certainly not forged – they were identified as being stolen from the Air Ministry, Bush House, and Young was sent to prison for eight months.

Clara Goldstein, a forty-year-old club proprietress, was arrested by Detective Sergeant Fisher for receiving a mink coat and clothing coupons valued at £3,000, and Stephen Raymond, a metal worker from Finsbury, and Joseph MacDonald, a labourer from Scotland, were arrested by Detective Sergeant Rawlings of the Flying Squad for being concerned together in stealing postal packages in the course of transmission; in addition, the proceeds of a West End shopbreaking were found in their possession.

Detective Sergeant Sid Ray of 'D' Division was entrusted with the arrest of Frank Thompson Sawdon, a fifty-nine-year-old dealer, for stealing a wireless valued £40 from a dwelling house, and Detective Constable Robertson made excellent arrests of two twenty-two-year-old drivers for a smash and grab at 8 Earls Court Road where jewellery valued at £100 was stolen.

After Gosling had been promoted to detective inspector (second class) during the summer of 1947 and Inspector Burgess was posted to Flying Squad duties on 21 December 1947, Gosling took Burgess' place on the Ghost Squad. Burgess had found his stay on the Ghost Squad to be tremendously stressful; he had half a dozen informants to run and often they would be picked up as suspected persons very late at night and Burgess would have to go out and vouch for them. He had to submit reports in respect of them and was working eighty hours a week, with seldom a day off. Burgess was glad to go; as he said, "My heart was not in it".

The vacancy left by Gosling was filled by Detective Sergeant Alfred Stanley Baker, the same day. Oddly, Baker was a second class sergeant, unlike Gosling who had been promoted from first class sergeant.

Baker was born in 1910 in Cardiff. He started his working life on the land, but seeing little prospect of advancement in the farming industry, he joined the Metropolitan Police on 28 December 1931 and was posted to 'E' Division. His first eleven years of service were spent on that Division and during that time he was awarded two commissioner's and five District commendations. To be awarded any commendations must be regarded as good, but compared with his contemporaries this was not a spectacular record. Nevertheless, he was posted to the Flying Squad and almost two years to the day of his posting was promoted to detective sergeant (second class) and retained on the Squad. He probably thought it was high time that he was promoted, because he had passed the examination for second class sergeant eight years previously. However, he appeared to prosper on the Squad and during his four year posting there he collected another thirteen commendations, twelve of which were awarded by the commissioner. After spending twelve months on 'H' Division, Baker was posted back to the Flying Squad and straight on to the Ghost Squad.

⋆   ⋆   ⋆

A twenty-two-year-old seaman was arrested by Detective Sergeant Carter of 'E' Division for receiving stolen clothing coupons; in addition, clothing valued at £2,000 was found in his possession, for which he was unable to account. Lillian Harris, a thirty-seven-year-old tailoress, was able to give an explanation of the Persian Lamb coat and the mink tie valued at £700 which Detective Inspector Judge from the Flying Squad found in her possession. Shame-facedly, she admitted smuggling it into the country from New York. When Judge submitted his report to Customs and Excise, the case of the smuggled coat was the last Ghost Squad arrest of the year.

During 1947 the squad had carried out 186 arrests and recovered property to the value of £50,231 4s 0d – over double the amount recovered the previous year. Informants were paid out £1,038 from the Informants Fund and, it was stated, "on the whole, played the game", and the squad officers charged incidental expenses of £545 3s 3d. It was money well spent, since some of the most dangerous criminals were now behind bars.

A constant battle with bureaucracy still raged over the supply of vehicles to the squad. They received strong backing from the Yard hierarchy, but the suppliers of the vehicles still dragged their heels. The Ghost Squad 'borrowed' a taxi until, six months later, their duplicity was discovered. They hired disreputable old cars and, on one occasion, a horse-drawn van, complete with peep-holes in the sides. But in spite of this, the results were exceptional. "This small squad has certainly justified its formation," stated the detective superintendent at C1, and William Rawlings, the Deputy Commander (Crime), concurred. "The personnel are hard workers," he wrote, "and possess many useful contacts. These have to be continually cultivated and the amount of money spent to this end is not excessive when the results achieved are considered... This squad has positively established itself as an asset of the Force, and of the CID in particular."

If Rawlings considered that to be a good return, what would be achieved in 1948 would leave it in the shade.

CHAPTER 6

The Ghost Squad's Best Year

The year commenced with the nationalisation of the railways; three months later, electricity would follow suit. Wages and prices were frozen, and in Sir Stafford Cripps' first budget tobacco and drinks duties were raised. In April the milk ration would be raised to three and a half pints per week; in September 1949, it would be cut again, to two and a half pints . On 5 July the National Health Service was founded and three weeks after that saw the end of bread rationing. Did this herald the beginning of the end of austerity? Not really.

★   ★   ★

Although the Ghost Squad would receive a string of glittering prizes throughout the year, a student of their arrests would have been excused for thinking, initially, that 1948 would be a damp squib for the unit.

Morris Kilingman had been circulated as being wanted for two months for two cases of larceny (trick) and obtaining £325. He was arrested by Detective Sergeant Driscoll of the Flying Squad, and when Kilingman appeared at Marlborough Street Magistrates' Court, he asked for three other offences to be taken into consideration and was sentenced to a total of twelve months' imprisonment and ordered to pay £25 costs. It rid the streets of a troublesome criminal, but he was hardly Ghost Squad fodder. Much the same could be said of Hilda Kosofsky, who was found in possession of a fur coat valued at £450. She may have been a friend of Lillian Harris, who had been arrested five days previously. If so, she could have received pertinent advice from her friend, since she too admitted smuggling the coat from New York; but the case failed to excite HM Customs, who simply confiscated it. The new addition to the squad, Sergeant Baker, made his debut by arresting six persons for receiving 400 fountain pens valued at

Percy Worth MBE, Chief Constable
of the CID and originator of the
Ghost Squad

Sir Ronald Howe CVO, MC, Assistant Commissioner
(Crime) and supporter of the Ghost Squad

Sir Harold Scott,
GCVO, KCB, KBE,
Commissioner of the
Metropolitan Police and
nervous backer of the
Ghost Squad

Jack Capstick – 'Charley Artful'

Henry 'Nobby' Clark (1924)

Henry Clark (1985)

John Gosling – 'The Yokel'

John Gosling,
in retirement

Gosling watching a suspect
(early 1950s)

Mathew Brinnand
– 'The Ferret'

John Jamieson

Mathew Brinnand (1989)

Jack Capstick's retirement party:
John Gosling (*left*), Jack Capstick
(*centre*), Walter 'Pedlar' Palmer
(*right*)

Percy Burgess

Tommy Butler
(*left*), a shy
suspect, George
Burton (*right*)

An Austin 16

A 1948 Wolseley – in far better condition, as is the Austin in the above illustration, than the cars used by the Special Duty Squad

The silver
cigarette case
presented to
Gosling by the
Honourable
Charles Wynn

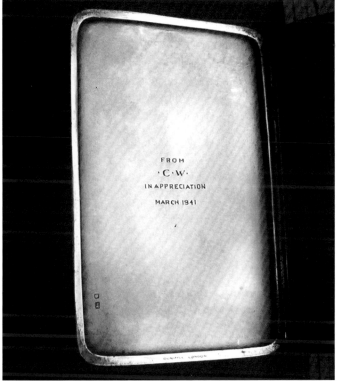

The cigarette case's
inscription

Some of the combatants in 'The Battle of Heathrow' who went on to assist the Ghost Squad: *left to right*, Det. Sgt. Micky Dowse, Det. Sgt. 'Bob' Acott, DFC, Det. Con. Donald MacMillan, Det. Sgt. Allan 'Jock' Brodie, DFC, Det. Sgt. George Draper, Det. Sgt. Johnny Franklyn

John and Marjorie Gosling on holiday at Dovercourt Bay, *circa* 1950

Det. Sgt. Charley Hewett, also from 'The Battle of Heathrow'

£700. Unfortunately, only Ismail Tropper was sentenced to six months' imprisonment; all the other prisoners (including Tropper's eighty-three-year-old grandmother) were acquitted. Two persons were arrested by Detective Sergeants Marr and Brodie of the Flying Squad; one of the prisoners was sixty-year-old Harry Benjamin, a furrier from Stoke Newington. An ermine coat valued at £1,451, the proceeds of a housebreaking at Kings Cross, was found in Benjamin's possession; both Benjamin and his co-accused were acquitted. Two months later Benjamin was arrested again, this time by Detective Inspector Judge of the Flying Squad. On this occasion there had been a larceny in a dwelling house at Streatham Hill and a fur coat, jewellery and other property, valued together at £1,388 13s 0d, had been stolen; part of the proceeds, worth £695 10s 0d, was found in Benjamin's possession. Again, he was acquitted. Perhaps Benjamin felt he was being persecuted; or possibly he thanked providence for the British jury system.

Detective Sergeant Driscoll of the Flying Squad arrested Jacob James Pletcher for being in unlawful possession of ten shirts and 200 clothing coupons; the magistrates at Bow Street Court fined him £15. It was a step in the right direction, but not by much.

Much better was the arrest of a gang from Dagenham who were found in possession of property valued at £1,500 from a housebreaking on 'Y' Division. Detective Inspector Jackson of the Flying Squad arrested Ronald Harris, a machinist from Dagenham, John Thomas Harris, a driver from Brentwood, Thomas Kenneth Thomas, a plasterer from Bow and Alexander McMirtrie, a labourer. Ronald Harris was sentenced to six months' imprisonment, John Harris and Thomas both to eighteen months' imprisonment and McMirtrie to two years' hard labour. The wife of one of the defendants was acquitted.

And even better than that was the arrest two days later of Harry Taylor, a street trader, and Ernest Edward Nunney and Charles John Gibbs, both lorry drivers, for robbery with violence at the sub-Post Office, Normans Mead, Willesden and for stealing £465. Eight days later the prisoners had Ronald Kemp, a general dealer, added to their ranks and the officers had recovered £300 of the loot. The arrests were carried out by Detective Inspector Little from 'X' Division, assisted by Detective Constable Robertson. This was the seventh occasion Robertson had assisted the Ghost Squad and for his work in this case he would be commended by the commissioner. So, in fact, would George Burton, who was monitoring the snout in the shadows. Meanwhile, Nunney was sentenced to five years' penal servitude, Gibbs (recently released from imprisonment for a smash and grab) to four years' penal servitude and Taylor and Kemp – possibly the look-out man and driver – received sentences of imprisonment: eighteen months in Taylor's case and fifteen months in Kemp's.

Annie Lewin, aged forty-six, who gave her profession as an assembler, and Thomas Blogg, fifty-eight, a plumber, both living at the same address in Bow, plus Patrick Blogg, aged twenty-eight, a labourer who declined to provide his address, were arrested by Detective Sergeant Fisher of the Flying Squad, after tapestry valued at £1,400, the proceeds of a warehousebreaking on 'G' Division, was found in their possession. The older Blogg received two years' imprisonment, the younger Blogg three years' penal servitude and Annie Lewin walked free from the Old Bailey, having agreed to be bound over in the sum of £5 to be of good behaviour for a period of two years. This was the latest in a series of Ghost Squad arrests made by Detective Sergeant Arthur James Fisher, for which he was commended both by the commissioner and Old Street Metropolitan Magistrates' Court. It was the most recent in a long line of commendations; five years previously he had been commended by the commissioner for arresting three criminals, one of whom was armed. This was Fisher's introduction to the Flying Squad, where he had been posted after seventeen years service, as a detective sergeant (first class), and he was absolutely suited to Ghost Squad work.

Detective Sergeant Bradford of the Flying Squad arrested two men for receiving a stolen car part; both were discharged. Three days later, Detective Inspector Jackson of the Flying Squad arrested two men for being in possession of jewellery valued at £318, the proceeds of a housebreaking. Then they were further charged with receiving a bracelet valued at £1,000. Nobody was particularly surprised when both were acquitted; juries thoroughly dislike convicting men (who may or may not be receivers of stolen property) who are seventy years of age. Although Thomas Rodway was also aged seventy when he was arrested by Detective Constable Robertson for receiving a quantity of pork and a pair of Avery scales, Rodway did plead guilty and the court exercised their prerogative of mercy, by fining him £10.

Following a shopbreaking at Blackheath Road in South-east London where car parts valued at £600 were stolen, Detective Sergeant Rawlings and his Flying Squad team raided premises in Islington. Of the three arrests carried out, only William Gray, aged forty-four, was convicted. He was fined £100; a lady living at the same address and a forty-four-year-old dealer were acquitted. Not a very satisfactory conclusion for Rawlings who the next day arrested Israel Marcus Schiffman aged forty-seven from Clapton, who was in possession of fifteen watches worth £150; Clerkenwell Magistrates Court decided that the proper penalty for receiving the watches should be a fine of just £5. Four days later, watches continued to figure in the Ghost squad return of work. Detective Sergeant Law and Detective Constable George Baldwin from Tottenham Court Road police station arrested John H Edwards, a forty-year-old jeweller, also from Tottenham Court Road, for receiving forty-two gold watches and a quantity of jewellery worth £570. At Marlborough Street Magistrates' Court, Edwards was fined £580. Archibald Rose, the forty-eight-year-old licensee of The Green Man public house, Blackheath, together with Benjamin Rose, a gown manufacturer aged forty from Shoreditch, were arrested by Detective Inspector Jackson and his Flying Squad team. The men were in possession of ten watches valued at £60; Greenwich Magistrates' Court fined them £50.

A snout led John Gosling to a draughty barn at Honour Farm, Bovingdon, Hertfordshire, where 1,000 yards of tapestry valued at £1,500 reposed; it had been stolen from a lorry somewhere between Chester and London. Gosling, anxious to get indoors during that freezing February, lost no time in contacting Detective Sergeant Driscoll of the Flying Squad in order to pass the matter over to him. Horace Edward Wood, a forty-four-year-old bookmaker, was arrested for receiving the material and went to prison for six months.

A lorry containing cartons of tea valued at £1,400 was stolen from a lorry park in Stepney on 11 February. Ten days later, Gosling received a telephone call from an informant, who told him he had been approached by a rival gang who knew the whereabouts of the stolen lorry and wanted him to assist in stealing it from the thieves – this was quite a common occurrence. So Gosling made his way from his home in Surrey to Cable Street in the East End of London and quickly found the abandoned lorry. But he stared in dismay at the long line of railway arches where his informant had told him the tea was stored. Fortunately, nineteen chests of the tea were found in the second railway arch that he squeezed his bulk into; they were part-proceeds of the load and were valued at £700. Gosling found a nearby pub with a helpful landlord and, telephoning the Yard for some assistance, he settled down in the living room which gave an excellent view of the railway arch. Nothing happened that night and nothing the following day. The next morning, a lorry drove into Cable Street and backed up to the arch. The doors of the arch were opened and the men from the lorry started loading the tea on to the back of the vehicle. Half-way through, Gosling and Detective Inspector Judge of the Flying Squad and his men interrupted the loading and arrested the men: James Stanley Ashead, a thirty-eight-year-old fish porter, George Alfred Hadley, a thirty-four-year-old fitter's mate and Elias Joseph Broad, a thirty-four-year-old coffee stall proprietor. They received eighteen months, fifteen months' imprisonment and three years' penal servitude respectively for their trouble; a fourth man was acquitted.

William George Leonard, aged thirty-four, a dealer from Kingston, was arrested for receiving 3,600 yards of art silk valued at £600, which had been stolen from Richmond. He was probably fortunate to be fined £100 with ten guineas costs. The arresting officer was Detective Sergeant 'Titch' Freeman of the Flying Squad and it was now that he started getting involved with Ghost Squad arrests. It was also around this time that Divisional Detective Inspector Claud Baker left the Ghost Squad. He had been in charge of the Ghost Squad for just eight months – three months longer than Jamieson had held the post but still a very short engagement. Why he left is not known; he returned to Flying Squad duties. It appeared that being the head of the prestigious Ghost Squad was something of a poisoned chalice; a new leader would not appear for another five months. During this interim period Gosling took over as temporary head of the unit, with Detective Sergeants Burton and Baker as the only other accredited members of the squad.

Two platinum and diamond rings, plus a wristlet watch, valued at £800 were stolen from 12 Cheyne Walk, Hendon by means of housebreaking, and on 17 February Reginald Emmanuel Levy, a forty-two-year-old commercial traveller, was found in possession of them; dealt with for receiving, he was sentenced to two years' imprisonment at the County of London Sessions.

Detective Sergeant 'Pedlar' Palmer now joined Sergeant Freeman in a quest to assist the Ghost Squad; however, the two men they arrested for receiving rolls of cloth, which had been stolen from Stoke Newington, were discharged, as was a forty-year-old manufacturer who was charged with receiving a carpet which had been stolen from a vehicle at Tottenham Court Road. He was well-known to Gosling, who had sent him away for four years fifteen years previously, and who went along with Detective Sergeant Rawlings from the Flying Squad. There was an element of doubt in the court hearing, and although the magistrate told the prisoner that he was "a clever and confirmed liar", he was given the benefit of the doubt. However, it was some consolation that Gosling later pulled him in again for another job, and this time he went down for eighteen months.

Detective Sergeant Elliott of the Flying Squad was no luckier when he arrested a fifty-one-year-old resident of Dolphin Square for receiving nylon stockings valued at £3,000; his case, too, was thrown out. The Ghost Squad's Sergeant Baker was rather more fortunate after he arrested Salehapshai Jaffarji, a thirty-six-year-old street trader. He appeared at the County of London Sessions and was sentenced to nine months' imprisonment for receiving 430 stolen fountain pens, an odd coincidence considering Baker's lack of success with the fountain pen receivers of exactly one month previously.

Alfred Tyne, aged thirty-nine and a tobacconist, was arrested on 18 March for breaking into a warehouse six days previously at 20 Bell Street, NW1 to steal cigarettes valued at £1,884 15s 10d. Tyne was part of a three-man gang; two weeks later John William Dunne, a thirty-two-year-old blacksmith, was arrested by Police Constable 359 'X' Fairbanks and both men were sentenced to twenty-one months' hard labour; the third member of the team was not caught.

Not so fortunate was Louis Anthony Wilson, a thirty-nine-year-old garage proprietor; he was caught by Detective Sergeant Winters of the Flying Squad, having been found in possession of a mink coat valued at £1,000, stolen eight days previously by means of housebreaking at 22 Hillsborough Court, NW8, and was weighed off at the County of London Sessions with two years' imprisonment. Simply because property had been positively identified as being the proceeds of crime did not automatically mean that anyone in possession of those items was guilty of feloniously receiving them, as in the case of the thirty-seven-year-old dealer who was arrested by Detective Sergeants Freeman and Palmer on 5 May in possession of four diamond brooches and a gold perfume flask, valued at £950, stolen by means of housebreaking a week previously. Six weeks later, the dealer walked out of the Old Bailey a free man.

Sidney Charles Gregg, a twenty-eight-year-old lorry driver, was caught by Detective Sergeant Alexander of 'Z' Division for being a suspected person and loitering with intent to commit a felony, as well as being in possession of housebreaking implements by night. After remanding him in custody for a week, Lambeth Magistrates decided that because Gregg had not taken the final step in his burglarious expedition, he should be bound over in the sum of £5 to keep the peace for twelve months. On the other hand, George Wain, a twenty-eight-year-old driver mechanic, had taken a step too far and was arrested by Detective Sergeant Roberts of 'Y' Division for a shopbreaking at 4-6 New Road, Edmonton. The quantity of ladies' clothing which was stolen, valued at £93 15s 0d, was recovered intact and Wain went to prison for twelve months.

Chaya James, a forty-two-year-old club proprietor with a criminal record which commenced in 1928, and Phillip James Gallagher, a thirty-seven-year-old driver whose criminal career had begun when he was fifteen, were arrested by Detective Sergeant Brodie of the Flying Squad on 16 April for stealing a Persian carpet and two rugs, valued together at £425, from Messrs Perry, London Ltd. They appeared at court the following day and were each sentenced to six months' hard labour.

Handbags valued at £1,100 were recovered intact following a factorybreaking in Dalston; so was the gang responsible. Robert Abrahams, a thirty-two-year-old bookmaker's clerk, John Forbes Cromb, a fitter aged fifty-six, and John Barker, a fifty-eight-year-old cabinet maker, received twenty-one months' imprisonment and three and four years' penal servitude respectively. In another part of London at roughly the same time, Albert Edward Finch, a thirty-nine-year-old coalman, and Richard John Beck, a thirty-four-year-old signalman, both from Harrow, were arrested by Detective Sergeant Anderson of the Flying Squad for receiving 100 handbags valued at £200. Both appeared at Wealdstone

Magistrates' Court and Finch was sentenced to three months' imprisonment while Beck received concurrent sentences of one and four months.

For unlawfully having $410 in his possession when he was arrested by Detective Sergeant Brodie of the Flying Squad, Phillip Morgan, a forty-four-year-old caterer a long way from his home in Belfast, was fined £50 with ten guineas costs at Marlborough Street Magistrates' Court. Frederick George Donovan, a thirty-year-old greengrocer from Southwark, was arrested by Detective Sergeant McKay of the Flying Squad for being in possession of a quantity of shoes valued at £200 and stolen in transit from the railway. At the County of London Sessions he was leniently dealt with when he was bound over to keep the peace in the sum of £10 for two years. And Detective Sergeant Acott of the Flying Squad arrested James Cardash, a radio dealer from Edgware, for the unlawful possession of 701 clothing coupons – he was fined £100.

Sergeant Baker was still continuing his lacklustre career with the Ghost Squad; he arrested a married couple from Sussex Gardens, W2, for receiving a quantity of jewellery – at the County of London Sessions the following month the husband, who had been in custody since his arrest, was acquitted and his wife was bound over in the sum of £5 to be of good behaviour for the next three years.

When Detective Sergeants Driscoll and Bridges arrested John Fleming for being found on enclosed premises for an unlawful purpose and being found in possession of housebreaking implements – to wit, a jemmy, two pieces of mica, four picklocks and other burglarious paraphernalia – because they had arrested him during daylight hours, the onus was on them to prove evil intent. They did, and Fleming was sentenced to two months' hard labour.

The tireless Detective Sergeant Brodie of the Flying Squad ran into a rather rough patch; he arrested a thirty-six-year-old furrier from Finchley Road in possession of $1,200; the case was discharged, as was that of a fifty-two-year-old licensee from North London arrested for receiving twelve bottles of whisky and two rolls of cloth. The bale of cloth valued at £100 found in the possession of Benjamin John Stokes and his wife, Elsie Elizabeth, both aged twenty-seven from Finsbury, by Detective Sergeant Coles of the Flying Squad, did result in a conviction; Benjamin was fined £10 with the option of two months' imprisonment if he failed to pay and Elsie was fined £5 or one month's imprisonment. The option of a fine was not proffered to James Clark, a forty-eight-year-old stoker, when he appeared at Lambeth Magistrates' Court. Detective Sergeant Ogden of the Flying Squad had found him in possession of two ladies' costumes worth £20, and Clark was sentenced to two months' imprisonment.

Ronald Patrick Curtis, a twenty-one-year-old street trader from West Ham, Frederick Craven, a forty-one-year-old dealer, and Ernest Arthur Bishop, a fifty-year-old driver, both from Leytonstone, were arrested by Detective Inspector Jackson of the Flying Squad for being concerned in a factorybreaking at West Ham, stealing property valued at £600 and for receiving the property. At Stratford Magistrates' Court, Curtis was sentenced to three months, Craven to six months and Bishop to one month's imprisonment. And a week later, another Flying Squad team, led by Detective Sergeant Russan, arrested Daniel Hanlon, a thirty-two-year-old labourer, Christopher McCarthy, a twenty-nine-year-old painter, and Patrick Hayes, a twenty-five-year-old labourer, for receiving jewellery worth £100; all were sentenced to two months' imprisonment at Marylebone Magistrates' Court.

It was about this time that the Flying Squad was given its own identity. Separated from C1 Department, it was now officially known as C8 Department, a designation it would hold for the next forty years. And because it was a new department, it was under the control of a detective superintendent, Bill 'The Cherub' Chapman, with twenty-six years service. With Detective Chief Inspector Bob 'Mr. Memory' Lee as his deputy, Chapman lost no time in increasing the Flying Squad personnel to eighty and upgrading the fleet to twenty-seven cars, three taxis and four vans. This made little difference to the working of the Ghost Squad; some really excellent information put a team of villains away for some time. George Harry Donovan, a forty-nine-year-old builder, Charles George Westlake a twenty-seven-year-old labourer, Albert Ernest Doran, an ice-cream salesman aged twenty-eight, and Ernest Sanderson, a lorry driver aged thirty-three, all of them from the Paddington area, were arrested by Detective Sergeant Anderson and his Flying Squad team after they were found in possession of three tons of stolen lead and 250 gallons of petrol, valued at £425. Donovan was sentenced to two concurrent terms of four years' penal servitude and fined £100, Westlake to eighteen months' imprisonment and Doran to nine months. Sanderson was bound over in the sum of £5 for two years.

George Burton needed Flying Squad assistance when he arrested three men in North London for receiving an iron safe; only Patrick Edmund O'Connor, a twenty-nine-year-old labourer, went down, for six months; the others walked. The assistance which Burton received one month later was from Detective Sergeants Palmer and Freeman, practically part of the Ghost Squad team, when he visited a flat in Mason Street, South-east London and arrested Patrick Daly, a thirty-six-year-old labourer, together with a lady living in a nearby flat, who were found in possession of thirty-eight wristlet watches and three pocket watches, the proceeds of a shopbreaking on 'L' Division and worth £300. The lady was discharged from Lambeth Magistrates' Court; Daly wended his way to the County of London Sessions, where he was sentenced to eighteen months' imprisonment. These details were recorded by Detective Constable Robertson who had left 'X' Division a week previously and was now not only posted to the Flying Squad; to all intents and purposes, he was also a member of the Ghost Squad. Four days after Patrick Daly's arrest, Alfred Daly, a thirty-two-year-old porter from Southwark, was arrested by Robertson; he joined his kinsman in the dock and he too was sentenced to eighteen months. Robertson was commended by the commissioner for his action in this case.

The Ghost Squad's new member, Robert James Robertson, was born in Lanarkshire just after the First World War started in 1914; after working as a farm labourer he joined the Metropolitan Police, just two days after the commencement of the Second World War. Posted to 'X' Division, there he served as a uniform police constable and an aid to CID until he volunteered for war service with the RAF. He served as a Flight Sergeant from 1942 until demobilisation in 1945, whereupon he rejoined the police and was posted back to 'X' Division. He was commended by the commissioner for ability in a case of larceny and one week later he was appointed to the CID. He was commended again by the commissioner for initiative in a case of receiving and had worked solidly for the Ghost Squad; at the time of his arrival on the Ghost Squad, he had effected fourteen arrests for them.

Divisional Detective Inspector Henry Stuttard arrived on 21 July, having been posted in from 'L' Division, to take over the running of the squad. Stuttard had been born in 1903 at Nelson, Lancashire and after a period of labouring he joined the Metropolitan Police in 1924, when he was posted to 'H' Division. Like Wensley before him, he loved the East End and its inhabitants. It was there that he spent the first ten years of his service and as an aid to CID and a detective constable he would build up an impressive number of contacts in the underworld who would still faithfully serve him, years later. He was also awarded seven commissioner's commendations, including monetary awards for good police work, before he was promoted to detective sergeant (second class) and posted to 'K' Division. The posting lasted just two years before he was promoted to detective sergeant (first class) and transferred to the Flying Squad.

In a bare three-year posting on the Squad, Stuttard notched up an astonishing further seventeen commissioner's commendations, including a high commendation on 28 February 1938 for courage and tenacity in effecting the arrest of a violent criminal for officebreaking and was additionally awarded £5 from the Bow Street Police Court Reward Fund. Two more of his commendations were for arrests of persons in possession of explosives and another was for arresting a man for robbery.

Stuttard was promoted to detective inspector (second class) in 1939 and was posted to 'V' Division. Six more commissioner's commendations followed, and seven years later Stuttard was promoted to divisional detective inspector and was posted to 'L' Division. After two years service at Brixton Stuttard was transferred to the Flying Squad and was given command of the Ghost Squad. At five feet ten, he was a rugged looking individual who said very little; but what he did say, as John Swain would later remark, "was with strength and meaning". He totally decried the use of force or the use of a truncheon on a prisoner, except in the direst of emergencies. Since he and Capstick had served on the Flying Squad at the same time, it is quite possible that their divergent ideas on how to bring about the arrest of criminals meant that they had little to do with each other.

The day prior to Stuttard's arrival, Victor Mannings, a fifty-six-year-old mechanic from Peckham, was arrested for a house-breaking at Chatham, where a quantity of ladies' clothing was stolen, valued at £150 and recovered intact. It is possible that Mannings was dealt with for receiving, because when he appeared at court, he was fined just £10. What was important about the case was that the arresting officer was Detective Sergeant Jim Moyle from 'L' Division; he had worked with Stuttard on that division and it would not be too long before Moyle was called up to be an important member of the Ghost Squad. In fact, within two days of Mannings' arrest, two more men were arrested for the same offence at Queen's Road, Peckham by Stuttard and Moyle; both were later discharged at court. Within a few days, the same two officers arrested Louis Cushieri, a thirty-eight-year-old furniture dealer from Goodge Street, W1, for receiving a quantity of cloth and dresses, valued at £250; Cushieri was fined £25 and a second man was discharged.

A combined operation between Detective Inspector Iredale of 'P' Division and Detective Sergeant Tiddy of the Flying Squad led to the arrest of Joseph Peter Cavedashi, a lorry driver aged twenty-six, and Percy Comissar, a thirty-three-year-old wireless and electrical dealer. Cavedashi lived in Peckham, which was where there had been the theft from a vehicle of 3,000 wireless valves and other property, valued at £1,462 10s 0d, all of which were found in the possession of the arrested men. Three months later at the County of London Sessions, both were sentenced to eighteen months' imprisonment.

Every arrest which has been mentioned so far in this book was as the direct result of information provided by a Ghost Squad snout. The one which follows, was not.

On 29 July a very professional gang of violent robbers (they were working under the direction of gangland boss Jack Spot, although this was never proved) staged a coup in a warehouse at the newly opened London Heathrow Airport. The prize was considerable. A consignment of gold bullion worth half a million pounds was being flown in from South America, in the warehouse safe was jewellery valued at £13,900, and other goods worth £224,000 were also stacked in the premises. The plan was this: the robbers had an inside man who had agreed to add pheno-barbitone tablets to the guards' coffee and, once the guards were drugged, to open the doors of the converted aircraft hangar to admit the robbers – for this he would be paid £500. In fact, he put such a large quantity of the drug in the coffee that the dose would have proved fatal to anyone who drank it.

But the coffee was not drunk by the guards or by anybody else – Detective Sergeants Charlie Hewett, George Draper and John Matthews of the Flying Squad had deputised for them. As the robbers, their faces obscured with stockings and their hands covered with gloves or socks, entered the warehouse and saw the 'guards' sprawled across their table, supposedly unconscious, the keys to the safe were taken from Hewett's pocket. As soon as the keys were inserted in the safe, the fourteen Flying Squad officers who had secreted themselves behind bales and packing cases emerged and a battle royal commenced. The thieves had a variety of weapons, an iron bar, a cosh, a broken bottle and giant wirecutters which they used with telling effect on the Squad officers. The Flying Squad had their truncheons, which were used to even better effect, and although four of the gang managed to escape, eight others were left unconscious on the tarmac outside the warehouse. Shocking injuries were inflicted on both sides, and one of the gang received wounds which were so severe that he was unable to join his seven co-defendants in the dock upon their initial appearance at Uxbridge Magistrates' Court because he was hospitalised.

At the Old Bailey on 17 September, having pleaded guilty to robbery with violence, Edward William Hughes, aged forty-eight, a bookmaker from Brixton (and, allegedly, the possessor of 'a weak heart') was sentenced to twelve years' penal servitude. Sammy Ross, a thirty-four-year-old bookseller, also from Brixton – and the leader of the gang – received eleven years' penal servitude. Alfred Roome – 'Big Alfie' – a forty-two-year-old clerk from Chadwell Heath (also known as 'The Ilford Kid'), had been responsible for a savage attack on the head of the Flying Squad and was the gang member who had been hospitalised as a result. Sentenced to ten years' penal servitude, he collapsed in the dock and was carried off to the cells, sobbing. As a result of this very un-robber-like display of emotion, Ross decreed that Roome should be ostracised in prison. Jimmy Wood, a thirty-seven-year-old car dealer from Manor Park, was sentenced to nine years' penal servitude. His brother George (who also liked to be called George or John Wallis), a costermonger aged twenty-six from the same address as his brother, was sentenced to eight years' penal servitude, as were George Thomas Smith, a twenty-eight-year-old labourer from Brixton, and Sidney Cook, a twenty-eight-year-old motor dealer – he was carrying a car's starting handle at the time of his arrest. William Henry Ainsworth, a thirty-nine-year-old dealer from Dagenham, received five years' penal servitude.

This was a really excellent piece of work – except that it was not a Ghost Squad case. The arrests had come about as a result of Anthony Walsh, whom the gang had recruited as the inside man, blurting out details of the plot to the security manager at the airport – hence the intervention of the Flying Squad. He was dealt with separately and was bound over in the sum of £10 to be of good behaviour for a period of two years.

But it was these names which were included by Stuttard on the Ghost Squad return of arrests, simply because he – and every other available Flying Squad officer – had been present. It was quite indefensible to have done this; the Ghost Squad already had a reputation second to none for police work – they did not need to embellish their returns of work with the efforts of others.

Walter McLean, a groom aged thirty of no fixed abode, was stopped in Marylebone Road by Detective Inspector MacDonald of the Flying Squad. McLean was in possession of a camera and other property which were identified as being the part-proceeds of a housebreaking at Church Farm Lane, East Wittering, Sussex. He had not been alone in this enterprise; the Ghost Squad snouts got to work and two days later Richard Argyle Carew, a masseur aged thirty-three – his criminal career had commenced fifteen years previously – and, like his companion, of no fixed abode, was also stopped in Marylebone Road, again by Inspector MacDonald. He was found to be in possession of a stopwatch, also identified as part of the property stolen from East Wittering. McLean was sentenced to three years' penal servitude, Carew to two years' imprisonment. John Robert Mayo, a forty-year-old street trader from Islington, was also arrested by Detective Inspector MacDonald for receiving five rolls of cloth valued at £100; he was fined £50 or three months' imprisonment. And Mark Richard White, a nurseryman aged forty of Bedford, must have clutched at the magistrates' heartstrings after he appeared in the dock charged with receiving thirteen tons of coal; he was fined just £5.

Alfred Michael Carroll, a clerk aged twenty-four of no fixed address, was arrested by Detective Sergeants Driscoll and Bridger of the Flying Squad in possession of a £100 sable cape. Taken to Gerald Road police station, Carroll admitted stealing the cape that morning from 91 Winchester Street, W1; he also admitted one or two other offences and was sentenced to six months' hard labour. Nine days later, the same two officers arrested Thomas Patrick English, aged twenty-three from Stepney, together with William John Parker, a nineteen-year-old soldier from the Worcestershire Regiment. They were in unlawful possession of cloth and trousers valued at £150, the result of a factorybreaking at Bethnal Green Road where property valued at £500 had been stolen. The following day, those officers arrested Edward English, brother of Thomas, and at Thames Magistrates' Court it may be assumed that the English brothers pleaded guilty to receiving the property because they were each fined £25 or forty-two days' imprisonment in default. Parker, being a member of a disciplined profession, should have known better and was sentenced to three months' hard labour.

The Ghost Squad informants continued to work overtime; Samuel Harris, a sixty-nine-year-old dealer from Golders Green, was arrested by Detective Sergeant Gullett of the Flying Squad for stealing a £250 ring – he was wanted at Blackpool and was detained until an escort collected him. Detective Constable Robertson arrested Thomas Frederick Magee for stealing an Austin car, and West London Magistrates' Court fined him £40 with £10 costs for doing so. Alexander Sydney Francis Cracknell, a thirty-year-old engineer of the Hartland Hotel, Brighton, was arrested in central London by Detective Sergeant Acott of the Flying Squad for stealing property from a house at Lea Green. He was detained at Cannon Row police station and it was intended to hand him over to an escort from 'R' Division, where the housebreaking had occurred; however, it was also discovered that he was wanted at Brighton for a series of cases of false pretences committed there during the previous two weeks. Cracknell was sentenced to twelve months' imprisonment. And Detective Sergeants Peter Vibart and Barney Gay of the Flying Squad arrested James Henry Alfred Smith, aged twenty-three, a labourer, and his brother, Ronald Frank Smith, aged eighteen, a soldier with the Royal Corps of Signals. Their address in Wandsworth Road, Battersea was extremely close to the scene of a smash and grab at 123 South Lambeth Road where clothing was stolen; the older Smith was sentenced to nine months' imprisonment two weeks later at the County of London Sessions whilst his sibling received three years' Borstal detention. Now it was the turn of the Ghost Squad operatives to get to work.

Inspector Stuttard, together with his 'L' Division sidekick, Sergeant Moyle, arrested Thomas Melvin, a fifty-two-year-old dealer of Stoke-on-Trent, together with George Craddock aged thirty-eight, also a dealer from South-east London, for factorybreaking at Stoke-on-Trent and stealing crates of cutlery valued at £500; both were sentenced to two years' imprisonment.

Henry McGuire, a kitchen porter aged twenty-six, Charles Berry Kennedy, a ship's foreman aged twenty-three, and the rather oddly-named Robert Peacock Allison, a twenty-two-year-old porter, were in possession of two saws, a pair of pliers and a jemmy which they were industriously using at 12.30 in the morning of 28 August as they were breaking into the shop premises of Messrs. Alexander, 94 Rye Lane, Peckham and stealing a quantity of clothing and cloth valued at £850. Unfortunately for them, Inspector Stuttard, Sergeant Burton and Detective Constable Robertson were close enough to arrest the lot of them, and McGuire was sentenced to eighteen months' imprisonment, with Kennedy and Allison receiving fifteen and six months respectively; Robertson was commended by the commissioner for his work in this case. Four days later, this time on the other side of London, the same officers (with the assistance of colleagues from the Flying Squad) arrested Henry Charles Hawkins, a thirty-nine-year-old driver, Leslie Walter Bobbett, of similar age and occupation, and Edward Albert Brett, a dealer aged thirty-seven, for receiving a quantity of men's suits and other clothing valued at £900. Both Brett and Bobbett were sentenced to three months' hard labour, while Hawkins received one month's hard labour. Two women – a housewife and a domestic – who were arrested with them, had their cases discharged.

A bonded warehouse at Dover was broken into and cigarettes and 100 cases of whisky valued at £10,000 were stolen; a few days later John Gosling was woken by an early morning telephone call from one of his most active informants. It led Gosling to a South London villain who, in turn, offered to tell Gosling the general area of the whereabouts of the stolen property. After a long, wearying search, Gosling arrived in Stotfold, Bedfordshire where he and Burton arrested Arthur Flood, a forty-nine-year-old tobacconist from that area, together with James Bidwell aged thirty-three, a manager from Letchworth, and recovered a large quantity of cigarettes which Flood had secreted in a disused cottage two miles away from his shop. Two days later, Rubin

William Quain, a forty-five-year-old property owner from Tredigar Road, Bow, was arrested by Detective Inspector MacDonald of the Flying Squad in connection with the same offence. Harold King, a forty-five-year-old shopkeeper of Stotfold was arrested by Gosling and Sergeant Freeman for receiving 45,000 of the stolen cigarettes and the same two officers arrested Herbert Elliott, a forty-nine-year-old shopkeeper from Clifton, Bedfordshire, for receiving 15,000 stolen Players cigarettes. Although a thirty-five-year-old director from Stotfold was also arrested for receiving stolen cigarettes valued at £200, his case was discharged at court. As for the others, Bidwell was bound over to keep the peace in the sum of £5 for two years together with £15 costs. King was fined £25 with twenty guineas costs and Elliot was fined £50. Flood – whom Gosling had suspected of a similar type of offence before the war in Camden Town – was sentenced to six months' hard labour and Quain received three years' penal servitude at Bedford Quarter Sessions. The whisky was not recovered; cigarettes valued at £7,000 were.

Detective Sergeant Driscoll and other officers of the Flying Squad kept careful observation on a twenty-nine-year-old shop fitter from Stoke Newington who had ventured south to New Cross Road, Peckham, before arresting him. He was found to be in possession of three rings and a brooch which the officers felt were unlawfully obtained, a view which was unfortunately not shared by the bench at Lambeth Magistrates' Court.

Another observation carried out by Detective Sergeants Foster and Anderson of the Flying Squad resulted in the arrest of Thomas Victor Outram, a thirty-year-old labourer, George Powell, a forty-year-old driver, both from North Kensington, and James Friston, also a driver, aged thirty-six from Paddington. They were charged with receiving a quantity of steel plates valued at £400 and the following month all of them were sentenced to fifteen months' imprisonment; a forty-three-year-old company director arrested with them walked free from court. So did a twenty-five-year-old 'model designer' from Muswell Hill; he was found in possession of £638 which Sergeant Burton and Detective Constable Robertson of the Ghost Squad deemed to be unlawful, but the prisoner managed to convince the justices at Marylebone Magistrates' Court otherwise. Scarcely any better was the case of colourfully named Delia Napoleon, a twenty-seven-year-old machinist who had first come to the notice of the police four years previously. Detective Sergeant Palmer discovered that she was in unlawful possession of jewellery worth £200 in Old Compton Street, but the magistrate at Bow Street decided that this matter would be best disposed of with a fine of twenty shillings.

★   ★   ★

It would be difficult (although not impossible) to find a more repellent example of the so-called gentry than Peter Martin Jenkins. Born in 1917, Jenkins came from a well to do family; he was educated at, remarkably, both Harrow and Winchester and possessed good looks and a stable background. However, he had deserted from the army twice, before first coming to the attention of the police in 1936; then he really went off the rails with a vengeance. In December 1937 he was part of a four-man gang – they became known as 'The Mayfair Playboys' – who booked a suite at the prestigious Hyde Park Hotel under a false name and invited the director of a Bond Street jewellers to bring a selection of jewellery along to the hotel for inspection. The director did just that, only to be savagely attacked by Jenkins, who coshed him to the ground, leaving him in a pool of blood, before decamping with the jewellery valued at £16,000.

He and his associates were soon caught, and when they appeared at the Old Bailey in February 1938 Lord Hewart, the Lord Chief Justice, had this to say, before passing sentence:

> The word education has been used about each of you. If I believed that you really were educated men, it would be necessary for me, on that account, to be more severe. Probably, all that is meant is that somebody has spent money in providing you with certain conventional opportunities of education. The results are not impressive.

As the leader of the gang, Jenkins received the heaviest punishment; seven years' penal servitude and twenty strokes of the cat o'nine tails. His three associates were then sentenced, respectively, to five years' penal servitude and fifteen strokes of the cat o'nine tails, three years' penal servitude and eighteen months' hard labour. In his long legal career, including sitting as Lord Chief Justice from 1922-1940, it was the only time that Lord Hewart had ever ordered prisoners to be whipped.

Prison for Jenkins was not the reformative exercise that one would have hoped for; scarcely had he been released when in 1945 he was stopped in the street by Detective Inspector Bob Higgins (later to become deputy head of the Flying Squad) and questioned about the parcel he was carrying. The parcel contained a stolen fur coat, and after Higgins had requested details of its provenance, Jenkins, with all of his customary arrogance, replied that he had "found it up a tree". It was not the wisest reply to make to a detective of Higgins' calibre, especially when it was repeated in court; it led to three years' penal servitude for Jenkins.

So at the relatively early age of thirty-one, Jenkins had already served a total of ten years' penal servitude, as well as getting 'a bashing' (as receiving the cat o'nine tails was inelegantly referred to by the underworld); and it would be reasonable to assume that Jenkins might have thought it was time to change his ways. Not a bit of it.

Gosling heard that Jenkins had teamed up with Harry Mann (who had only just been released from his two-year sentence for housebreaking, courtesy of Gosling) and he, together with Detective Sergeants Freeman and Palmer, kept the duo under observation in the vicinity of Grosvenor Road, Muswell Hill. Both Jenkins and Mann were arrested for being suspected persons, loitering with intent to commit a felony, to wit, housebreaking; surprisingly, given their past convictions, both were bound over in their own recognizance in the sum of £10 for two years. The arrest occurred on 15 July.

Shortly afterwards, Sir Joshua Reynolds' unfinished portrait of Georgiana Cavendish, Duchess of Devonshire, valued at £5,000, was stolen, having been cut from its frame in the Kensington flat belonging to George Josslyn L'Estrange Howard, the 11th Earl of Carlisle.

Gosling heard from an informant that Jenkins had been hovering on the edge of the Earl's social circle and next, that Harry Mann was offering the painting for £1,000; rather easily, given their association and arrest of two months previously, he was able to put two and two together.

Gosling found a talented and believable 'buyer' to negotiate the sale of the painting, measuring four by two and a half feet, which Jenkins, incredibly, carried around, rolled up in a car rug; after three 'dummy runs', the two thieves finally produced the genuine article at Harrow at nine o'clock in the morning of 11 September. The 'buyer's' car sped away and Detective Inspector Robinson and Detective Sergeant Dowse of the Flying Squad made the arrests; the portrait was deemed to be the genuine article at an art gallery at Hay Hill, W1, and both Jenkins and Mann appeared at the Old Bailey and were each sentenced to four years' penal servitude.

It was said that the theft had come about after Jenkins had cultivated the friendship of one of the Earl's relatives. That may or may not be true, but this case really was the end of Jenkins – he later died of alcohol abuse in a lodging house. Mann went on to bigger things; following his release, he and a gang of four others knocked on the door of a house in Golders Green, attacked and tied up the German maid and ransacked the house. He was sentenced to fourteen years' imprisonment.

One of the arresting officers in the Jenkins case, Detective Sergeant Micky Dowse, had only just resumed work; during 'The Battle of Heathrow' six weeks earlier he had been quite badly injured, having been hit with a pair of giant wirecutters as well as being coshed. A popular Welsh singer on the Squad, he later sadly contracted tuberculosis.

★ ★ ★

Percival Trotter, a forty-year-old driver, discovered that his criminal convictions, which commenced in 1940, counted against him after he was arrested by Detective Sergeant Holcombe from 'X' Division for receiving a wireless set worth £33; he was sentenced to six weeks' imprisonment. Robert Briggs, a forty-four-year-old french polisher from Bethnal Green, together with Charles Radden, a thirty-one-year-old lorry driver of no fixed abode, were arrested by Detective Sergeant Munnie from the Flying Squad for receiving three bedroom suites to the value of £300. Perhaps Radden's homelessness touched the heartstrings of the bench at North London Magistrates' Court, because he was bound over in the sum of forty shillings to keep the peace for twelve months. The same leniency was not extended to Briggs, who was sentenced to six months' imprisonment. And, as was so often the case, a furrier charged with receiving a fur cape and a fur tie walked free from court, having been given the benefit of the doubt.

Stuttard had never lost his appetite for leading from the front; together with Detective Inspector Macdonald he arrested John Walter Maffia, aged forty-four, and George Albert Fry, aged fifty-nine, on 18 September for receiving various amounts of stolen property valued at £350, and both were bound over in the sum of £10 for a period of two years; a third man was discharged. But if those results were disappointing, the arrests carried out during the early hours of the following day by the same officers were not.

Several lorries arrived at railway sidings at Cricklewood and six men alighted from the first lorry, followed by three men from a second lorry who climbed an embankment and vanished among the rolling stock. During the next half-hour the men slid carpets and cases of whisky, valued together at a staggering £15,000, down the embankment to where the lorries were parked. As the men descended the slope to load the booty into the lorries, so lights in a nearby builder's yard came on and Stuttard and MacDonald and their men rushed at the thieves. One of the men managed to jump into a lorry and drove off, with four of his accomplices on board. The four others were caught and unwisely offered resistance, as their battered appearance revealed the following day at Hendon Magistrates' Court. The court was told that when arrested, the various comments from Henry William Bissell, aged twenty-four, a general dealer, William Dennis Tripp, aged twenty-seven, John William Capon, aged twenty-four, and Charles Alexander Hasber, aged thirty-four, were as follows: "Alright, I admit it; we were caught," "Somebody must have split on us. Where did you all come from?" "We're caught; what is there to say?" and "There is nothing to say – you got us bang to rights."

All four men were accurate in their assertions, and it was a matter viewed very gravely by the courts; Bissell was sentenced to six years' penal servitude and Hasber to five years' penal servitude. Capon and Tripp each received two years' imprisonment.

Beatrice Kettle, a fifty-seven-year-old cafe proprietress, and her daughter, thirty-seven-year-old Daisy May Kettle, a waitress, both of Bethnal Green Road, were arrested by Detective Inspector Periam of the Flying Squad for receiving cigarettes valued at £50. Old Street Magistrates felt the daughter was the more culpable and they fined her £25, whilst her mother was fined £15. The arresting officer, Philip Graeme Periam, had joined the police in 1928 and had spent twenty years, almost to the day, working at divisional duties before arriving at the Flying Squad with eleven commissioner's commendations to his credit. He, too, would become involved in further Ghost Squad arrests.

Alexander Sydney Francis Cracknall, with a criminal record stretching back ten years, was fingered by a Ghost Squad informant as living in Salcombe, Devon, which was where he was arrested by officers of that constabulary. He had been circulated as being wanted for false pretences and larceny by officers at Worthing and was duly handed over to them. Further information from the Ghost Squad snouts was farmed out to 'L' Division; Bastiaan Hendrekus Nossent, aged twenty-three and a Dutch national, and Ivor George Bittner, a twenty-seven-year-old labourer, both of no fixed abode, were arrested by Detective Sergeant Mullins and Detective Constable Garment for stealing 220 bedsheets from James Hayes & Co., 129 Coldharbour Lane, Camberwell. Nossent received a ticking-off and was bound over to keep the peace in the sum of £5 for two years, whereas Bittner was sentenced to fifteen months' imprisonment.

James William Smith, aged thirty-eight, and Richard McCann, aged thirty-two, were both described as 'dealers'. When they were arrested in possession of watches valued at £1,000 by Detective Sergeant Gullett and three other members of his Flying Squad team, Smith struck the better deal – he was discharged after he gave evidence against McCann, who was fined £100 with £21 costs.

When Joseph Adelman, a grocer aged forty of Edgware, Middlesex, received a visit from Detective Sergeant Wallis from the Flying Squad, he was initially arrested for receiving a quantity of rice, allegedly stolen. Not so; Hendon Magistrates discharged him but fined him £150 with ten guineas costs against Adelman's Stores Ltd. for failing to keep proper records. And Leonard Alfred Castell, a thirty-year-old shop manager from Islington, was arrested, also by Detective Sergeant Wallis, because a shop at 325 Edgware Road, Paddington had been broken into and cigarettes and cigars had been stolen to the value of £400. These items had been recovered intact at Mr Castell's premises, and after a series of remands at Marylebone Magistrates' Court he was fined £50 and was allowed seven days to pay.

When Lucy Edna Smith, aged twenty-six, a housewife from Shepherds Bush, was arrested with her husband, Walter, aged thirty-two and a coal porter, for being in possession of a quantity of cloth, gloves and a camera, valued at £400 by Detective Sergeants Hewett and Gentle of the Flying Squad, it was Mrs Smith who walked free from court five weeks later, having been bound over for a period of two years; her husband went down for eighteen months for receiving. The same two officers had even less luck when they arrested a forty-one-year-old licensee and a twenty-nine-year-old driver for receiving eleven cases of whisky valued at £260, because after appearing at the Old Bailey both men were acquitted.

It was at this time that Detective Sergeant Baker and the Ghost Squad parted company; given the little he had achieved, it seemed no great loss. In fact, in his memoirs Gosling stated that following his promotion to detective inspector, the vacancy left by him for a sergeant had been filled on the Ghost Squad by Detective Sergeant Palmer, and to all intents and purposes it probably was. Certainly he made no mention of Baker who was posted to 'Y' Division. Officially, Baker's place was taken by Detective Sergeant Moyle.

Calvin James Moyle was born in 1909 at Plymouth, Devon. He served in the British Army with the Royal Army Service Corps as a fitter for six years before joining the Metropolitan Police in June 1931; within six months he was awarded his first commissioner's commendation, for stopping a runaway horse. It was then that he was transferred to 'L' Division and three years later he was appointed detective constable and posted to 'E' Division. At six feet tall, with his Army background, he was well able to take care of himself; during his four-and-a-half-year stay on 'E' Division, one of the four commissioner's commendations that he was awarded was for courage and devotion to duty, whilst effecting the off-duty arrest of a number of hooligans who had been causing a disturbance.

On Christmas Day 1939 he was posted to the Flying Squad and three years later he was promoted to detective sergeant (second class) and was retained on the Squad for a further four years. During that time he clocked up another thirteen commissioner's commendations, three of which – perhaps surprisingly – were with his predecessor on the Ghost Squad, Alfred Baker.

Moyle was promoted detective sergeant (first class) and one week later, in May 1946, he was posted back to 'L' Division. Just two and a half years and seven commissioner's commendations later, he was back on the Squad again and straight on to the Ghost Squad.

* * *

Joseph Daniel Powers, a thirty-five-year-old car dealer from South Kensington, discovered that his fifteen-year-old criminal record counted against him after Detective Sergeant Foster and his Flying Squad team arrested him for obtaining a car by means of false pretences; he was sentenced to twenty-one months' imprisonment.

Benjamin Rosenfield, a forty-six-year-old tobacconist from Hackney, was found in possession of stolen cigarettes valued at £5,000 by Detective Sergeant Bradbury of the Flying Squad (later, as a detective chief inspector, he would run the office set aside for the investigation into the great train robbery); three months later at the Old Bailey, Rosenfield was sentenced to two years' imprisonment.

When the Ghost Squad personnel received information that two fourteen-year-old boys were responsible for the larceny of brass items, they decided that this was not a case for which they should task the Flying Squad and instead farmed it out to Detective Constable Huntley from Peckham police station; both boys had the matter discharged at Lambeth Juvenile Court. The Special Duties Squad concentrated on more pertinent matters, and as the young Peckham desperadoes were bracing themselves for a confrontation at the Juvenile Court, the Squad's informants came up with something far more suitable.

A large quantity of tapestry worth £1,200 was stolen by means of a warehousebreaking at Newark, Nottinghamshire and gradually it made its way down to Stoke Newington where on 9 October it was found in possession of Jack Greenberg, a thirty-three-year-old commercial traveller, who was arrested by Detective Sergeants Walker, Wallace and Munsie of the Flying Squad. Two days later the same officers arrested Samuel Greenberg, a thirty-seven-year-old linen merchant from Walthamstow. Jack was sentenced to nine months' imprisonment, Samuel to fifteen months, and the wife of one of the brothers was discharged at court five weeks after her arrest.

Percy Friend, a dealer of Chertsey, Surrey, was arrested for a factorybreaking at 58 Acklam Road, North Kensington where a quantity of material and ladies' dresses, valued together at £800, was stolen. Since Mr Friend was sixty-five years of age at the time of the offence, unless he possessed powers of athleticism which the arresting officers failed to disclose, it is highly likely that he was dealt with for receiving the stolen property, which would in some way account for him being bound over in the sum of £10 for two years at the County of London Sessions. Binding over seemed to be the order of the day; Harry Thomas Millard, a driver from Camberwell and Leonard Southgate, a fruiterer from Peckham, both aged twenty-two, were arrested by Detective Sergeant Brodie and officers from the Flying Squad for stealing a van and its contents valued at £1,000; both were bound over in the sum of £25 for two years and were ordered to pay £20 costs. Ernest Elias Wood, a forty-one-year-old butcher from Kingsbury, was arrested by Detective Sergeants Probert and Cherry of the Flying Squad. Wood was not bound over for receiving stolen meat valued at £2,443 but was undoubtedly fortunate to be fined £500 or three months' imprisonment in default.

Back to 'L' Division again, and this time Detective Sergeant Sharman, in charge of the 'L' Division 'Q' Car, arrested a thirty-nine-year-old shopkeeper from Ladbroke Grove for receiving eight parcels of curtaining plus twelve extra pieces of curtaining and was probably peeved when the case against the shopkeeper was discharged. However, this was just a blip, since he had much better luck in arresting Peter Cyril Johnson, a twenty-one-year-old seaman, Joseph Chandler, a dealer aged twenty-one and Neville Baldwin, an eighteen-year-old street trader, for stealing whisky valued at £1,500. Johnson was sentenced to two years' imprisonment, Chandler to twelve months and Baldwin to three years' Borstal detention. A thirty-nine-year-old fruiterer from Walthamstow was discharged. Three days later Sergeant Sharman struck again, arresting Jacob Sampson, a fifty-one-year-old shop manager from Bayswater, for receiving fifty suits worth £600; he received nine months' imprisonment. Cyril Aspella, a thirty-six-year-old waistcoat maker from Acre Lane, was far more fortunate than Mr. Sampson when he was arrested a few days later by Detective Sergeants Ogden and Grant of the Flying Squad for receiving a quantity of gents' suiting valued at £150; at the County of London Sessions he was fined £30.

Albert Henson, a forty-year-old lorry driver, was arrested by Detective Sergeant Anderson and Detective Constable MacMillan for stealing two bales of cloth worth £100;

Marylebone Magistrates fined him £10 or one month's imprisonment. A thirty-four-year-old fish and chip shop proprietress from Islington was arrested by Detective Sergeants Foster and Anderson for receiving fifty gallons of cottonseed frying oil valued at £80. Quite possibly the bench at Marylebone Magistrates' Court believed that increasing the North London public's consumption of fish and chips would improve flagging morale, and the lady was discharged.

A little judicious night-work sent Detective Sergeants Palmer and Acott to Haverstock Hill, NW3, where they arrested Thomas Phillip McCarron, a twenty-four-year-old plasterer's mate, for being a suspected person, loitering with intent to break into shops. Rather surprisingly, he was fined twenty shillings. A week later, enjoying more night-work, Detective Sergeant Bradbury of the Flying Squad and his team kept observation at Cambridge Crescent where they arrested Patrick Hussey, a labourer, Christopher Brennan and John Joseph Kennedy, all aged twenty-one and all from the same address at Lisson Street, Paddington, in the act of attempting to break into a shop and possessing housebreaking implements by night; even more surprisingly, all were bound over in the sum of £10 for two years. Three days later, the same skills at night-work resulted in the arrest of Kenneth George Neart, a twenty-six-year-old engineer from Willesden. He was caught in the act at 1.30 in the morning at King's Grove, Peckham for officebreaking, attempting to steal £850 from a safe and possessing housebreaking implements by night. He was by no means as fortunate as his counterparts from Haverstock Hill or Lisson Street; at the County of London Sessions exactly one month later Neart was sentenced to twenty-one months' imprisonment. Far more fortunate was the arresting officer from 'L' Division, who had featured so prominently in the arrest of the Peckham juveniles; less than two years later Detective Constable Bob Huntley would be posted to the Flying Squad for a total of ten years. Huntley would go on to receive twenty-six commissioner's commendations, be awarded the British Empire Medal for gallantry after disarming a gunman, the Queen's Police Medal for distinguished service and retire after over thirty-six years' service, as Commander of the Bomb Squad.

Keeping more conventional hours, Detective Sergeant Boshell of the Flying Squad arrested Laurence Daniel Attridge, a thirty-year-old builder from Collier Row Lane, Romford, for receiving a fur coat and a quantity of ladies' garments; he was sentenced to eighteen months' imprisonment at Chelmsford. And ladies' clothing featured again, this time valued at £600, when Detective Sergeant Anderson and his team arrested James Henry Waterhouse, a fruit salesman, and Rose Margaret Ridewood, a newsagent, both aged forty-one, for receiving feminine garments stolen by means of a housebreaking on 'D' Division. Waterhouse was sentenced to a total of six months' imprisonment and felt this rather excessive; he appealed and was released on bail, but his appeal was dismissed and he was ordered to pay seven guineas costs and to complete his sentence. Prudently, Mrs. Ridewood considered her punishment of a £100 fine or three months' imprisonment in default to be just about right. The same thoughts were probably in the mind of Henry John Bird, aged fifty-three, after he was arrested by Detective Constable Donald MacMillan for receiving two clothing coupon books; he was fined £25 or three months' imprisonment. And Morris Grossman, a forty-seven-year-old general dealer from Stoke Newington, may have thought that the fine of £300 with ten guineas costs for receiving twenty-two gold watches valued at £200 was a trifle severe; but since his criminal career had started over thirty years previously, it may have been a good result for him.

Receiving furs continued to be popular in the run-up to Christmas; Harry Waterman, a thirty-year-old hairdresser, was charged with receiving a £300 fur coat and was sentenced to twelve months' imprisonment at the County of London Sessions; his co-accused, a thirty-one-year-old housewife with an exotic-sounding Neapolitan name, was acquitted. The following day, Detective Inspector Periam and his Flying Squad officers swooped on Karter Singh Opel, a thirty-seven-year-old wholesaler from Stepney, together with James Thomas Patrick Quirk, from Canning Town. A shopbreaking at Chatham had resulted in furs valued at £3,000 being stolen; the two men were found in possession of £1,000 worth of them. At the Old Bailey the following February Opel was sentenced to nine months' imprisonment and Quirk to eighteen months. Five days later Inspector Periam struck again; he arrested Ontonio Cruz (a Spaniard) and Vittoria Spizzo (an Italian) for a shopbreaking at Stowmarket, Suffolk. Furs valued at £1,800 had been stolen; these were recovered intact and six weeks later both men were sentenced to two years' imprisonment at East Suffolk Quarter

Sessions; the bench commended Periam for his work, as did the commissioner.

In fact, any commodity was fair game for the thieves and receivers; following a warehousebreaking on 'X' Division where cutlery valued at £2,000 was stolen, Detective Inspector MacDonald and other Flying Squad officers arrested Alfred Edward George Bottoms, a twenty-seven-year-old counterhand from Cricklewood who was in possession of the part-proceeds, valued at £1,700. He was sentenced to twelve months' imprisonment. James Donoghue, a forty-year-old street trader, and Eddie Duff, aged forty-two, a costermonger, were found in possession of stolen cloth worth £500 by Detective Sergeant Anderson of the Flying Squad. Donoghue, whose criminal career started in 1927, was sentenced to fifteen months' imprisonment and Duff, who received his first conviction at the age of sixteen, was sentenced to nine months.

A twenty-six-year-old carpenter made use of two different names, possibly to evade apprehension, because he was circulated as being wanted for an offence of inflicting grievous bodily harm. He could have saved himself the trouble; arrested by Detective Sergeant Parker of 'X' Division, his case was discharged at West London Magistrates' Court. Harry George Parkinson Clarke's criminal career had started in 1931; a thirty-nine-year-old sales manager, he was arrested by Detective Sergeant Acott of the Flying Squad for unlawful possession of 222 pairs of nylons valued at £222. Convicted on two charges at the County of London Sessions, he was fined £150 with twenty guineas costs, plus another £50 fine or three and three months' imprisonment, consecutive.

Edith Elizabeth Talbot, a fifty-two-year-old cafe proprietress from Islington, was arrested by a Flying Squad team, led by Detective Inspector Cole. She was in possession of a quantity of ladies' coats, costumes and dresses, valued at £800 and stolen from Messrs Fisher, Renwick, a railway depot repository, as well as from a shopbreaking in her area; for five counts of receiving she was sentenced to nine months' imprisonment at the County of London Sessions the following March. Next, it was the turn of Walter Harold Gill Morrish, a twenty-one-year-old ambulance attendant, who was arrested by Detectives Sergeants Anderson, Foster and Detective Constable MacMillan of the Flying Squad for storebreaking and stealing wireless sets valued at £100.

Shortly afterwards, Ronald Page, an eighteen-year-old labourer, was arrested by the same officers for the same offence. Both appeared at court on 13 January 1949 when Morrish was sentenced to fifteen months' imprisonment and Page was sent to Borstal detention for three years. On the same day, a sixty-six-year-old market salesman and a forty-year-old tailor who had been charged with receiving one of the stolen wireless sets were acquitted.

Lewis Phillip Beck, aged sixty-five, and his son, Phillip Adam Beck, aged twenty-four, both jewellers of the same address in north London, were arrested together with Rufus Cardash, a thirty-five-year-old traveller from the Euston Road, by Flying Squad officers Detective Sergeants Brodie and Franklyn for receiving seventy ladies' cocktail watches worth £700. Lewis Beck's criminal record commenced in 1938 and Cardash's in 1936; the junior Beck had no previous convictions. So they were very lucky to be dealt with so leniently. Cardash was fined £750 with £25 costs, or three months' imprisonment in default. Lewis Beck was also fined £750 with £25 costs or one month's imprisonment in default, and his son was fined £250 with £25 costs or twenty-one days' imprisonment in default.

James Patrick Cavanagh was a forty-eight-year-old builder from North Kensington who was described as an expert housebreaker and one who had been the subject of many police enquiries during the previous few months. It took a Ghost Squad informant to nudge Detective Sergeant Acott of the Flying Squad in his general direction, and Acott arrested him for a housebreaking on 'S' Division where furs valued at £910 were stolen. Property from the housebreaking valued at £692 was recovered and in addition, Cavanagh's son, Patrick Walter, a driver aged twenty, and Edith Connelly, a seventy-one-year-old housewife, also of North Kensington, were similarly arrested. The following February at the Old Bailey, the senior Cavanagh was found guilty of receiving the property; he was sentenced to three years' penal servitude. His son was sentenced to Borstal detention and the elderly lady was bound over in the sum of £5 for two years.

At the age of fifty-one, Stanley Gillman, a draper of Hornsey, had no previous convictions. He was foolish indeed to have received clothing stolen from the Fisher, Renwick, British Railways depot and also from a shopbreaking on nearby 'N'

Division, which totalled £600 in value; he was arrested by Detective Sergeant Probert of the Flying Squad and was sentenced to twelve months' imprisonment.

A week before Christmas, Detective Sergeants Muncie, Walker and Walters of the Flying Squad arrested Sydney Crapper, aged forty-three, a shop proprietor, for receiving stolen sheets, Joseph Edward Carroll, a twenty-six-year-old labourer, and James Joseph Walsh, a thirty-five-year-old salesman, both for stealing ten suits and an overcoat valued at £120 and Walsh alone for stealing suits and shirts valued at £50. All received imprisonment at West London Magistrates' Court: Crapper got two months' imprisonment and a fine of £5 or an extra month's imprisonment in default. Walsh was sentenced to three months' imprisonment and Carroll to two months. Nathan Kurtz, a forty-four-year-old tailor, and Morris Marks, a tailor's presser aged twenty-eight, both of the same address in Finchley, were rather more fortunate when they were arrested by a different Flying Squad team, comprised of Detective Sergeants Anderson and Forsyth, plus Detective Constable MacMillan, two days later. They had received stolen cloth valued at £300. Early in the New Year Marks was fined £10, whilst the rather more culpable Kurtz was fined £250 with twenty-five guineas costs or three months' imprisonment in default.

Three men and a woman, all from the same address in West London, were arrested by Detective Sergeants Walker and Wallis of the Flying Squad for receiving a quantity of National Savings Certificates valued at £500, the proceeds of a housebreaking at Edgware. The case produced a less than a satisfactory conclusion: the woman and one of the men had their cases discharged at West London Magistrates' Court, and her husband and the other defendant failed to appear.

Frederick Ernest William Willison, a twenty-eight-year-old labourer, rather had his Christmas spoilt when he was arrested in London and handed over to an escort, since he was wanted for storebreaking in Bognor Regis.

The year came to a close when Patrick Joseph Gilmore, a twenty-nine-year-old chef, and Reginald Nelson Bause Markham, a twenty-three-year-old hairdresser, were arrested on Christmas Day for shopbreaking with intent at 60 Old Compton Street. They were remanded to Marlborough Street Magistrates' Court until New Year's Day 1949. Perhaps the magistrates thought that their actions were the result of youthful impetuosity or that by missing Christmas they had suffered enough. Each was sentenced to one day's imprisonment. This meant that they were detained until the court rose that day; and on the first day of 1949 the case list cannot have been too long.

It was a fitting end to an action-packed year. The Ghost Squad had been responsible for 252 arrests – almost half as many arrests again as in the first year's operations – and had recovered property to the value of £81,374 14s 0d, in excess of half as much again as the previous year. Informants, who had been paid £1,628 from the Informants Fund and received a share of the £8,000 from insurance companies and loss adjusters, had been worth every penny. When one considers that for five months the Ghost Squad had been without a divisional detective inspector to lead it, these results were nothing less than fabulous.

At the beginning of the year, Capstick, who had been deputising for Howe, requested a second vehicle for the Ghost Squad. It is not now entirely clear how he set out the request, but he probably suggested that it was for a temporary period only. The following day, a Humber was delivered to the Ghost Squad. Three months later, B6 (Traffic) Department demanded the return of the vehicle. Detective Superintendent Chapman, the head of the Flying Squad, promptly refused. A furious row broke out between the departments until two months after the refusal Gosling submitted a report, complaining that one car for the squad was clearly inadequate, and the Ghost Squad was eventually permitted to keep the vehicle. Of necessity, the vehicles were continually swapped around. By the end of the year, two Wolseley cars had been allocated to the Ghost Squad, but Stuttard stated that the time was ripe for a further vehicle to be added to the fleet in order to cope with the increasing workload and mentioned that a report to that effect would be submitted in the near future. In addition, Stuttard praised the valuable assistance given by Flying Squad officers, namely Detective Sergeants Freeman and Palmer, as well as Detective Constable Robertson.

The report for the year's work read:

The work of the personnel has been very praiseworthy. They are hard workers; do not work to the clock and I feel very confident that with the excellent team spirit which prevails among them they will go from strength to strength.

Detective Superintendent Chapman wholeheartedly agreed, and his praise was echoed by the Deputy Commander, William Rawlings, who noted:

> In 1948 the Special Duty Squad has maintained its efficiency and usefulness. The number of arrests for which it has been responsible and the amount of property recovered shows a decided increase on the year 1947. Many Divisions and some Provincial Forces have benefitted by their endeavours.
>
> Detective Inspector Stuttard has proved himself an excellent leader of this small band, the members of which are untiring in their efforts to unearth the persons who commit crime in the Metropolis. They maintain their high standards of informants and the improvement in 1948 over 1947 has only cost the additional small sum of £590. In my opinion, this is a satisfactory years' work by this particular squad.

Howe passed the report on to the Commissioner to see. Sir Harold Scott put his seal on the past twelve months' work when he wrote: "The Special Duty Squad are to be congratulated on an excellent year's work".

The Ghost Squad were riding on the crest of a wave. During the year they had averaged arrests at the rate of five per week. They had the personal backing of the commissioner. Nothing could go wrong.

Could it?

CHAPTER 7

Apocalypse

n March 1949 clothes rationing came to an end. In Cripps' second budget, Income Tax relief was put in place and beer and wine duties were reduced. However, on the downside, butter was still beyond the means of most families. On 1 May the gas industry was nationalised, and five weeks later the dock strike forced the Government to use troops to unload goods. In mid-September the pound was devalued by 30% against the dollar. One cheering piece of news from America was that Sir Laurence Olivier's *Hamlet* was the first British film to win the Oscar for 'Best Film'. Soap rationing ended the following year, and although one year later the meat ration would be cut once again and would remain in place until 1954, the year when ration books would finally be abolished, it seemed as though Britain was slowly – very slowly – starting to emerge from post-war austerity.

★   ★   ★

Mark Miller, a forty-three-year-old dressmaker from Colindale, succumbed to temptation (as he had fifteen years previously) and received stolen cloth valued at £500. He was the first of the year's arrests for the Ghost Squad after Detective Sergeant Fisher and Detective Constable MacMillan of the Flying Squad paid him a visit; Miller was fined £250 and twenty-five guineas costs or three months' imprisonment in default.

In fact, at the beginning of 1949 the Flying Squad would be making themselves very busy indeed on behalf of the Ghost Squad informants. Next, Detective Sergeant Munsie arrested Robert Wass, a thirty-eight-year-old labourer of Camden Town, for receiving three and a half tons of lead piping worth £400. Wass had led a blameless life until then; he was sentenced to fifteen months' imprisonment. Hyman Levine, a forty-one-year-old tailor of Maida Vale, had similarly steered clear of the law;

that is, until Detective Sergeant Hewett arrested him for receiving two rolls of lining and a roll of overcoat material, valued at £130; Levine was fined £30. Another first-timer to fall foul of the Flying Squad was Andrew Zani, a sixty-two-year-old cafe proprietor from Paddington. Detective Inspector MacDonald and Detective Sergeant Veasey discovered he was in possession of a quantity of stolen tea worth £30 and, what was more, that he had contravened the Aliens Order. He was fined £15 with five guineas costs on the first charge and bound over in the sum of £10 for a period of twelve months on the second. Isadore Galizer, a forty-two year old general dealer from Clapham Common, had also avoided contact with the authorities – until Detective Sergeants Foster and Anderson entered his premises and discovered that he was in possession of a quantity of stolen silk stockings valued at £120. Galizer was offered the choice of paying a fine of £120 with the option of three months' imprisonment if he did not. Arthur Victor Lee, a thirty-two-year-old catering accountant, and Benedict Yafrate, a twenty-eight-year-old waiter, on the other hand, were no strangers to the world of crime; they were arrested by Detective Sergeants Brodie and Franklyn for housebreaking with intent and Lee was sentenced to three concurrent terms of fifteen months' imprisonment, with Yafrate receiving nine months at the County of London Sessions. Robertson had also made an input into this case; he, Brodie and Franklyn were commended by the commissioner.

Now it was the turn of the Special Duties Squad to get involved; Detective Sergeant Palmer and Detective Constable Robertson visited Hendon Stadium on 19 January and arrested William Walton, a thirty-eight-year-old dealer, for loitering with intent to pick pockets. The following day at Hendon Magistrates' Court, Walton, who had been known to the police since 1931, received the maximum penalty for the offence: three months' hard labour. Three days later, Arthur Jacobs who, like Walton, was aged thirty-eight and had also been acquainted with the police since 1931, was arrested at White City Stadium for going one step further and actually stealing £5 from a punter's pocket; he was sentenced to three months' imprisonment.

More conventional Ghost Squad work recommenced the following day, when Cyril Packer, a twenty-nine-year-old credit dealer from Conway Street, NW1, together with Blume Goodcovitch, a forty-five-year-old housewife from Beehive Lane,

Ilford, and her husband Alexander, aged forty, a shopkeeper, were arrested for receiving 120 pairs of nylon stockings valued at £120; in addition, Alexander Goodcovitch was further charged with receiving a further fifty-six pairs of nylons. For some reason, Packer and Blume Goodcovitch appeared at West London Magistrates' Court where Packer was fined £50 with five guineas costs and Mrs. Goodcovitch was fined £75 with ten guineas costs, whereas Alexander Goodcovitch appeared at Old Street Magistrates' Court and was fined £100 with ten guineas costs.

The Flying Squad returned to assist and they had plenty to occupy them. Alec Hancock, unemployed and aged fifty, was arrested by Detective Inspector Periam and Detective Sergeant Williams at Regent's Park for unlawfully acquiring two suit lengths and was sentenced to three months' imprisonment. Three days later, the same two officers arrested two men for being in possession of a lorry and its contents valued at £960 which had disappeared from Kennington nine days previously, and shortly afterwards they arrested Thomas Lee, a twenty-five-year-old slater far from his home in Chatham. Lee was wanted for a shopbreaking in Kent where property valued at £1,000 had been stolen, and five weeks later at Maidstone Quarter Sessions he was sentenced to three years' penal servitude.

Peter Patrick Peedell, a thirty-nine-year-old labourer, was also arrested for a shopbreaking, in this case where clothing valued at £344 had been stolen. Part of the proceeds, worth £228, was found in his possession, and he was given the choice by Detective Sergeants Munsie and Walters of which way to jump. Peedell chose the receiving charge, a wise course of action, because he was fined £6 or one month's imprisonment in default.

George Chaloner, a thirty-six-year-old hotel manager of Sussex Gardens, W2, was arrested by Detective Sergeant Hewett and Detective Constable Gentle for being in unlawful possession of twenty-four pairs of nylons, for which he was fined £25 or two months' imprisonment as an alternative. The following day, the same officers arrested a forty-three-year-old managing director for receiving 1,977 yards of poplin and eighteen rolls of cretonne material, valued at £1,000. Obviously, being a director of a company carried more weight than being a labourer or unemployed, because his case was thrown out of court. Unperturbed, the two officers arrested Reginald Garrett, a twenty-four-year-old street trader, together with Lawrence

William Wood, two years older than his associate and also a street trader, the following day. They were charged with stealing or alternatively receiving a lorry, valued at £1,400 plus its contents, rationed goods worth £150. Three weeks later they appeared at Middlesex Sessions where Garrett was bound over in the sum of £10 for a period of two years; Wood was sentenced to three and six months' imprisonment, to run consecutively. Hyman Fidler, another street trader aged twenty-five, was arrested by Sergeant Hewett shortly afterwards; he was in possession of seventy-two pairs of nylons and at the County of London Sessions he was fined £10 with five guineas costs.

A twenty-nine-year-old builder from the Old Brompton Road, Chelsea was found to be in possession of cameras valued at £700, the proceeds of a shopbreaking; he was acquitted at the County of London Sessions. And in another part of the capital, a window cleaner whose criminal career had commenced eight years previously when he was eighteen was found by Detective Inspector MacDonald and Detective Sergeant Veasey of the Flying Squad to be in possession of two cameras valued at £200; these were the proceeds of an officebreaking. In a curious twist to the running of the Ghost Squad, the window cleaner failed to answer his bail at court and a warrant for his arrest was issued. Two months later he was arrested by Detective Sergeant Palmer and Detective Constable Robertson; why it was necessary for two officers from an undercover squad to effect such a mundane arrest is not clear. In any event, ten days later, the man was acquitted of the charge at the County of London Sessions.

Peter Deary, a forty-five-year-old broker from Forest Gate was arrested by Detective Inspector Periam for receiving thirty ladies rings valued at £750. He was detained, awaiting escort to Chatham, where the rings originated. A forty-five-year-old banker and a nineteen-year-old shop assistant were charged with receiving thirty-seven wristlet watches worth £370 – both were discharged.

It appeared the courts were getting a little soft on sentencing for receiving soft goods (or apparatus pertaining thereto) – when Alec Bookbinder, a thirty-five-year-old traveller, was found by Flying Squad officers in possession of a stolen 'Supreme' cloth cutting machine valued at £90, he was fined £35 and three guineas costs. He was offered two months' imprisonment in default of payment, but paid the fine. So did Mary Rosner, a thirty-five-year-old housewife from Leytonstone, after she was fined £50 or three months' imprisonment, having been arrested by Detective Sergeants Munsie and Walters for possession of 114 pairs of nylons. When Marven Thomas Clack, a labourer aged thirty-eight, was arrested by two of the Ghost Squad team, Detective Sergeant Freeman and Detective Constable Robertson, for receiving two bales of silk and a length of cloth, it appeared that the court took little notice of his criminal career which had commenced in 1932; he was fined £10. And when George Lee Haaker, a thirty-two-year-old pilot of the Mayfair Hotel, Berkeley Street, W1, was arrested by Flying Squad officers for receiving 238 pairs of nylons, quite possibly Bow Street Magistrates did take note of his unblemished career and war record, because he was fined £100 or six months' imprisonment in default.

But if the courts were taking a lenient view of housewives and labourers receiving a few nylons, they were nevertheless taking a harder line on more determined criminals. Robert Bimpson, aged twenty-five, and David Wells, aged twenty-four, both labourers of no fixed address, were arrested by Detective Inspector Periam and his Flying Squad team for housebreaking, where a fur coat and jewellery to the value of £850 were stolen; Bimpson was sentenced to eighteen months' imprisonment and Wells to twelve months.

The following day, Periam's counterpart, Detective Inspector MacDonald, arrested Alfred Kitchener Bennett, a twenty-six-year-old fruiterer from Plaistow, and two days after that Francis George Stanley Martin, a lorry driver aged thirty-nine from nearby Stratford. Both were charged with stealing a lorry and its load – seven and a half tons of butter – valued together at £1,850, both were remanded in custody and at the Old Bailey almost a month later Bennett was sentenced to eight months' hard labour while Martin received two years' imprisonment.

Walter William Sampson, a twenty-two-year-old miner, and Henry Jeffrey Douglas Jackson, aged twenty-nine, were arrested by Detective Sergeant Hewett after being found in possession of three fur coats and a quantity of jewellery, valued at £800. Because the men were unable to give a satisfactory explanation, they were charged with receiving the goods. However, when they appeared at Clerkenwell Magistrates' Court, the police offered no evidence to the charge; they were handed over instead to officers from Hertfordshire Constabulary, who knew exactly where the property had originated from.

A tip-off from a snout left no time for Detective Sergeants Palmer and Freeman plus Detective Constable Robertson to alert other officers; they hurried to Duke Street, Marylebone where they arrested a club secretary, Edward Marro, aged forty, and Robert Sydney Newton, also aged forty and a lorry driver from Norwich. They were found to be in possession of four sacks of meat, five crates of rabbits and six crates of eggs. Marro was sentenced to three months' imprisonment and ordered to pay five guineas costs and Newton two months' imprisonment and ordered to pay two guineas costs.

John Raymond Halmshaw had been known to the police since he was fourteen; now, aged twenty-five and a motor mechanic from Kentish Town, he was arrested by Detective Inspector Periam and his team for housebreaking and receiving clothing valued at £75. Less than a month later, at Essex Quarter Sessions, he was sentenced to two years' imprisonment.

It must have been a considerable number of handkerchiefs to have been worth £250, but that was what Frederick Stocks, a general dealer aged thirty-nine, Jack Waters, a thirty-seven-year-old caterer, and Frederick Charles Swift, an interior decorator aged thirty-one, had in their possession when they were arrested by Detective Sergeants Wilson and Stevens. It was sufficient, three months later at the County of London Sessions, to send Stocks and Waters to prison for fifteen months each and Swift for nine.

The courts have always taken a severe view of postmen who steal property entrusted to them. Although forty-year-old Arthur Stanley Jay had no previous convictions, it mattered little to the magistrates at Marylebone. One week after his arrest by a Flying Squad team for the larceny of a postal packet, Jay was sentenced to a total of six months' imprisonment. That may have been considered to be a just punishment; however, it was astonishing was when Detective Inspector Periam arrested Leonard Hyman, a twenty-one-year-old lighterman of no fixed address, for being a suspected person, loitering with intent for the purposes of housebreaking, possessing a firearm and stealing clothing. It is highly likely that a few Flying Squad jaws dropped after Hyman was leniently bound over in the sum of £10 for twelve months.

Lieutenant Donald Bridwell, aged thirty-one, and Sergeant Francis W Angell, aged forty-one, both of 97 Park Street, W1 and both serving members of the United States Air Force, were found in possession of 445 pairs of nylons by Detective Sergeant Hewett and Detective Constable Gentle of the Flying Squad; they were handed over to the USAF Provost Marshall.

More nylons featured when Peter Belak, a twenty-eight-year-old toolmaker from Hampstead, was arrested by Detective Sergeant Acott for being in unlawful possession of 363 pairs of them and was given fourteen days to pay a fine of £200 or be sentenced to six months' imprisonment in default. A smuggled mink coat, also seized, was handed over to HM Customs & Excise – Belak, who until then had no previous convictions, was not prosecuted for that offence. Neither was the forty-eight-year-old traveller who was arrested with him, and whose criminal career stretched back twenty-five years; the case against him was discharged. And after Mendel Hollander, a forty-five-year-old hosier from Stepney, was arrested by Detective Sergeant Taylor for receiving 291 pairs of nylons, he was fined £250 and ordered to pay twenty-five guineas costs; the charges against the seventy-five-year-old shop assistant who was arrested with him were dropped. Another seventy-five-year-old, this one a tailor, who was arrested by Detective Inspector Periam for receiving a fifteen guinea ring, was similarly discharged. The same officer, with the assistance of Detective Sergeant Williams and Detective Constable Grose, arrested Uszer Shapira, a fifty-two-year-old dealer from Stoke Newington who was in possession of twelve watches. It appeared that they were uncustomed goods; the prisoner appeared at Clerkenwell Magistrates' Court and was fined £26 8s 0d and ordered to pay five guineas costs.

Once again, a shop owner and a driver were arrested for being in possession of stolen goods; in this case, Thomas William Duffy, a forty-seven-year-old fruiterer, was supplied with eighty dozen eggs and thirty pounds of meat by Walter Albert Davey, aged thirty-nine, and, like Duffy, a resident of Stoke Newington. Arrested by Detective Sergeant Taylor of the Flying Squad, both men appeared before Tottenham Magistrates' Court and Duffy, whose criminal record commenced in 1918, was fined £25 with three guineas costs; Davey was fined a similar amount, plus an extra £15 costs. The property in the case was described as being stolen from 'some person or persons unknown', as were the thirty-two tyres and inner tubes seized by Detective Sergeant Moyle when he arrested Leonard Ernest Orchard, a thirty-nine-year-old garage proprietor from Kensal Green, a week later. Appearing at Willesden Magistrates' Court, Orchard was fined £20 with five guineas costs.

On 12 April members of the Ghost Squad – Detective Sergeants Moyle and Burton – had to move quickly and liaise with Detective Sergeant Taylor of the Flying Squad to arrest James William Malin, aged thirty-seven, and Charles John Taylor, aged forty-one, both furniture porters and both with criminal records (Taylor's going back to 1926), for receiving three tables and three sideboards, valued at £110. Malin was sentenced to twenty-eight days' imprisonment and Taylor to three months.

Even more impressive than Taylor's criminal pedigree was that of a wizened fifty-nine-year-old dealer who was arrested by Detective Constable Robertson at Walthamstow for being a suspected person, loitering with intent to pick pockets. The prisoner's criminal career had commenced in 1914, the year when Robertson was born, but the evidence against him was insufficient to impress the bench at Stratford Magistrates' Court and the case against him was thrown out.

As if to make up for this rather ignominious defeat, Ghost Squad information was passed over to Robertson's former stamping ground, 'X' Division, and it was there that the crew of that division's 'Q' Car arrested Frederick Andrews, aged thirty, Arthur Burns, aged twenty-six, and Robert Charles Crawford, aged thirty. All hailed from Cardiff, and it transpired that the police of that city wished to question them regarding a safe-blowing at the city's Ministry of Agriculture office where cash and petrol coupons to the value of £200 had been stolen. In fact, when they were arrested, the safe-breaking impedimenta were still in their possession.

Donald George Scobie was arrested by Detective Inspector MacDonald and Detective Sergeant Bill Marchant and found it difficult to explain why a labourer of no fixed abode would require a gents dressing set; he was sentenced to two months' imprisonment. Walter Swaine, aged twenty-nine, and Michael William Cavanagh, aged twenty-eight, also found certain difficulties in explaining to Detective Constable Robertson why two tyre fitters would lawfully be in possession of sixteen pairs of shoes; each were fined £10 and given seven days to pay.

Robert Cox, aged fifty-five, who described himself as both a lorry driver and a greengrocer of, rather unusually, no fixed abode, was arrested in Plaistow by Sergeant Burton for stealing a lorry and its load of plywood, valued at £1,800. Almost as if to commemorate a criminal career which had commenced at the age of fifteen, when Cox appeared at the Old Bailey one month later, he received fifteen months' imprisonment.

The case which follows demonstrates both a classic Ghost Squad investigation and the remarkable tenacity displayed by Detective Sergeant Jim Moyle throughout.

The safe at a Post Office at Blandford, Dorset was blown at two o'clock on a Sunday morning and £12,000 cash, postal orders, insurance stamps and petrol coupons were stolen. The persons responsible were Arthur Burke – also known as Richard Davidson – aged thirty-five, a dealer from Hunstanton, Norfolk, and James Dickson, also aged thirty-five, an American and an explosives expert; and both were very clever thieves. The men had arrived in Blandford separately, one by train, the other by car. With their haul, the two men left the scene of the crime in a saloon car. Burke took Dickson to a railway station where he boarded a train to London; in the meantime, Burke switched cars and completed his journey to London in a sports car, so if anyone had seen his departure from the Post Office in the saloon, there would be nothing to connect him with his arrival in London in a sports model. There, they made their only mistake; they put their trust in a slimy garage proprietor whose garage in Maida Vale they used as a repository for the loot, a service for which they agreed to pay him £100 when they retrieved it the following day. But the garage proprietor decided to help himself to some of the stolen postal orders, which he then offered for sale; unfortunately, the man he offered them to was one of Gosling's best informants.

Gosling tasked Moyle to keep observation on the garage proprietor and followed him into central London until he met Burke and Dickson at the Cumberland Hotel, Marble Arch. The men split up after a drink, so Moyle followed Burke all the way to the Bournemouth area; Moyle was tailing Burke so closely he was unable to inform Gosling of his whereabouts for three days. Eventually, Dickson met Burke in Bournemouth, and now Moyle informed Gosling and a team of detectives including George Burton was sent to assist. A microphone was lowered into the fireplace of the men's hotel room, a canopy was erected over a manhole cover in the street outside the hotel with a detective keeping observation inside it, telephone calls were intercepted and, at the same time, garages were warned to look out for the stolen petrol coupons.

A week later, the two men travelled north and Moyle followed, but after he trailed them into Hunstanton, he lost them. However, Moyle remained where he was, and that night the County Council Offices in March, Cambridgeshire were broken into and the safe was blown; cash and more petrol coupons were stolen. Dickson returned to Hunstanton alone; he went to a premises which Moyle had seen the two men visit previously, to hide the cash and, with the assistance of officers from the Norfolk Constabulary, Moyle arrested Dickson. Dickson was now kept incommunicado; Moyle moved into his hotel room and when Burke telephoned from London asking for a share of the cash, Moyle, mimicking Dickson's American accent, told him he would telegraph £100 to a London Post Office. As he went to collect the money, Burke was arrested.

The garage proprietor was arrested and was given an ultimatum: give evidence for the prosecution or join the others in the dock. He decided to adopt the first option but proved to be as slippery with the Ghost Squad as he had been with his former associates and retracted his statement during his testimony. However, there was sufficient evidence to send Burke and Dickson down for ten years and Moyle and Burton were two of the officers who were commended by the commissioner.

It was back to more mundane matters for the Ghost Squad; Percy Hobbs, a twenty-seven-year-old labourer, was arrested by Detective Constable Farrant of the Flying Squad for deserting from the Royal Corps of Signals and was handed to a military escort; Sarah Fishman, a fifty-four-year-old housewife from Moscow Road, W2, was arrested by Flying Squad officers for harbouring 180 pairs of nylons and dealing in uncustomed goods and was fined a total of £225 and ten guineas costs; and Allan Frank Bernett, a caterer aged twenty-three, was arrested, also by Flying Squad officers, for receiving four hundredweight of butter, worth £35, and was fined £15 with five guineas costs.

But it was about this time – 4 June 1949 – that there was a subtle change in the Ghost Squad tactics. More of the Ghost Squad personnel started making arrests, far more than had done so previously.

The proceeds of a larceny from a vehicle in Mortimer Street, off Tottenham Court Road – 260 yards of silk valued at £90 – resulted in Palmer and Robertson paying a visit to David Diamond, a thirty-five-year-old street trader. Charged with receiving the material, Diamond was sentenced to six months' imprisonment at Marlborough Street Magistrates' Court. Next, it was the turn of Ghost Squad operatives Gosling and Burton to assist Detective Inspector MacDonald of the Flying Squad in arresting Leonard Charles Cunnington, a twenty-five-year-old seaman from Islington, for stealing – or, alternatively receiving – pens valued at £1,368, of which the part-proceeds, valued at £560, were found in Cunnington's possession. He probably opted for the latter option; he was sentenced to one month's imprisonment.

Four days later, Walter Clifford Burridge, a labourer aged thirty-seven of no fixed abode, was arrested by Robertson for unlawful possession of a clock, radio sets, jewellery and clothing, worth £100. Notwithstanding the fact that Burridge's criminal record had commenced twelve years previously, the bench at Marylebone Magistrates' Court bound him over in the sum of £25 to be of good behaviour for a period of two years.

On 22 June Robertson arrested William Albert Harold Ward, a stoker aged forty-one from Paddington, for receiving a suitcase containing a fur cape and other clothing, valued at £120. Further intelligence must have been received because the following day Robertson arrested John Albert Spencer, aged forty-two, and Thomas Welsh, aged twenty-nine, both labourers and both of no fixed abode, for stealing the suitcase. For his part in the transaction Ward was fined £10; both Spencer and Welsh were sentenced to eighteen months' imprisonment. Robertson lingered in the Paddington area a little longer; two days later he and Palmer arrested George Waugh, a thirty-four-year-old lorry driver, and Edward William Carr, a dealer aged twenty-five, both from Paddington, for larceny of corrugated iron sheds, and both men were sentenced to six months' imprisonment.

On 30 June Palmer and Robertson arrested Edward George Smith (who was first brought to the notice of the police at the age of sixteen), a thirty-nine-year-old livestock dealer from Hanwell, for stealing twenty-nine pieces of silverware and a carpet. It was 'a carpet' (or three months' imprisonment) which Smith was promised if he failed to pay the £100 fine which was imposed on him at Ealing Magistrates' Court. Within a week the same two officers struck again, arresting Gilbert Lee Searle, a thirty-nine-year-old electrical engineer who hoped to enhance his stock by receiving electrical goods valued at £105; West London Magistrates' Court fined him £30 plus five guineas costs. Whilst Robertson was dealing with the prisoner, Palmer was called to assist Burton in South London to apprehend John Mack, a thirty-five-year-old labourer. Mack, who had commenced his criminal career fifteen years previously, was arrested for a housebreaking in Dorking, Surrey and stealing property valued at £250. Six weeks later at Surrey Quarter Sessions he was sentenced to six months' imprisonment.

Two days later, a thirty-one-year-old salesman was arrested for receiving Postal Orders, National Savings Certificates and Post Office date stamps, valued together at £1,700, and made the mistake of giving a false address in Notting Hill. It guaranteed he would be committed in custody to stand his trial at the Old Bailey. On 18 July Moyle arrested a gown manufacturer from East Ham for receiving thirty panels of lining material worth £1,000; it was probably coincidental that his address was yards away from East Ham Magistrates' Court, where the bench dismissed the case, saying there was, "an element of doubt".

Stuttard had been promoted to detective chief inspector on 1 July and was retained on the Ghost Squad; no chair-bound warrior he, on 19 July Stuttard led a raid on the premises of William Vincent, a thirty-nine-year-old cabinet maker from Brick Lane, and seized a quantity of stolen oak timber valued at £800. The arrest was officially carried out by Detective Sergeant Hewett and when cautioned, Vincent, with unintentional humour, replied, "I suppose I'm lumbered". Old Street Magistrates' Court fined Vincent £75 with ten guineas costs or three months' imprisonment – both the fines and costs were paid. And three more arrests were carried out by Palmer and Robertson on 30 July for factorybreaking at West Hampstead and the larceny of a large amount of plastic panelling worth £1,500.

During that two-month period, just one arrest was carried out on behalf of the Ghost Squad informants and that was by the Flying Squad; Detective Sergeants Vibart and Gay arrested Norman Peter Wood, a thirty-year-old radio mechanic, for receiving a stolen 1½ litre Riley car worth £950; he was sentenced to six months' imprisonment at North London Magistrates' Court.

Several more Flying Squad arrests were made after the two-month period; Charles John Clay, a fifty-two-year-old shoe repairer from Shoreditch, was arrested by Detective Inspector Hilton for receiving 770 wireless valves valued at £750. However, eight days later Hilton made a further arrest: Patrick William Murray, a thirty-three-year-old lorry driver, also from Shoreditch, who was charged with stealing 800 of the wireless valves. At Old Street Magistrates' Court on 24 August Clay was fined £20 with the option of six weeks' imprisonment; Murray was committed to the County of London Sessions for sentence. And two days later, Detective Sergeant Hewett arrested Charles James Bull, a timber porter aged thirty-two, for larceny of timber, as a servant, valued at £200, who admitted, "I've been a fool"; he also appeared at Old Street Magistrates' Court, where he was fined £10 or two months' imprisonment in default.

The Special Duty Squad wiped up three fraudsmen for larceny (trick), and six days later Gosling led a team to arrest a forty-eight-year-old hosier for receiving 600 pairs of stolen nylon stockings. Two weeks later Moyle and Burton arrested Peter Stanley Boon, a twenty-two-year-old packer, Bernard Lloyd, also twenty-two, and Thomas Brown, a thirty-one-year-old porter, for a shopbreaking at Hazelmere; they were handed over to an escort from Godalming, Surrey.

Detective Sergeant Hewett of the Flying Squad continued his run of arrests, all of which dealt with the acquisition of varying amounts of timber, with fluctuating degrees of success. He arrested two timber merchants aged sixty-four and seventy-one respectively, for receiving a quantity of timber worth £50, plus a quantity of plywood. Then came the arrest of a twenty-seven-year-old fish curer from Bethnal Green, who was in possession of 250 cubic feet of timber valued at £220. Old Street Magistrates decided that there was insufficient evidence against him and dismissed the case. Finally, James Newman, a twenty-nine-year-old labourer from Bethnal Green, was arrested for larceny of timber worth £10 – he was fined £5 or given twenty-eight days' imprisonment.

In fact, Detective Sergeant Charlie Hewett has figured prominently in the Ghost Squad arrest casebook, as has Detective Constable Don MacMillan. Although they appear not to have carried out Ghost Squad arrests together, nevertheless they served on the Flying Squad as a team, and were known as

'Chas and Mac'. Hewett had often been used for undercover work; he also acted very bravely during 'The Battle of Heathrow'. He was chosen to act the part of one of the 'drugged' security guards who was robbed of the safe keys, after being savagely kicked, gagged and tied up by one of the gang, Alfred Roome. During the ensuing fracas, Roome gravely assaulted the Squad leader and in turn was beaten by Hewett so badly that he was hospitalised. Whilst Hewett was meting out punishment to Roome, another member of the gang tried to attack him; in defending his partner, MacMillan had his nose badly broken.

Victor Jose Howe, a thirty-one-year-old salesman of no fixed abode, was stopped in the street in possession of a quantity of jewellery valued at £175 by Detective Inspector Periam and his Flying Squad team. The onus was on Howe to prove that the items had been lawfully obtained, but he failed to do so and was remanded at Marylebone Magistrates' Court for a week until 15 September. During the interim period, a little more intelligence was gleaned as to the provenance of the items found in his possession; at the remand hearing no evidence was offered, Howe was re-arrested and taken to Wembley police station where he was charged with housebreaking.

Palmer and Robertson made their way to Ascot racecourse on 22 September and there arrested Frederick Walter Rose – his criminal career had started thirty years previously – and Charles William Wood, both aged forty-six, for being suspected persons, loitering with intent to pick race-goers' pockets; both were conditionally discharged for a period of three years. Rather less fortunate was Ivor Rothsey, aged fifty-four, who the following day at Ascot was arrested by Robertson for the same offence; he was sentenced to one month's imprisonment. As Robertson was busy carrying out his arrest, Gosling, Moyle and Burton were also busy arresting two men, with help from the Flying Squad, for larceny and receiving a lorry carrying a load of silks and other fabrics valued at £18,000. This case was described by Gosling in his memoirs as 'The Squad's last case', although that was slightly inaccurate; it was certainly the Ghost Squad's last big case.

Gosling had been called from his bed at 3.30 that morning by a trusted informant, whom he met an hour later in Whitehall. They drove off north, right out of London, and as they passed a pub in Elstree, the snout directed Gosling's attention to an eight-wheeled lorry which, from the height of the springs, Gosling could see was empty. The informant explained that the lorry had travelled down from Manchester and had been left locked and immobilised at a lorry park at Caledonian Road; but despite there being two night-watchmen in charge, it had nevertheless been stolen. On they went until they reached Hemel Hampstead, Hertfordshire, and at a gateway the snout pointed out a number of roughly built pigsties, part of Crossways Farm, Tavistock Green. Telling Gosling to "help himself", the snout departed and, looking inside one of the pigsties, Gosling saw the lorry's load, an enormous amount of silk. After questioning the owner of the property, Mr. Maurice, it was clear to Gosling that the man was a dupe of the thieves; he telephoned Moyle and Burton, who arrived an hour later, as did Detective Sergeant Hewett of the Flying Squad. The owner produced a rent book in respect of the rented pigsty and gave a description of the two men, who had told him they lived in London Colney, plus their car. Although Gosling believed the address on the rent book was bogus – it was – he instructed Burton and Moyle to take Maurice to the London Colney area to establish that the address given was definitely false. As they drove towards that area, the owner of the farm suddenly spotted a Riley car parked outside a pub and stated that that was the car which belonged to the men. Burton gave Maurice a ten shilling note and told him to go into the pub, buy the men some drinks and engage them in conversation, while he listened at the door. Maurice did so and Burton recorded a very incriminating conversation by the two suspects: Leonard Edward Varney, aged thirty-nine from Palmer's Green, and Ernest Henry King, aged thirty-five from Friern Barnet, both of them fuel merchants.

Brought back to the farm, they were shown the property and cautioned, to which King replied, "That's done it". At Caledonian Road police station, Varney asked, "How did you know we were at that pub?" and King commented, "We've got some good friends, somewhere". They needed them; the men instructed top barristers, including Derek Curtis Bennett QC, to mount a spirited defence at the Old Bailey, but they nevertheless went away for long periods. On 30 December 1949 – almost exactly four years since the preliminary meeting of the Ghost Squad had been called – Gosling, Burton and Moyle were commended by the commissioner for their ability in this case. It was the one and only time that these three officers were collectively recognised for their work on the Special Duties Squad.

On 4 October Palmer and Robertson arrested a forty-year-old labourer from a hostel in Buckinghamshire for unlawful possession of $400, and three days later the same officers arrested William Colquhoun, a thirty-seven-year-old seaman, for stealing 130 pairs of nylons. At Bow Street Magistrates' Court he was fined the rather unwieldy sum of £364 13s 3d or the option of six months' imprisonment. Colquhoun was given no time to pay and was committed to Wormwood Scrubs. Jack Phillips, a carpenter aged forty of no fixed abode, and Neville Brown, aged thirty-eight from Sheffield, were arrested by Palmer and Robertson, together with officers from the Surrey Constabulary, for breaking and entering a house in Leatherhead and stealing jewellery and clothing; they were charged and appeared at Dorking Magistrates' Court.

And on 25 October Moyle and Burton stopped Walter Samuel Eardley, aged forty-one, a clerk of no fixed abode. He was in possession of two cameras and other property, believed to have been the proceeds of a shopbreaking at 29 Duke Street, W1 and he was charged and appeared at Bow Street Magistrates' Court.

It was not the most phenomenal arrest carried out by the Ghost Squad personnel, but it is worth mentioning because it was the last arrest they ever made.

CHAPTER 8

Post-Mortem

T hus did the Ghost Squad come abruptly to an end in October 1949; after Stuttard's optimistic report on the squad's activities in 1948 – it contained the best results ever – and the commissioner's hearty congratulations at the beginning of 1949, there was not one further word entered on the Ghost Squad file. On 3 October Stuttard was transferred to C1 Department and he could certainly have provided a report and details of the year's arrests, for the commissioner, who had initially authorised the squad, was still in office at the time of its demise and had been so interested in the squad's progress at the beginning of the year, but Stuttard did not. In his memoirs Gosling stated that he stayed with the Ghost Squad for three months 'to tidy up a number of loose ends', but the records show that on the same day that Stuttard was posted from the Ghost Squad, so was Gosling, who was transferred to 'D' Division. Of course, Gosling could have been transferred 'on paper' and remained behind tidying up the loose ends, but it raises the question of why was he posted at all, especially when Burton, Moyle and Robertson continued working as the Special Duty Squad, carrying out five more arrests. And if Gosling did remain for three months, why did he not submit the return of arrests and a closing report? In Gosling's private papers there are some scrawled statistics for 1949 by 25 November of that year, but those figures were never submitted. It was almost as though no one was interested in the results which had been obtained, that the Squad had become an embarrassment, something to be swept under the carpet, a subject not to be mentioned.

* * *

In trying to determine why the Ghost Squad ceased to exist, the books which mention the unit throw very little light on the rationale behind the decision.

Capstick, in his memoirs, *Given in Evidence* (John Long, 1960), fulsomely praises the Ghost Squad but gives no clues as to its demise. In their rather hagiographic account of *The Flying Squad* (Arthur Barker Ltd., 1968), Norman Lucas and Bernard Scarlett state that the authorities claimed the Ghost Squad's work was completed and that as the crime wave was being contained the Ghost Squad's activities should cease and their type of work should once again be carried out in a more conventional manner by the Flying Squad. Gosling, in his book *The Ghost Squad* (W H Allen, 1959), concurs with this view. The former commissioner, Sir Harold Scott, penned his memoirs in 1954 and in a reference to the Ghost Squad stated that the unit had been formed prior to the formation of the Flying Squad, conveniently forgetting that on the previous page he had correctly stated that the Flying Squad was formed in 1919. He added that five years after the demise of the Ghost Squad, 'a little group of officers continues to act in this way'; although who these officers were, is difficult to say.

In his book, *East-End Underworld* (Routledge & Keegan Paul Ltd., 1981), Raphael Samuel leans heavily on the reminiscences of one Arthur Harding, a vicious and thoroughly unpleasant East End criminal, who claimed, incredibly, that he worked as an informant for the Ghost Squad. Harding stated that his estimation of the police fell a tremendous amount and that he found they were crooked from top to bottom. In fact, Harding never held the police in any kind of esteem; he loathed them, especially Frederick Porter Wensley, the creator of the Flying Squad, and was wont to make allegations of impropriety against the police at the drop of a hat. Little that Harding says can be relied upon without the strictest verification.

James Morton's books, *Bent Coppers* and *Supergrasses and Informants* (Little, Brown & Co. 1993 & 1995), mention the Ghost Squad with varying degrees of accuracy. Matthew Brinnand is mistakenly referred to as 'Brinn' and the Ghost Squad personnel are described as being four young officers, or officers who were either new to the Force or from a different division, sent to mix with the underworld, posing as criminals to report back their findings. Morton also mentions the case of the kidnapped bank manager in 1947. In getting the name wrong of the Flying Squad officer who deputised for the bank manager – it was Detective Sergeant William Deans, not William Davies –

Morton makes the mistake of accepting the same information as Neil Darbyshire in his book, *The Flying Squad* (Headline Book Publishing plc, 1993). However, both are wrong in another respect: this case was not generated by the Ghost Squad. Darbyshire also states that four relatively junior detectives were given carte blanche to roam wherever and whenever they chose and would not be obliged to explain themselves to any senior officers except Worth and Howe, who were barely interested in the fine details.

Statements such as these merit closer examination. In fact, at the time of the creation of the unit these 'youthful officers' were aged forty-two, forty-three, forty and thirty-six. As for being 'junior officers' – a divisional detective inspector, a detective inspector (second class), a detective sergeant (first class) and a detective sergeant (second class) – they had a total of over seventy-two years' service. Not be obliged to explain themselves to any senior officers except Worth and Howe? No, except for Detective Superintendent Thompson of C1 Department, the Deputy Commander (Crime) William Rawlings, the Deputy Assistant Commissioner (Crime) Hugh Young and the Commissioner, Sir Harold Scott, that's all. And they were barely interested in the fine details? Not according to the carefully set out reports, listing the number and types of arrests, the property recovered, the cases cleared up and the expenditure of the squad which were submitted through all of the officers mentioned above, right up to the commissioner.

Darbyshire further states that the Yard had never published the precise amount paid in any one year to informants, but says it was clear in 1947 that the Metropolitan Police Receiver thought the total excessive. This assumption is nonsense. Apart from the Receiver's initial hostile reaction to the AC(C)'s impertinence for daring to demand a car for the unit, the Ghost Squad file was never forwarded to him again. In any event, the expenditure of £1,038 during 1947 – which was a grant from the Home Office and nothing to do with the Receiver – was considered to be well spent by the very senior officers who supervised the Ghost Squad.

However, in his book, *Scotland Yard – The Inside Story* (Hutchinson & Co. Ltd, 1948), Stanley Firmin stated that the scheme had proved highly successful but that it was open to question whether it had yet achieved as much, or could achieve as much, as the old system in which every single Scotland Yard man was his own undercover agent, with a dozen long-known and well-tested informants as his own special string to call on should the occasion offer. Firmin was a former crime reporter and therefore some of his hyperbole can be excused; if every Scotland Yard officer had been his own undercover agent, with a string of informants at his beck and call, there would have been no need for a Special Duty Squad. Furthermore, the book was only published in 1948; in judging a unit which had barely got underway, Firmin's comments must be regarded as speculative.

Robert Murphy's book, *Smash and Grab* (Faber & Faber, 1993), describes Gosling as being a maverick detective whose career with the Ghost Squad failed to win him the promotion he expected. Mr. Murphy was obviously unaware that Gosling, promoted to the rank of detective inspector whilst serving on the Ghost Squad in 1947, was further promoted to the rank of detective superintendent six and a half years later.

There will always be those who enthusiastically advocate the notion that the spectre of corruption hangs over élite police units; it was suggested that the gang leader Billy Hill had 'got the Ghost Squad in his pocket'. Not deeply enough or for long enough, it would appear. In August 1947 he was arrested for warehouse-breaking and, claiming that he had been fitted up, he failed to appear at court and absconded to South Africa. However, he returned two months later, gave himself up and was sentenced to three years' imprisonment.

The suggestion that reward money was shared between the Ghost Squad officers and their informants was hinted at by both Darbyshire and Morton; the latter also stated that some officers were thought to be getting too close to their criminal counterparts for their own and the Force's good. But who is supposed to have made these allegations? Neither Morton nor Derbyshire is able to offer a source. Samuel suggests that arrests were followed by complaints about the police embellishing or fabricating evidence. But by whom? All of these allegations are highly presumptive, so let me pose the question: were the Ghost Squad officers crooked?

I think it highly unlikely, for this simple reason: four of the Yard's top crime-busters would hardly have been hand-picked for a unit where integrity was paramount if any suspicion of impropriety existed about them. Sir Ronald Howe was no fool;

he knew how much the Squad's success depended upon the veracity of the four men he had chosen. He would have reviewed their records before selecting them. He would have seen that all four men, in common with many other successful detectives, had allegations of misconduct lodged against them; he also knew that they had been completely exonerated. And because Sir Ronald was experienced in the ways of criminal investigation, he also knew that malicious allegations were made by criminals in order to have the officers transferred (as had happened during the Second World War, to Clark) and to weaken their cases in court. "I know you all," Howe had told the men at their initial briefing, "and I know you will not let us down." And they did not.

No official allegations of impropriety were made in respect of the Ghost Squad. Had they been, they would have been rigorously followed up; they were not matters which could have been simply brushed under the carpet. When allegations of misconduct were made against Clark and Stapeley, and later with the arrests of Compton and Cooper, such accusations were scrupulously investigated.

One theory put forward to me was that Compton and Cooper brought about the downfall of the Ghost Squad. This cannot be true – the facts simply do not come together.

Just one arrest was made on behalf of the Ghost Squad by the two officers together. Another was made by Cooper alone, and Compton carried out a further arrest in company with two other Flying Squad officers. Nothing can be read into that. Between the period of the first Ghost Squad arrest – 9 January 1946 – and Cooper and Compton being returned to uniform – 4 November 1947 – fifty-one individual Flying Squad officers had acted on 146 occasions to bring about the arrest of 176 prisoners. Compton and Cooper were involved on three occasions in the arrest of four prisoners, none of whom were the officers' so-called 'victims' in their subsequent trial.

So the facts simply do not add up; if it had been thought that these two officers had acted in anyway corruptly in the running of the Ghost Squad during their tenure on the Flying Squad, which came to an abrupt halt in early 1947, it would have meant that the officers running the Ghost Squad, plus their informants who were supplying the information, would have been seriously compromised. Had that been the case, it is a matter of common sense that the authorities would not have permitted the Ghost Squad to run for another two years.

★ ★ ★

Many people thought the squad was disbanded because they had achieved what they had set out to do. Certainly, the crime figures had gone down. In 1946 indictable offences numbered 127,796; in 1947 they fell to 127,458, in 1948 to 126,597 and finally, in the year of the Ghost Squad's demise, to 106,077. And by 1949 the Metropolitan Police had marginally increased its strength to 15,768. With 1,426 CID Officers in place, it was considered that they were slightly over-strength.

Some of the commonest factors thought to contribute to the demise of the unit were as follows: that the Yard hierarchy thought that running informants was rather distasteful; that Divisional CID chiefs were complaining that all of the best Ghost Squad work was going to the Flying Squad instead of their men; and that because the crime figures had been reduced and the manpower levels had increased, the commissioner decided that the Ghost Squad had run its course.

The very pertinent opinion of George Price, who worked with the Ghost Squad on the Percy Street clothing coupon case, was contained in a letter to me dated 24 April 1996:

> Friends from the Flying Squad and Ghost Squad told me they could not function as was intended – remaining anonymous and passing over the administrative work to Division. There was invariably a clash of interests and eventually they cut out Divisions and worked with the Flying Squad, but there, if anything, greater acrimony prevailed and the informants were ducking and diving from one to the other and the two elitist squads could not agree as to methods. As the Ghost Squad was far smaller and more recent, that was the one that had to go. The idea was great but like so many other operations, there were too many snags in the application.

Price's judgment is, I believe, very sound; as is the view taken by the late former Detective Superintendent Bob Higgins, in a letter to me dated 6 February 1994:

So far as my memory goes, it was discontinued because it was
felt that they had done what they set out to do and the general
opinion of the divisional detective inspectors (DDIs) was that
it should be discontinued ... The opinion of the DDIs would
be taken and they suggested the squad should be disbanded.

This concurs with John Gosling's opinion.

John Swain was a detective constable posted to C1
Department in 1949. In a letter dated 14 March 2002, Swain –
later to be a detective chief superintendent on the Flying Squad
and awarded the Queen's Police Medal for distinguished service
– recalled that:

I would like to think that the Ghost Squad was run as such an
undercover unit should be run. Those who worked on it, did
not talk about it. Additionally, fringe workers like myself and
others, co-opted to work on 'something' connected with that
team did not discuss it with others. The Ghost Squad was
never wound up, as such; it just quietly disappeared. Their
office was taken over by C1 officers.

Doubtless, there is an element of truth in all of these theories. In
1946, Divisional officers carried out 102 Ghost Squad arrests,
with the Flying Squad contributing to sixty-three arrests; and in
both cases, Ghost Squad personnel were sometimes involved.
Just three arrests were conducted by the Ghost Squad alone. The
following year the ratio had shifted. Fifty-three arrests were made
by Divisional officers and 137 by the Flying Squad, and again, in
both cases there was sometimes Ghost Squad participation. In
1948 the ratio shifted once again; twenty-eight arrests were made
by Divisional officers (with no Ghost Squad involvement), 190
by the Flying Squad (with some commitment by the Ghost
Squad) and thirty by the Ghost Squad alone. But by 1949, there
was a complete turnaround. In the ten months of the Squad's
operations, just four arrests were carried out by Divisional
officers. Sixty-two arrests were made by the Flying Squad with
minimal Ghost Squad involvement, and fifty-two arrests were
made solely by the Ghost Squad.

This gives the impression that the Ghost Squad did not wish to
farm out their information to divisions and that they provided the
Flying Squad with work they did not want to carry out

themselves. But this was a squad which had emphatically been told from its inception that they must not get concerned in arrests themselves. Of course, it was inevitable that on occasion they would be involved, but as the Ghost Squad's time drew to a close, it appeared that by personally making arrests for inconsequential offences, they were courting recognition – and of course possible exposure for their informants.

But nevertheless, question marks are raised. Why did Capstick and Clark leave the unit after only one year? In replacing Capstick, why did Jamieson stay only four and a half months? Claud Baker lasted longer – eight months – but why, after he left, was there a gap of five months? He was still part of C1 Department and was not promoted until almost eighteen months later. As Burgess replaced Clark he only lasted eleven months, and as Alfred Baker replaced Gosling he remained for just ten months. Well, it will be remembered that in Deputy Commander William Rawlings' report dated 2 January 1947 he did stipulate that officers should be changed if they became stale or if they ran into a bad patch; perhaps that's the answer.

There is one other possible explanation of the demise of the Ghost Squad that has never before been considered: that it simply ran out of steam.

By the time the last Ghost Squad arrest had been carried out on 25 October 1949, the total for the year was 118. Compare that with the figures by the same date in 1946 – 145 arrests. In 1947, there had been 144 arrests by that date and in 1948, 200. It seemed the unit was flagging, and although there were some superb arrests – in the case of the theft of a lorry and its load of silks and fabrics, valued at £18,000 by Gosling, and the case of the two safe-blowers, which took Moyle and Burton all over England, south of the Wash – there were others which were less than spectacular: the arrest of a man who had failed to surrender to bail (and was later acquitted), arrests of suspected persons (among whom another had his case dismissed) and the arrest for larceny of timber valued at £10 for which the miscreant was fined £5. It seemed that many of these arrests were carried out almost from desperation. Perhaps the Ghost Squad informants were exhausted as well, especially Gosling's snouts; after all, he had used the same ones on many occasions throughout the Ghost Squad's reign. Did they feel that exposure threatened? It is possible, especially since informants as well as other Ghost Squad members would meet at Gosling's home address to discuss forthcoming cases. But to those who, faced with a conundrum, like all the loose ends neatly tied up (as indeed I do) there can only be disappointment. Whether the end of the Ghost Squad was as the result of one profound factor above all others or, as is more likely, a combination of reasons, it will always be a matter of speculation amongst Ghost Squad theorists. But it is pointless looking for assistance in the Special Duty Squad file; the last entry shows 'PA' – signifying that the papers should be 'put away' – and they were.

★   ★   ★

So let us take a look at the results achieved by the Ghost Squad. For the first three years of its existence, the Squad were responsible for 609 arrests and the recovery of stolen property to the value of £155,732 12s 6½d; there is no argument about that. During 1948, Gosling stated in his memoirs, the Ghost Squad recovered property worth £7,000 more than in the previous two years combined, making a total of £81,374; this is correct. It is at this point that Gosling's figures start to go awry. He also stated that in the first nine months of 1949 180 arrests were made and property valued at £91,164 was recovered, this representing an excess of £17,000 over the previous year's figures. According to Gosling's memoirs, during the Ghost Squad's lifetime this brought the number of arrests up to 789, the number of cases solved to 1,506 and the amount of property recovered to £253,896.

Gosling's figures do not bear close investigation. In fact, during 1949 118 arrests were carried out, not 180, and the value of the property recovered is difficult to estimate. If the figures for 1948 had been exceeded by £17,000 as Gosling claimed, the total figure for the property recovered in 1949 would have been £98,374, not £91,164. However, the true figure probably falls far short of that amount. The records which were kept for the last year of the Ghost Squad's operations were in a shocking state. One of the worst offenders was Detective Sergeant Freeman, whose often incomprehensible scrawl left a great deal to be desired. The number of cases solved cannot be computed. Even if there had been a feedback from officers conducting their cases once the matters had been dealt with at court, there would have been nobody left in the Ghost Squad office to record them. In addition, the value of property stolen and the amount recovered was often not filled in. The best figure for recovered property I can find for 1949 – and I stress, this is on the figures available to me – was £56,941 15s 0d, or almost two-thirds of Gosling's figures. Perhaps he had access to records which I did not, or conceivably the most generous explanation is that arithmetic was not Gosling's strong suit.

According to the details made available to me, during the lifetime of the Ghost Squad, 727 persons were arrested – that is fact. If my figures regarding the amount of recovered stolen property are accepted as accurate – and I fully accept that they may not be, because of the lack of information entered into the Ghost Squad return of arrests for 1949 – my accumulated total is £212,674, or £41,222 less than Gosling's account. It could well be that Gosling adopted a little journalistic licence because these figures appeared in his memoirs rather than being used for accounting purposes for Scotland Yard, but at the end of the day – with a discrepancy of sixty-two arrests and a possible inconsistency in recovered stolen property of just over £41,000 – it really doesn't matter.

In less than four years, this élite group, composed of four men – and often fewer – earning no overtime whatsoever in respect of the enormously long hours they worked and claiming derisory out-of-pocket expenses, produced results which were nothing short of fabulous. It was not done for the glory; out of the eleven officers officially posted to the Ghost Squad over a period of almost four years, five collected a total of thirteen commissioner's commendations (which works out to just over half a commendation per officer per year), and the other six officers were not commended at all. They had recovered property worth by today's standards something in the region of £6 million, but more importantly, they had done what they set out to do. They had split the criminal gangs and sown the seeds of distrust amongst the underworld; none of them knew who amongst their members could be trusted any longer.

CHAPTER 9

A Modern Day Ghost Squad?

Could the Ghost Squad exist today? In my opinion it should, especially with crime figures once again going right through the ceiling; for the twelve months up to May 2010 there were 828,685 crimes committed in London, as opposed to 128,954 at the time of the Ghost Squad's formation – this in spite of the fact that the numbers of police in the capital have trebled since 1945 and that technology in the battle against crime has improved immeasurably.

The reality is that such a resurrection would face insurmountable difficulties. I believe, as I always have done, that informants, properly used, are one of the strongest weapons in the battle against crime. The reason why the Ghost Squad could not exist today is because of the breakdown in the Criminal Investigation Department over the past forty years of the basic principles concerning investigation and the day-to-day running of informants; what follows explains why.

★　★　★

Practices in the CID (including the running of informants) changed in 1972 when Sir Robert Mark GBE became commissioner; he was determined to root out corruption in the CID and, in fairness to him, there was dishonesty in that department which needed to be tackled and eradicated. However, in doing so Mark replaced the senior officers within the CID with uniform officers who, if they possessed any experience of investigative work, had done it so long ago that it was now nothing more than a dim and distant memory. In fact, most of them possessed no CID experience whatsoever. So in order to make the whole system of informant-running more accountable, the correct details of the informant had to be registered with the Deputy Assistant Commissioner (Crime), who also stated that he would personally supervise the payment of all rewards in excess of £500. In addition, rewards from insurance companies and loss adjusters were channelled into the DAC's office, so that payments to informants were made through the Yard; and it was a reckless officer indeed who tried to approach the insurance company direct, on behalf of his informant. Insurance companies are never very keen on paying out, and on several occasions officers who tried to circumvent the system were gleefully grassed up to the Yard; this led to officers being returned to uniform or sacked.

If this had been the extent of a much-needed shake up, few detectives – honest ones – would have quibbled about the identity of their informants being known to one very senior officer and the information being kept under lock and key at the Yard. But that was not the only change in dealing with informants that was about to descend on the Metropolitan Police CID.

At the same time, a whole series of unworkable rules and regulations were unleashed regarding meeting offenders on bail; many informants were indeed on bail and wished to impart information in order to lighten their burden. Police were told that persons subject to bail conditions could only be met at a police station and this had to be sanctioned in advance by an officer of no lesser rank than superintendent; in addition, a whole series of reports and entries in official books had to be submitted, signed and counter-signed. For blindingly obvious reasons, many informants were less than happy about the risk of their being seen by their associates venturing into police stations. Many officers contrived to bump into them 'accidentally' in the street or a pub, but in that eventuality even more paperwork was generated and any officer who 'accidentally' neglected to record an 'accidental' meeting could look forward to a one-way ticket to the uniform department.

But that was not all. In his endeavours to stamp out corruption, Mark had introduced 'interchange' – the swapping of personnel between the CID and uniform. As the years passed, an enormous amount of expertise was lost because 'career detectives' were disappearing through retirement or resignation, and a great many officers were injected into the CID from uniform with no experience of investigative work, especially at inspector and chief inspector level. Quite often, these postings were due to the officer's gender, colour or sexual orientation, not because he or she possessed any expertise in crime fighting – which most conspicuously did not; it was done to add something of interest on their CVs as they rose through the ranks and to display to the world what a caring, sharing police service the Metropolitan Police was. And as investigations into criminal offences deteriorated, so too did the running of informants.

One mercifully short-run incentive during the 1970s and '80s was the attempt to penetrate gangs of football hooligans with young police officers. Since this type of offence was dealt with under the heading of 'public order', the scheme was run by uniform officers with the rank of chief inspector, who usually possessed little or no experience of covert operations. The shaven-headed, earringed young constables presented a sorry picture at court. Few had any idea about how to behave when compromised in serious criminality, any more than they possessed experience of attending Magistrates' Courts, let alone Crown Courts. Due to their inability to collect and record evidence coherently and deliver it at court, their testimony was ripped to shreds by experienced barristers, leaving their jeering clients free to swagger from court. One such senior (so-called) supervising officer, between the arrests being carried out and the debacle at court, had been promoted to superintendent. "Great fun!" he chuckled. "Wouldn't have missed it for the world!" His sentiments were not echoed by his young charges, who were undoubtedly wondering what on earth they had got themselves into, as they miserably awaited the outcome of an internal investigation into allegations of perjury and attempting to pervert the course of justice.

Probably the most headline-catching case of botched informant-handling in recent years was the case of 'Witness Bromley'. Damilola Taylor was a ten-year-old African boy who was stabbed to death in South London, so it was clear from the start that this would be a high-profile case. 'Witness Bromley' was a fourteen-year-old girl who claimed to have witnessed the murder and could identify those who had participated in the attack; so far then, so good. It therefore seems incomprehensible that the officer in charge of the case decided that the best person to debrief the girl was a woman police constable with no experience in that sphere of police work. Under the WPC's supervision, 'Bromley' was taken for taxi rides and visited amusement arcades, was promised holidays, given a pet and showered with hundreds of pounds worth of mobile phone cards. Placed in a hotel with her mother, the pair ran up a bill for meals, drinks and phone calls amounting to £4,133 – in just one week. Asked to leave the hotel, she promptly set fire to the bathroom. A reward of £50,000 was on offer to the person who brought the victim's killers to justice; Bromley was told by the WPC that she would be more or less guaranteed to get the money if she said that she had actually witnessed the attack rather than having relied on second-hand information.

Armed with this incredible advice, 'Bromley' did just that; except that she changed her version of events time and time again. It is little wonder that at the trial of the youths accused of the murder, the Judge Mr. Justice Hooper described 'Bromley' as, "an inveterate liar and a troublemaker with a fertile imagination", and the accused were acquitted.

* * *

One of the greatest weapons against crime was the use of the Resident Informant – later to become colloquially known as a Supergrass – a practice which had originated in the 1970s. It commenced with one Derek Creighton Smalls – known to his friends (and he would soon possess few enough of them) as 'Bertie' – who, after being arrested for a high-value bank robbery, decided to broker a deal whereby he would name and give evidence against his co-accused, providing he was allowed to walk free from court. That was what happened; Smalls was a free man and his associates were sentenced to a total of 308 years' imprisonment. The judiciary were outraged that a guilty man could escape punishment, and for all future cases a tariff was laid down – initially, one of five years' imprisonment – to accommodate those who gave evidence against their fellow robbers. Apart from identifying gang members to the police, specifying the offences which they had committed and detailing the whereabouts of property the gang had stolen, Supergrasses were useful in other ways. They split gangs with their treachery, making each gang member distrust the others and be wary of trusting them in the future, thus making them less effective. In fact, it went even further than that; Supergrasses informed on their family members as well. One propped up his brother, his father and later, having really acquired the taste for grassing, his mother. As far as police were concerned, the situation could not have been better. The underworld was in turmoil; when a gang of robbers were arrested, it was often the case that they were lining up to become Supergrasses. According to the amount of information at their disposal, it was a matter of 'first come, first served'. Armed robbers who spent too long agonising over the decision of whether or not to 'Do a Bertie' (as the practice had become known) were often doomed to disappointment after their associates overtook them in the grassing stakes. Unsolved crimes, which had often been forgotten, were cleared up, firearms and stolen property were recovered and many of the criminals who had had the finger pointed at them by a Supergrass even pleaded guilty at court.

However, it did lead to sloppy practices by some officers who treated the Supergrasses almost like friends, completely forgetting that these were criminals who had committed some of the worst depredations in the criminal calendar: shooting their victims, squirting ammonia in their eyes, pouring petrol over them. Where a tight grip should have been kept on the Supergrasses, all too often the reins were left slack. It led to some near-incredible behaviour by the officers handling them: drinking with them in pubs, in areas where the Supergrasses were known (and, what was more, known to be informing), taking them to police sports clubs and, most deplorable of all, introducing them to their wives and families when they took the Supergrasses home for Sunday lunch. It led to some deeply regrettable and embarrassing incidents, and it is only surprising that there were not more.

After some of the debacles of the seventies and eighties, the rules of running and debriefing Supergrasses were tightened up – not before time, but not, it transpired, quite enough. In the early 1990s the Flying Squad arranged for a highly dangerous armed robber to be allowed out of prison whilst serving a sentence, to participate in what was intended to be the dry run for an armed robbery, in order that when the robbery was carried out his associates might be arrested. Of course, the 'dry run' was nothing of the kind; out of sight of the Squad officers, the robbery actually took place. From the prison cell to which he was returned, the Supergrass – for that was the status speedily bestowed upon the robber by the Police Complaints Investigation Bureau (CIB) – made a number of damaging allegations against the Flying Squad, not least that they had stolen his share of the proceeds of the robbery.

During the ensuing protracted investigations, both criminal and internal, the cunning and highly manipulative Supergrass, by now released from prison and ensconced in a safe house, completely ran rings around his minders supplied by CIB. Whilst he made detailed allegations of impropriety against a number of the Flying Squad officers, in which he alleged that they had stolen £250,000, he also managed to commit seventy vicious armed robberies which netted £100,000 during the space of six months, right under their noses of his CIB minders. After he whined that he was £2,600 in debt, CIB gormlessly paid off the arrears; the next day the Supergrass carried out another robbery, followed by another the following day.

With the aid of some incredibly stupid and gullible police officers, as well as a number of corrupt ones, some of whom went to prison and some of whom didn't, the Supergrass managed to destroy the North-East office of the Flying Squad. The name of Rigg Approach was so tainted it was closed down and relocated elsewhere. It is only remarkable that the whole of the Flying Squad was not disbanded.

Could anything worse happen to undermine the integrity of the police? Well, no, unless one counts the two Yardie members who were used as police informants, one of whom carried out a series of armed robberies, drug dealing, extortion rackets and running a chain of prostitutes, once again right under the noses of his handlers, whilst the other raped and murdered a young woman.

★   ★   ★

Something quite clearly had to be done – but what? It appeared that the British Army in Northern Ireland might have the answer. Military Intelligence had formed a breakaway section – it was known as the Force Research Unit or FRU – which was responsible for running informants in the Province. The agent who collected intelligence in respect of various terrorist organisations was given a four-figure number to identify him and was only referred to by that number. His real identity was kept securely locked away. He was trained in resistance to interrogation and anti-surveillance techniques and taught a sophisticated version of Kipling's 'Kim's Game', so as to be able to memorise objects, incidents, statements, names and faces without having to resort to making written notes. The agent was provided with 'handlers' – many of them had come to the unit from Special Forces – and he would be met at agreed times and varying locations for debriefing purposes. This would be carried out by means of a 'rolling pick-up'; as soon as it was clear on the street, he would be collected by a nondescript car (with interchangeable number plates) which barely stopped moving, and with an armed back-up car in tow the agent would be taken to one of several safe houses to be debriefed using a tape recorder. Later, after the information had been checked by the handlers and if possible verified and even improved or expanded upon, the recording would be transcribed on to contact sheets for dissemination to the various interested agencies. In fact, this worked very well. Every piece of paperwork was typed and dealt with in a secure unit. The handlers – although they dealt with more than one agent – did nothing else other than informant-handling; no criminal investigation, arrests, interviews, preparation of cases or court attendance, like their police CID counterparts on the mainland. If an agent needed to impart information urgently there was a dedicated switchboard which operated on a twenty-four-hour basis, and because the handlers either lived at the barracks or nearby, the matter could be addressed immediately. And the anonymity of the agent was paramount. When information was received as to the identity of a terrorist who was responsible for a bombing or a murder, the Royal Ulster Constabulary officers would simply be told the name of the suspect, what he was wanted for and be instructed, "Go and arrest him."

All this worked very well until one such agent was arrested and it was discovered that he had been indulging in serious criminality; in addition, he alleged that his handlers were also deeply involved in these matters. The threat of prosecution hung over members of the unit for years; the agent, after admitting twenty terrorist offences which included five cases of conspiracy to murder, went to prison for ten years.

Back on the mainland, this system was attempted with restricted success. Dossiers of informants were kept with the local, divisional detective chief inspector in filing cabinets which were often left unlocked, 'handlers' (with often limited or no experience in dealing with informants) were appointed and the system of 'contact sheets' was started so that everything which transpired between the informant and his handler was recorded. It was something like the scheme which had been used in Northern Ireland – but with nothing like the same amount of security. Thus were informants' identities and activities handed over to junior CID typists, whose ability to keep their mouths shut was often on a par with their typing skill, and the ensuing paperwork was left on CID officers' desks for all to see. With more and more people in the know regarding the true identities of informants, the risk of exposure was higher than ever before.

It was not long before defence lawyers – thanks to inexperienced, loose-lipped 'detectives' – got to hear of this detailed documentation which pertained to every informant in police circles, and they wanted access to it. Although requests to be told the true identity of an informant would be refused by the courts, the lawyers quickly realised that they could get round this obstacle by suggesting that informants should not have their identity protected, because they were acting as *agents provocateurs*. The threat alone of unmasking an informant would often be sufficient for the Crown Prosecution Service to abandon the trial.

The whole system of running informants had gone into freefall, not only in the Metropolitan Police but also nationwide. Two Police Forces decided that 'experts' in running sources should approach every arrested person to see if they wished to become informants. Due to the fact that these approaches were inevitably rebuffed, because of the officers' lack of expertise and the paucity of the rewards on offer, this 'Keystone Cops' approach surprisingly did actually produce some limited results. Prisoners were so disconcerted by these clumsy tactics that not knowing who to trust amongst their peers produced a rather disruptive effect in criminal circles. On the downside, some of these would-be informants decided to sell their experiences to the media, for undoubtedly more profit (and at substantially less risk to themselves), by plaintively complaining about the efforts which were being made to 'entrap' them.

In Worth's report for the Ghost Squad, he suggested that in isolated cases a tried and proven informant could be paid a reward even when, through no fault that could be attributed to him, the job had failed to materialise. An amended version of this concept was tried sixty years later; one Police Force thought that making payment advances to informants before any result at all had been achieved would inspire them to provide compelling intelligence, and another believed that informants should be paid retainers rather than paying them for results.

And so it went on; one knee-jerk reaction after another was tried before being rejected for its sheer silliness. One idea was to ask the informant to sign a contract in which they would promise not to indulge in criminality whilst they were providing information. Another was not to hand over the full reward but rather to 'drip-feed' it to the informant, so that his associates would not embarrassingly question him as to how he had suddenly come into a significant amount of money. It appears that nobody had suggested that in that eventuality the informant could simply have replied, "I stole it". The best wheeze was to suggest providing counselling if the informant suddenly felt traumatised about the people he had grassed up.

The latest Home Office offensive is known as CHIS (pronounced 'chiz'), an acronym for Covert Human Intelligence Sources. No individual officers run their own informants. There are two distinct groups of officers: those who gather and evaluate intelligence from an informant and those (oblivious of the identity of the informant) who act on that information. Those are the bare bones of this system, which, it appears, has been advanced to cover everybody's back.

In the real world, an informant can provide information which at the time of imparting it is accurate. However, criminals can and do change their minds, so the disposition of stolen property can be changed, often at the last moment; the venue where an armed robbery is going to be carried out can also be varied. Under the CHIS system, when that happens, could the informant contact his handler in time? Would the handler be on duty, and if not, could the officer responsible for carrying out the observation, search or arrest be contacted? And if the handler could be reached, would it be possible to carry out a meaningful risk-assessment to cater sufficiently for the change of plan?

All this has to be taken into account, and more. How will action taken as a result of the information received impact upon the local community, especially if that community is racially diverse? What are the ethical, personal or operational risks which are likely to result? But above all else, what is the justification for the action? Is it a matter that is proportional, accountable and necessary?

At the end of the day, there is the debrief; when an operation has resulted in the biggest fuck-up since the flood, wide-eyed, inexperienced officers can mop their perspiring brows and whimper the phrase so beloved of senior management: "Lessons have been learned".

*   *   *

It's all a far cry from the time when the Ghost Squad was formed. AC(C) Howe made it quite clear that never would the officers be required to identify their informants; that was the way it had always been and would continue to be for thirty years thereafter. Now, with the proliferation of paperwork, the exposure of an informant's identity is more likely than it has ever been. Nor does it end there. Whenever the services of undercover officers are required, the participation of an informant in a crime is needed, an observation needs to be mounted, or an informant recruited, the same prodigious amount of paperwork is generated, in which officers ponder, theorise and agonise over decisions on whether or not to proceed with a course of action, before passing the whole equation on to an officer of more senior rank for him to imitate the junior officer's actions before making a decision. And whilst that whole excruciating process is enacted, the crime has been committed, the stolen property has been disposed of and the potential informant has become fed up and gone home.

*   *   *

Controversial Gosling may have been, but as he remarked, "If every policeman in the Metropolitan Police worked to rule, they wouldn't catch two thieves out of a hundred". Many officers who have run informants believe that the best informant is the one who works with the officer who recruited him; that the officer is in constant contact with the informant and can react at a moment's notice to changes in the information; and that the officer who is in a position to prompt a snout into action, can also – because of his experience as a detective – tell an informant when to pull back and, most importantly, can protect the identity of a snout. This last is paramount. I ran informants all through my service, and not one was ever compromised or even suspected.

"I don't think that some of my unorthodox methods made me a lot of friends in high places," Gosling once said, referring to the hierarchy at Scotland Yard, "but they got the job done."

They did, as opposed to what is achieved by the huge amount of red tape which exists today, designed to protect everybody's backs – except that it doesn't. Hardly a week goes by without reports of the police being vilified for mistakes, born out of incompetence, inexperience or downright bone-idleness, which have led to the guilty being freed or the innocent killed, both of which are entirely preventable.

Add to this the massive, morale-shattering amounts of money paid to officers for a whole cross-section of complaints of discrimination, and it is little wonder that the Police Services are in such a parlous state. Once the most oft-heard police expression used to be "Alright – you're nicked"; it has now been replaced with "I can't believe you said that – that's *so* offensive!"

So no, the Ghost Squad could not exist today, even though it is needed now more than ever before; there are too many rulings and directives and too much correspondence. And there are too many people – gutless, inexperienced senior police officers, frightened members of the Crown Prosecution Service, but mainly defence lawyers – in the know.

But most of all, there's no more Goslings.

CHAPTER 10

The Aftermath

S o the Ghosts had scattered; what happened to them?
Promoted to the rank of deputy commander, Percy Worth, the originator of the scheme, retired after almost thirty-six years' service on 30 June 1946. Always an enthusiast of racetracks, he was appointed head of the Greyhound Tracks' Security and he employed former CID officers. Each of the (then) eighty greyhound tracks nationwide had a security officer – generally, an ex-detective – in charge, and Worth promoted excellent liaison with the local CID offices and the Flying Squad. He wrote the foreword to Gosling's memoirs in 1959 and died just after his seventy-fifth birthday in 1963.

★　★　★

The Commissioner, Sir Harold Scott, should be mentioned, since he sanctioned the emergence of the Ghost Squad. His policy of 'make do and mend' was perhaps necessary in the post-war years of austerity, but as the years went by it was felt that a more forceful commissioner would have demanded extra funding from the Home Office. But Sir Harold was not a dynamic leader; he was at heart a civil servant just like his masters in the Home Office. After he cooperated with the John Scott-Henderson QC enquiry into the Christie affair the enquiry came to the conclusion that Christie's confession to murdering Beryl Evans was false and that her husband, Timothy Evans, had been properly convicted and hanged. Sir Harold must have exhaled a sigh of relief when the committee announced decisively that no innocent man had been hanged nor was such a situation ever likely to occur. And when Neville George Clevely Heath was circulated as being wanted for the bestial murder of Margery Aimee Brownell Gardner, Sir Harold permitted the publication of Heath's name and description in the press but forbade the publication of photographs of Heath, in case identification became an issue at his trial. But before a suspect comes to trial he has first to be caught. The investigating officer had not the faintest idea as to Heath's whereabouts, so the psychotic and truly dangerous Neville Heath simply changed his name and ten days later at Bournemouth met a twenty-one year old former Wren, Doreen Margaret Marshall, and murdered her, just as brutally as he had Margery Gardner. After Heath had been hanged and questions were raised in the House regarding the decision not to publish Heath's photograph, the Home Secretary had little difficulty in assuring members that the decision taken was the correct one. Doreen Marshall's heartbroken parents would have begged to differ.

Sir Harold stood down in 1953, handing the reins as commissioner over to Sir John Nott-Bower, and after publishing several books died in 1969.

★   ★   ★

Sir Ronald Howe remained in the position of AC(C) for eight years before he was succeeded by Mr. R L (later Sir Richard) Jackson CBE. Sir Ronald then took up the post of deputy commissioner and served Sir John Nott-Bower KCVO, KPM for most of the new commissioner's term in office, retiring one year prior to Sir John. From his time as AC(C) until his retirement, Sir Ronald was the British representative on the International Criminal Police Commission (Interpol) and became a friend of the novelist and creator of James Bond, Ian Fleming. In return for a trip to Turkey, where the Interpol conference was being held in September 1955, Fleming graciously immortalised his friend as Assistant Commissioner Ronnie Vallance of the Yard in several of the Bond books.

After retirement, Sir Ronald wrote two books: his memoirs, *The Pursuit of Crime* (Arthur Barker Ltd., 1961), and *The Story of Scotland Yard* (Arthur Barker Ltd., 1965). Neither of the books mentioned the Ghost Squad. He became chairman of Group 4 Total Security, a post he held for sixteen years, before becoming the company's president; he died the following year, just prior to his eightieth birthday.

★   ★   ★

Following his promotion to detective chief inspector on 3 October 1949 Henry Stuttard was posted off the Flying Squad and transferred to C1 Department. There he dealt with serious and sensitive enquiries, many of which were on behalf of the Director of Public Prosecutions. John Swain remembered him with great affection, describing him as 'a rugged type of individual' and recalling the time when he and Stuttard had arrested a man who, on two occasions in South Africa, had attempted to murder his wife. When he was placed on board a ship at the London Basin to be returned to South Africa for trial, the prisoner shook hands with Stuttard and thanked him for the humane way in which he had been treated. Stuttard certainly was compassionate; when Swain, a very junior officer, repeatedly submitted a report to a deeply unpleasant detective inspector who on every occasion 'blue-pencilled' (or rejected) it, Stuttard took the report, which Swain had re-typed on three occasions, looked at it, saw it was absolutely perfect and signed it, telling Swain in the presence of the obnoxious inspector, "Don't ever take your reports back to that man, again". But most telling of all was the occasion when Swain encountered a bullying gang leader and his minions in a club who demanded, unsuccessfully, that Swain should buy them drinks. Recounting this incident in his memoirs, Swain told how he reported this to Stuttard the following day, who decided that this situation could be turned to the advantage of the police. He made a series of telephone calls, utilising his underworld contacts, until he finally had the gangster's telephone number. A no-nonsense meeting was arranged that evening and in the Globe public house in Whitcombe Street near Leicester Square, Stuttard, in the presence of the gangster and Swain, jumped up on a table and rapped his umbrella to gain the attention of the crowded bar. Indicating the gang leader, and referring to him as a 'rascal', Stuttard humorously informed the pub's clientele of the liberty the gang leader had taken with his young charge, told them that he (the gangster) was now very sorry and would buy everybody in the pub a drink, for as long as they wanted to stay. Jumping down from the table, Stuttard announced, "Mine's a large scotch, to start off with".

The assembled clientele of The Globe, including Stuttard and Swain, proceeded to consume drinks for the next two hours at the gang leader's expense. It is difficult if not impossible to imagine a

Scotland Yard detective chief inspector acting in such a fashion today.

Stuttard was promoted to detective superintendent Grade II on 14 September 1953 and continued working at C1 Department until his retirement on 12 June 1955. His was a career to be proud of. In over thirty-one years' service, he had notched up thirty-three commissioner's commendations, alone. He retired to his house in Barnfield Avenue, Kingston, Surrey and five years later he and his wife Nora moved to Seaton in Devon. He died on 5 June 1979, almost twenty-four years to the day after he had retired, aged seventy-five.

★   ★   ★

One month after John Jamieson left the Ghost Squad and was posted to 'D' Division, he was promoted to detective chief inspector. Two years later he attended the Senior Course at Ryton-on-Dunsmore Police College and two years after that he was promoted to detective superintendent Grade II. Before he left 'D' Division fifteen months later, following his promotion to detective superintendent Grade I, he had successfully investigated a string of murders during his eight-year stay.

Jamieson played a prominent role in the investigation of the murder of Stanley Setty, who had initially been reported as a missing person on 5 October 1949. Setty's dismembered body was later washed up on the mudflats at Tillingham Marshes, Essex. Donald Hume was later arrested for the murder but the jury failed to agree upon a verdict; he later pleaded guilty to being an accessory after the fact to murder and was sentenced to twelve years' imprisonment. After his release in February 1958, Hume admitted to the *Sunday Pictorial* that he had indeed murdered Setty. Wanted by the Yard for two armed robberies, he went to Switzerland in January 1959 where, during a botched hold-up, he shot and killed a taxi driver and was sentenced to life imprisonment. Jamieson also conducted the investigation into the murder of the celebrated cartoonist, Harry Saul Michaelson, who sketched so quickly he was dubbed 'One Minute Michaelson'. He was murdered when his flat was broken into and he was battered to death with a chair. Fingerprints were lifted from the chair, and when an aid to CID saw Harry Lewis behaving suspiciously in Scott Ellis Gardens, St. John's Wood (where Jamieson lived) he arrested him. Lewis' fingerprints matched those found on the chair, he confessed and was hanged at Pentonville Prison on the morning of 21 April 1949. His proceeds from the robbery? Just £5 8s 9d. Jamieson considered Michaelson to have been such a kindly man that if Lewis had asked him for the money, Michaelson would have willingly given it to him.

And when a young prostitute was brutally murdered, Jamieson took over the investigation, assisted by John Gosling, and quickly identified the killer, who shot himself before he could be arrested. So thorough was Jamieson's investigation and he accumulated such an abundance of overwhelming evidence, that when the coroner at the inquest asked what his action would have been if he had caught up with the suspect before he had shot himself, Jamieson simply replied, "I would have apprehended him and brought him back to London on a charge of murder".

Jamieson was worshipped by his staff and the year following his promotion he was transferred to C1 Department. Perhaps it was only a stop-gap; three months later he was posted to No 3 Area District Headquarters. In the Queen's Birthday Honours list two years later Jamieson was awarded the Queen's Police Medal for distinguished service. His final posting, to No 2 Area District Headquarters, came the following year, and after a brief three-month stay he retired on service aged fifty-nine. Jamieson had served over thirty-two and a half years and had been awarded twenty-nine commissioner's commendations. He died on 14 November 1974, just before his seventy-sixth birthday.

*　*　*

Claud Baker headed the Ghost Squad for just eight months before resuming duty at C1 Department. Within eighteen months he was promoted detective chief inspector. He conscripted John Swain, who had the ability to take down shorthand, to assist him in an investigation in which he supplied Swain with the necessary equipment: a cushion, a doctor's head lamp, a new notebook and a supply of pencils. The chairman of a company of civil engineers had reported an approach made by a man who purported to be a King's Messenger and stated that he could secure a lucrative contract for him with a Far Eastern company. The expected profits would amount to several million pounds and the 'King's Messenger'– in fact, a retired army officer – stated that the contract would be awarded to the chairman's company for a consideration of 10% of the profits. Therefore, it was Swain's job to sit on the cushion in a darkened cupboard in the chairman's office with the doctor's head lamp illuminating the notebook, and to take shorthand notes of the conversation between the two men. As the fraudster emerged from the company's offices into Victoria Street, so he was arrested by Baker; he was later convicted at the Old Bailey.

An enormously hard worker, Baker lasted another three years at the Yard, until he suffered a coronary thrombosis which was the cause of his premature retirement on 3 August 1952. Aged forty-seven, he had served just over twenty-seven years and had been awarded thirty-nine commissioner's commendations. He retired to 'Ingledene', The Street, Little Clacton, Essex but his retirement was short-lived. Sixteen months later, on 3 December 1953, he died.

★   ★   ★

After eleven months' service on the Ghost Squad Percy Burgess resumed Flying Squad duties for one month, before his third and final posting back to 'C' Division. He attended the Senior Course at Ryton-on-Dunsmore Police College during 1949 and within three months of passing it he was promoted to detective chief inspector and was posted to C1 Department. It lasted no time at all; three weeks later he was on his way to City Road police station. Burgess was still enthusiastic and as full of ideas as ever. In 1950 he submitted a report suggesting that between six and twelve dilapidated cars and vans should be bought up and used purely for observation purposes; he stated that this idea had already been successfully used during a wages snatch and when the vehicles were not needed they could be garaged at Lambeth. It seemed an excellent concept, but not to the hierarchy, who vetoed the idea.

After one year's service at City Road Burgess was posted to 'T' Division, and after six months he resigned, aged forty-six and with just over twenty-five years' service. He kept himself amazingly busy. He formed 'King's Detective Agency', ran two village shops, became a Child Welfare Officer for the London County Council and worked on cases for his son, David, who had a solicitor's practice. I corresponded briefly with his wife Elsie in

1998. At that time Burgess was in hospital with pneumonia and she had been unable to read him my letter; I hope she was able to, later. She told me that he had enjoyed his police service and following his retirement from the Metropolitan Police they had gone to Africa for three years where he had formed a police force for a diamond mine – a task she described, with masterly understatement, as "very onerous". He wrote an account of his African experiences, *Diamonds Unlimited* (John Long, 1960), and the year before he died he was interviewed and filmed at home by Testament Films for the programme *Bad Boys of the Blitz*.

Altogether, he was commended on forty-four occasions; he died of MRSA at the age of ninety-three.

*   *   *

Moyle stayed on the Flying Squad for two more years before, like so many of his contemporaries, attending the Junior Course at the Police College at Ryton-on-Dunsmore, Warwickshire for the first six months of 1951. Upon his return, he was promoted to detective inspector and posted to 'M' Division. Two years later he attended the Advanced Course and in January 1954 he was posted to 'C' Division. Later the same year he was promoted to detective chief inspector and four months later he was posted to C1 Department. It is surprising that Moyle never advanced any further up the promotion ladder, but on 4 January 1959, five years to the day after his promotion, he decided to call it a day. Aged forty-nine, he had served over twenty-seven-and-a-half years in the Metropolitan Police and had been commended by the commissioner on thirty-three occasions. His retirement lasted a creditable twenty-five years; he moved to Marine Parade, Hastings and died on 17 January 1974, aged seventy-four.

*   *   *

George Burton returned to more conventional duties on the Flying Squad, where he stayed for another seven years. He was awarded a total of thirteen further commissioner's commendations during this second tour on the Flying Squad and seven of these were with Moyle, with whom he continued to work after the Ghost Squad had finished. Now well into his forties, he was a keen and resolute Squad officer, arresting gangs specialising in the use of explosives, dangerous and persistent criminals and a set of conspirators to rob. In November 1956 he was posted to 'H' Division, just after collecting his twenty-ninth (and final) commissioner's commendation for ability and determination in effecting the arrest of a gang of troublesome housebreakers, and fifteen months later he went to 'Y' Division – a home posting for him. Did he want to leave the Squad? Almost certainly not, and why should he, when he was bringing in such impressive results? But it appears he did little else in his last three years of service – perhaps he was a little disgruntled at leaving the Squad.

A great thief-taker Burton certainly was, and one who could no doubt have reached an impressive rank in the Metropolitan Police. Alas, it was not to be. Academia was not his strongest point; he failed to pass the First-class Civil Servant's Examination time and time again, which would have opened the doors to further promotion. Apparently, situated above the building where the examination took place was a clock which chimed every hour, 'Will ye no' come back again?' and Burton took this to be an invitation reserved especially for him.

On 24 January 1960, with just over thirty years' exemplary service, Burton retired to the family home at Dorchester Avenue, N.13. He died, aged seventy-eight, on 10 October 1987.

CHAPTER 11

The Helpers

By the time Reggie Grose had left the Flying Squad, two months prior to the demise of the Ghost Squad, having been promoted to detective sergeant (second class), he had accumulated seventeen commendations. His next posting was to 'N' Division for a period of eleven years; during that time he would be moved to four offices on the division. His last posting was to 'H' Division which would last almost three years. In September 1963 he attended a first-year course in general principles of criminal law run by the East London College of Commerce. He achieved an attendance record of 75% but in May 1964 he failed the examination at the conclusion of the course; he resigned from the Metropolitan Police on 8 March 1964. The reason shown was 'service' – he had served for twenty-six years, three months and nine days; his certificate of service was marked 'exemplary' and he had been awarded twenty-four commendations – plus a George Medal, of course.

Reggie Grose was an irrepressible character; his sometimes outrageous behaviour (including the 'one-eared elephant' joke, when he would pull out one empty trouser pocket before threatening to unzip his fly) was the source of much amusement. Part of the Grose legend involved an incident where a police horse was appropriated from the stables at Harlesden police station; Grose was later found astride the animal, directing traffic at the Jubilee Clock junction in Harlesden High Street. Drink, needless to say, had played a contributory part in this escapade. Grose was later employed as a solicitor's clerk and although he appeared as a legal representative for arrested persons he never forgot his roots. After a thorough interview with a client, the names of co-conspirators, accomplices and receivers of stolen property would miraculously become apparent to the arresting officers, and once they were also arrested Reggie Grose would act for them as well. It seemed as though – as far as Grose was concerned – the Ghost Squad had never really gone away.

On one particular occasion a local villain alleged to police that during his absence his ex-wife had stolen a large amount of property from a club he was running. The wife and her family were all arrested, some of the stolen property was recovered and she and her relations admitted the offence, under the legal eye of Reggie Grose. But a week after they had been charged, the arresting officer, former Detective Sergeant 'Dick' West, received a telephone call from Grose stating that the estranged husband had approached his former wife, demanding money which purported to be on behalf of the police, in order for him to drop the charges against her. The husband duly made a statement of withdrawal and the whole matter was submitted to the Metropolitan Police Solicitors' Department. The accompanying report included a reference to information having been received that the club owner might try to extort money from his ex-wife by alleging that police wanted money to drop the charges and that in consequence the investigating officers were liable to be accused of serious impropriety.

The following day A10 (the police complaints department) burst into the CID office, only to be told that the matters of which the investigating officers were being accused were already the subject of a report to the solicitors' department. It was not really the result that the complaints officers had been anticipating. The ex-wife went to prison and nothing more was heard from the husband. "Nevertheless," as West later told me, "without the tip-off from Reg, I could quite unwittingly have walked into a hornets' nest, instead of which I emerged smelling of violets!"

I wrote to Grose on 15 October 1993 asking him for details of his activities on the Ghost Squad. For quite some time he had been suffering from multiple sclerosis; at one stage he had been completely paralysed, and the doctors thought this could have originated from his ill treatment as a prisoner of war. But his friend, Daphne Skillern, took my letter into him and he promised to reply to it when he felt well enough to do so. Sadly, that time never came; he died on 20 October, aged seventy-five. Notwithstanding his conviviality, Grose was a very private individual; his funeral wishes were that no announcement of his death should be made in the *Daily Telegraph* until after his funeral, that there should be no service, no flowers and that the only person who should attend was Daphne Skillern, his loyal friend for thirty-nine years.

★   ★   ★

After the Ghost Squad folded, Bob Acott stayed with the Flying Squad for another year until promotion took him to a succession of postings. By the time he was promoted to detective superintendent in 1960, when he was posted to the Murder Squad, he had been commended on nineteen occasions. In 1961 Acott conducted the investigation into what became known as 'The A6 Murder', for which James Hanratty, a twenty-four-year-old criminal who had just completed a term of corrective training, was hanged. Controversy over his conviction raged for years and there were three Home Office enquiries, the last of which was referred to the newly-appointed Criminal Cases Review Commission in 1997. In 2001, at his family's behest, Hanratty's body was exhumed, and the following year the Court of Appeal (Criminal Division) ruled that Hanratty's DNA profile fitted exactly the DNA found on items at the scene of the murder. The judges dismissed as 'fanciful' the assertions of the family's barrister, Michael Mansfield QC, that the items were contaminated. The proponents of Hanratty's supposed innocence continued to insist almost hysterically on his blamelessness; one of them who really should have known better informed me that Acott had planted the incriminating DNA at the time of the murder. When it was pointed out that DNA analysis was unknown in 1961 and would not be discovered for several more decades, I was mysteriously informed, "Acott knew!"

Acott retired with the rank of commander in 1969 and although he died before the incontrovertible ruling on Hanratty was handed down from the Court of Appeal and had been vilified during the whole campaign, he was finally vindicated.

* * *

Philip Periam left the Squad one month before Acott; his posting to 'P' Division lasted just two weeks before he was back on the Flying Squad again, this time for a three-and-a-half-year posting. He was awarded twenty-two commissioner's commendations for outstanding police work before promotion to detective superintendent and his final posting to 'R' Division. After four years he retired in August 1958; his retirement lasted thirty-four years and he died aged eighty-five.

* * *

Tom Bradford's second tour on the Flying Squad – including his Ghost Squad work – lasted six and a half years; promoted to the rank of detective superintendent in 1954, he spent just nine months with C1 Murder Squad before he was back on the Flying Squad again for a final two-year posting as deputy to the Squad chiefs, Guy Mahon and Reg Spooner. He retired in 1956 having been awarded thirty-eight commissioner's commendations and died almost exactly thirty-one years later, aged eighty.

* * *

Bill MacDonald remained on the Flying Squad for two and a half years after the closure of the Ghost Squad and then, after spending two years on 'Y' Division, was posted to C1 Murder Squad, having been promoted to detective superintendent. He learned his skills well; after his final posting to 'G' Division two years later he was ineligible, by reason of his rank, to receive any further commissioner's commendations – his total by then amounted to thirty-four. But because he had been commended at the Old Bailey for his ability in a difficult case of manslaughter, he was personally congratulated by Sir Richard Jackson, CBE, the Assistant Commissioner (Crime). He retired having served exactly thirty years to the day; he died aged seventy.

* * *

Charles Hewett's career had been a distinguished one; it was inevitable that he would become a copper. His great-grandfather, grandfather and father had all served in the Berkshire Constabulary, as had his father's brother and brother-in-law; in addition, another of his father's brothers had served in the City of London Police and another brother-in-law had served in the Surrey Constabulary. Hewett spent over six years with the Flying Squad, was promoted to detective sergeant (first class) and spent a four-year posting with C1 Murder Squad. Further promotion sent him to the Company Fraud Squad for three years, and with his commissioner's commendations totalling sixteen, his last four years were spent as a detective superintendent on 'M' Division. He served eighteen days longer than Bill MacDonald. Charley Hewett died of a massive stroke in 2003, aged eighty-eight.

* * *

Allan Brodie inexplicably left the Metropolitan Police in 1951, having served just eighteen years and having been awarded twelve commissioner's commendations; he served with the Malayan Police Service for six years during the 'Emergency' and provided distinguished service, just as he had during the Second World War. He retired to Aboyne, Scotland, as the proprietor of a fishing tackle and horn craft shop.

★   ★   ★

Arthur Fisher served three years on the Flying Squad and was posted to divisional duties for the rest of his service. Rather confusingly, his records show that he both passed and failed his examination for inspector on the same day in 1943, but whatever the case, he was never further promoted. He was supremely capable; the last of his forty-one commendations, for ability and persistence in arresting a gang of active housebreakers, was awarded ten weeks before his resignation, after twenty-six years' service, in June 1954.

★   ★   ★

Bill Judge's eight years service with the Flying Squad came to an end in 1950 and two years later, he was promoted to detective chief inspector. Serving on 'L', 'M' and 'B' Divisions, after over thirty-three years' service, he retired with the rank of detective superintendent. His last three years were spent at No. 1 District Headquarters; he had been commended on twenty-six occasions.

★   ★   ★

After his three tours with the Flying Squad totalling eleven years, Len Crawford left the Squad in 1949, never to return. After a short, six-month home posting on 'S' Division, he was promoted to detective chief inspector and during the rest of his ten years' service he served on 'Y' and 'G' Divisions. He achieved the rank of detective superintendent and retired in February 1959 after over thirty-two years' service. Crawford, who was tremendously admired by his officers, had been commended on thirty-three occasions, and his retirement was almost as long as his service; he died aged eighty-six.

★   ★   ★

'Pedlar' Palmer remained with the Flying Squad until 1951, which was when he received his thirty-fourth and final commendation before his last posting to 'J' Division. It was a pity that he was never promoted beyond the rank of detective sergeant (second class) because he was quite capable, but in those days, before being permitted to sit for the examination, it was necessary to pass the first-class Civil Service educational examination. It was not through want of trying; Palmer failed this examination on six occasions between 1938 and 1945. His last five years were spent quietly in this Metropolitan Police backwater, after the rough and tumble of police work in his previous years. He retired in 1956 and died aged seventy-four.

★ ★ ★

Palmer's partner, 'Titch' Freeman, who possessed the near-illegible handwriting, was slightly more fortunate than his friend; he managed to pass the Civil Service examination at his fifth attempt. He received his final – and thirty-sixth – commissioner's commendation on 4 March 1949. He made his last arrest for the Ghost Squad four days later, and two days after that he was dead. The cause was appendicitis followed by peritonitis. As a first class sergeant, his widow's pension, including an allowance for his fifteen-year-old daughter, of £4 11s 6d per week was not excessively generous.

CHAPTER 12

The Wrong 'uns

Following the quashing of Cooper and Compton's convictions in 1947, both were reinstated and returned to uniform. It was not long before Cooper was medically discharged after seventeen and a half years' service suffering from 'anxiety neurosis' – understandable, given the circumstances – but Compton appeared to be made of sterner stuff and stayed on with the rank of station sergeant (the uniform equivalent of detective sergeant, first class) to serve a total of over thirty-one years, leaving on a full pension with an 'exemplary' certificate of service; he died at the age of seventy-three, and Cooper at the age of eighty-five.

*   *   *

As Alfred Baker was posted from the Ghost Squad on 4 October 1948, he was immediately transferred to 'Y' Division. Three years later, on 31 August 1951, he was posted to 'S' Division as Police Constable 577 'S', having been reduced in rank to date from 23 July 1951. The offence for which he had been found guilty on a discipline board was:

Acting in a manner likely to bring discredit on the reputation of the Force by improperly using his position as a police officer in attempting to obtain information from constabulary officers concerning the prosecution of a private individual.

However, in *Police Orders* of 1 January 1952 this was cancelled. A reprimand was substituted and Baker was restored to the rank of detective sergeant (second class). The only difference that this made was to his pension; Baker had retired twelve days previously, one week short of completing twenty years' service, on the grounds of ill health. He vacated his Police Married Quarters at Morton Way, N.14 and eventually moved to Richmond, Surrey. He died on 30 October 1990 aged eighty.

*   *   *

If Freeman's handwriting was almost indecipherable (and Gosling's not much better) Robertson's writing skill was a model of excellence. Nor was that all; he had proved himself to be a hard worker and during a period of three weeks in 1949 had been commended for his ability by the commissioner on three occasions, once in a case of shopbreaking and twice for arresting housebreakers. As the Ghost Squad folded, Robertson stayed with the Flying Squad for three more years, collecting five more commissioner's commendations before he was promoted to detective sergeant (second class) and posted to 'D' Division. There, he was again commended by the commissioner, this time for ability and assistance in arresting 'two troublesome thieves'.

But questions were starting to be raised regarding Robertson's probity. It was not necessarily because (as was related to me) "he came to us from the Flying Squad, full of pomp and importance and supreme confidence". One officer renowned for his physical and moral courage described himself as "disturbed and terrified" at his actions during the one and only enquiry on which he accompanied Robertson (whom he referred to as 'The Evil Scotsman'), and resolved never to accompany him again.

This description appeared justified. On 28 March 1955 Robertson appeared on a disciplinary board at New Scotland Yard. He was charged that on 18 October 1954, at two separate addresses, he had failed to properly account for property which he had seized, namely four National Health insurance cards, thirty National Insurance stamps and twelve books of postage stamps, and that he failed to 'promptly and diligently' make enquiries in respect of two rings which he had taken possession of, which were suspected of being stolen. He was found guilty of all charges and was required to resign.

Robertson appealed to the Secretary of State, who four months later varied the punishment by substituting a reprimand and directed that Robertson be reinstated with the rank of detective sergeant (second class) as from the date of his punishment and ordered that for the purposes of his pay he was deemed to have served continuously as from that date. It was considered, not least by Robertson, to be quite a result, although within days he was transferred to his old stamping ground, 'X' Division. Robertson may have thought that this was going to be a golden year for him; however, there were still five months of 1955 left to run.

In January of that year, Robertson had been awarded his

thirteenth – and final – commissioner's commendation for initiative and determination in a case of housebreaking. Six months previously, a Maltese pimp named Joseph Grech had been arrested for housebreaking. A key which fitted the front door of the burgled premises and which had been found in Grech's possession was of no relevance to the case, said Grech, because it fitted the front door of his own premises. This explanation was disbelieved by the jury, who found him guilty, and Grech was sentenced to three years' imprisonment.

But from his prison cell Grech made a series of hugely damaging allegations against the police; the Commissioner Sir John Nott-Bower directed Detective Superintendent Herbert Hannam to investigate these accusations. Hannam was a brilliant detective, but he was not everybody's cup of tea, either inside or outside the police. He was known as 'Suits' because of his immaculate attire, spoke with a rather affected accent and smoked expensive cigars. Hannam had received a great deal of bad publicity, both from the judiciary and the press, during the case of Dr. John Bodkin Adams, who it was said had poisoned for gain elderly ladies in his care. The doctor was acquitted of murder, and Hannam, who had conducted the investigation, was vilified. However, Leonard 'Nipper' Read QPM, who went on to smash the Kray empire, was a detective constable when Hannam was a detective inspector and admired him greatly, learning an enormous amount from him regarding criminal investigation and presentation of cases at court. Read's admiration was not shared by Percy Hoskins, a Fleet Street crime reporter who described Hannam as being, "like a big chocolate Easter egg; beautiful on the outside, but fuck-all inside".

But now Hannam took up the cudgels, because what Grech had to say was this: that he had given an associate, Morris 'Spider' Page, the sum of £150 to pay to Robertson, the officer in charge of the case, to ensure that a locksmith manufactured a lock to fit his (Grech's) front door, to account for the key in his possession. An honest key-cutter who owned a premises in Praed Street was approached to do just that. In addition, it was alleged that a further £150 would be handed to Robertson in the event of an acquittal. Grech's solicitor was a man named Ben Canter, who had acted for the notorious Messina brothers, a group of vicious pimps who had been controlling prostitution in Soho since before the Second World War; in fact, investigations and prosecutions were still being instituted against them at the time of Hannam's investigations and would continue until the end of the decade. Grech also alleged that Robertson had coached Canter regarding questions which should be put at the trial; in addition, Robertson had accepted a certain Tony Micallef, who was related to the Messina family (and who would feature in 'The Gangbusters' investigations into Soho's Maltese Syndicate twenty years later) to stand as a surety to permit Grech bail.

So just nine weeks after the Secretary of State had reinstated him, Robertson was suspended from duty and appeared at the Old Bailey on 17 November, together with Canter and Page, before the Lord Chief Justice, Lord Goddard.

During the course of the trial Grech alleged that at Page's suggestion Robertson lent Grech the key which had been found in his possession, so that a lock could be made to fit it, but Grech had failed to bribe a senior officer at West End Central, Inspector Charles Reuben Jacobs, who wanted £500. In retaliation, Jacobs allegedly got two of his officers to say that they had seen Grech in the vicinity of the burgled premises, and this had resulted in his conviction.

Hannam gave evidence that during the investigation Canter had told him, "Don't hold it against Jock Robertson; he is a decent bloke and he only loaned us the key – 'Spider' fixed the rest" and also that Page had said that with regard to the spoils of the housebreaking, that Grech, " ...had a monkey out of the peter and some groins, but they were tripe".*

Canter found himself in serious difficulties when in cross-examination he was asked if he could imagine an honest policeman accepting somebody with Micallef's credentials as a surety; Robertson, too, faltered when Lord Goddard asked him pressing questions. Police Constable 197'D' David Pritchard (later detective chief inspector), then an aid to CID, was in court on another matter and heard Robertson say, "My Lord, you are being very hard on me". Goddard retorted that it was Robertson who had put himself in that position.

---

* Or in more prosaic language, " ...he had £500 out of the safe and some rings, but they were worthless".

The jury did not retire for very long before finding the three men guilty of conspiring with each other to pervert the due course of justice, and on 29 November 1955 Canter was sentenced to two years' imprisonment, as was Robertson who was also dismissed from the Force, with Page receiving fifteen months' imprisonment.

Following the court case, Pritchard recalled, "a few more CID at 'DP' (Paddington police station) were a little nervous but the majority were straight and hard working; one of the best was Leonard 'Nipper' Read". In fact, Read was one of the few CID officers who refused point-blank to contribute to Robertson's defence fund.

An internal investigation three months later resulted in Jacobs being found guilty of assisting a prostitute to find a premises, failing to disclose a man's previous convictions in court and failing to account for property from a man who had been arrested. Unsurprisingly, he was dismissed from the Force but he appealed to the High Court to have the decision of the discipline board overturned; however, it did him no good at all. Similarly, Robertson continued to protest his innocence for many years, but he was as unsuccessful as Grech had been.

This raises the question: were Robertson and Baker wrong 'uns before they were posted to Division; were they crooked whilst they were working with the Ghost Squad? It was alleged that Robertson had met Page whilst he was working with the Ghost Squad; this is possible, but the records show that Page was not arrested by Robertson or any other member of the unit.

I think it highly unlikely – in both cases – for three reasons: firstly, in his report for the commissioner dated 10 January 1949 Stuttard praised the work carried out by officers other than those officially attached to the unit, namely Detective Sergeants Freeman and Palmer, plus Detective Constable Robertson. I cannot believe that Stuttard would have done so if any doubt existed regarding Robertson's probity. Secondly, I believe that Baker was posted to division because placed in a position where he worked on his own he was useless. He had lasted on the Flying Squad less than ten months. And thirdly, Gosling simply would not have countenanced criminality which would have jeopardised the squad of which he said, "I was bitterly disappointed when it ended; naturally, I wish that the authorities had kept it going".

CHAPTER 13

Charley Artful

F ive months after leaving the Ghost Squad, Capstick, who had still been retained on C1 Department, was promoted first to detective chief inspector and two years after that to detective superintendent. For the next ten years until his retirement he would investigate some of the Yard's most baffling murders.

During a murder investigation in Wales Capstick pulled lines of black thread around the entrances to a field, a trick he had been taught by Alf Dance. When Capstick discovered that overnight some of the threads had been broken, it led to him to two buried bodies and the murderer.

Probably his most famous investigation of all was a series of ghastly murders, indecent assaults and abductions of young boys and girls in Blackburn, Lancashire. Returning home after two solid months of painstaking but fruitless work, Capstick was looking forward to a good night's sleep. It was not to be. The telephone rang at four o'clock in the morning; there had been another murder of a child. June Ann Devaney, not quite four years old, had been abducted from the hospital bed where she had been recovering from pneumonia, and been raped and brutally murdered. A Winchester bottle close by her cot was found to have fresh fingerprints on it. These prints were not on file, so Capstick informed the Chief Constable, Mr. C.G. Looms, that he intended to fingerprint every male in Blackburn between the ages of fourteen and ninety. The astonished police chief replied that there were 123,000 residents in the area and that the taking and checking of prints might take years. Capstick replied that he felt that every decent person in the area would agree to co-operate, and to inspire public confidence he would ask the local mayor to get the ball rolling by providing his fingerprints first.

It was a tremendous task, and as Capstick continued his investigations with separate lines of enquiry the fingerprints were rigorously checked against those found on the bottle. It paid off. Three months later, card number 46,253 was found to bear the identical prints – and with overwhelming evidence, meticulously assembled by Capstick, twenty-two-year-old Peter Griffiths was found guilty of the murder and hanged at Walton Prison on 19 November 1948. Griffiths had denied any involvement with the previous attacks on children and there was insufficient evidence to link him with them. But coincidentally or not, there were no more child murders in Blackburn.

Promoted to the rank of detective chief superintendent, Capstick took charge of the CID in the Metropolitan Police's No. 4 Area; as such, he could have relegated the investigation of murders and other serious offences to the senior officers under his control. To a certain extent he did, but as 'The Guv'nor' he had to be seen to be in charge of major investigations and he lent his expertise, which resulted in the successful conclusion to many of those cases. After three years in the rank Capstick retired, having served over thirty-two years. He was fifty-two years of age and he went to work for Garfield Weston Allied Bakeries, where he coordinated security for their fifty premises all over the United Kingdom. After three years of this employment, he looked forward to a long retirement with his wife Violet – always known as 'Babs' – and their three sons. He spent his leisure hours playing bowls at Norwood Sports Club and cultivating the beautiful roses which habitually adorned his buttonhole, but the strains and stresses of the job which he had loved had left their indelible mark on him. He did not live long enough to collect his state pension and died on 4 June 1968. He was a sad loss to the Force to whom he had devoted most of his adult life. His contribution to the police and to society, with his sheer hard work, informant-running and series of successes in murder investigations, surely merited an inclusion in the Honours' List. That he did not receive recognition was nothing short of a disgrace.

To add insult to injury, an appeal against conviction was heard almost fifty years after the conviction of Iain Hay Gordon for the murder of Patricia Curran, a judge's daughter, in Northern Ireland. Capstick had investigated the case, in which the injuries to Miss Curran's face were so frightful it was initially thought she had suffered a blast from a shotgun; in fact, she had been stabbed in the face thirty-seven times. At Gordon's trial at Belfast Assizes, Capstick had been fiercely cross-examined by H.A. M'Veigh QC for the defence, who alleged that Capstick's interview had not conformed with the Judges' Rules. However, the Lord Chief Justice of Northern Ireland, Lord MacDermott, ruled that the police procedure had been entirely proper. Gordon had been convicted of the murder, with the jury's verdict of 'guilty, but insane' and he had spent seven years in a mental hospital. Now, nearly half a century later, he appealed against conviction. There was no new evidence; the appeal relied upon destroying the credibility of Gordon's confession to Capstick. With Sir Louis Blom-Cooper QC for the appellant stating "Capstick was a liar", and Ronald Weatherup QC, appearing on behalf of the Director of Public Prosecutions, accepting that Gordon's confession had not been voluntary and that its contents were not a reliable account of what had occurred, it was hardly surprising that the Lord Chief Justice, Sir Robert Carswell, quashed the conviction.

This was followed by a television dramatisation of the investigation, which portrayed Capstick screaming questions at Gordon. Inexplicably, Capstick's original Liverpudlian accent had, for the purposes of the programme, been replaced with a broad Cockney one. It was an utter disgrace; Capstick deserves to be remembered for his impressive battle against crime rather than by a piece of cheap, sensationalist television.

CHAPTER 14

The Ferret

When Brinnand resigned in 1946, he left without a pension; after fifteen years and 205 days service he was awarded a gratuity of £191 1s 0d. This sum of money (approximately £8,000 by today's standards) was a useful amount but by no means sufficient to solve Brinnand's problems.

In 1943 Brinnand commenced an extra-marital relationship with a woman named Florence Kinghorn (née Clifford), and early the following year she gave birth to the first of their three children. Just prior to October 1946, Brinnand's wife found out about his affair with Mrs. Kinghorn and also that she – Mrs. Kinghorn – was then pregnant with Brinnand's second child, and this knowledge would ultimately lead to a divorce. Brinnand did not enjoy a harmonious relationship with his father-in-law, George Harrison, who in Brinnand's own words was in a position to do him 'great harm'. Would the 'great harm' have been reporting his extra-marital activities to the police? It almost certainly would have been, because in those days 'consorting with a woman, not your wife' was an offence leading to dismissal from the service; and this, in part, was backed up by Daisy, who later told her son that if Brinnand had not left the police when he did, he would have lost his superannuation.

So when Brinnand resigned from the police he also left Daisy and his son without any financial support whatsoever. Brinnand's father disowned him. The law at that time would not permit a woman to divorce her husband on the grounds of desertion until they had been separated for at least six years (although Daisy would certainly have had compelling grounds because of Brinnand's adultery), and during the late 1940s and '50s she worked as a telephonist for the Church Commissioners for England. She remarried in 1954, and Brinnand would never see Daisy again; the next time he saw his son John would be thirty-five years later.

Life for Brinnand after the Ghost Squad did not initially run smoothly. He now had Florence and his two sons (the second was born in 1947) to support. Initially, he took employment with Wimbledon Greyhound Stadium, of which the security was now under the control of his Ghost Squad mentor, Percy Worth. But the job did not last for Brinnand – he started drinking and gambling heavily and also had financial difficulties. He drifted from one race track to another, in London and Southend, carrying out fairly menial work.

But in the late 1940s he did find a permanent job. He worked as part of the unloading gang for the construction company which was building Crawley New Town; although he was unused to hard manual labour, he stuck at it for two or three years and drew the rewards – £30 per week, a fortune at that time.

In the early 1950s Brinnand and his family moved back to London and he secured employment as a park keeper, first at Tooting Bec then at Dulwich Park. In the mid-1950s he was called before a promotions board held at County Hall and, after giving the board, in his words, "a true explanation" as to how he came to leave the Metropolitan Police, he was promoted and placed in charge of a small park to the rear of the BBC at Hammersmith. About this time, his daughter was born and Brinnand also obtained his Royal Horticultural Society Instructors Certificate; this led to his becoming the horticultural instructor at the St. Nicolas Remand Centre in Enfield, where he would stay for the next two years.

So after spending almost ten years dealing with all matters horticultural, Brinnand suddenly ditched this way of life when he became Chief Security Officer at Reeves, the manufacturers of artistic paints and pencils. This was followed by working as the 'house detective' at the Savoy Hotel, and whilst he was so employed he opened an office in the Strand and commenced a part-time private investigation business. Gradually the part-time job grew and blossomed into a full-time one, and his post-police career really started to take off. Much of his work came from solicitors representing wealthy clients and well-established businesses, and he also conducted a number of investigations on behalf of the University of London into 'A' & 'O' level leakages. One of his more fascinating investigations was when he was employed by the firm of solicitors representing John Profumo, the former Secretary of State for War. Brinnand conducted a very searching enquiry on behalf of his clients and met all of the persons involved in what became known as 'The Profumo Affair'. Brinnand's business prospered and he provided his family with a good standard of living for a number of years.

By now Brinnand was in his sixties and the arduous work as a private investigator had begun to take its toll. Taking a more sedentary job, he became warden at Tooting Bec police station and finally security officer at Guys Medical School, from where he retired in 1976. After retirement, he assisted his second son in setting up an office-cleaning business, helping out with the clerical side of the operation.

In March 1981 a family reunion took place at 81B Trinity Road, South London. Present were Florence, their three children together with their respective partners, and his son from his first marriage, John, and his wife. It was the first time that Brinnand ever saw his four children together; it would never happen again. Whether or not his first wife Daisy was invited to the meeting is not known; in any event she did not attend and died of cancer four years later. Brinnand and his son from his first marriage never enjoyed a particularly close relationship but they did have occasional contact with each other over the ensuing years; and Brinnand did get to meet his three granddaughters.

His second family parted company from him in 1992; a lonely and bitter man, he died in the Welbeck Residential Home, Tooting Bec from bronchopneumonia and cancer of the prostate two years later, on 10 December, aged eighty-five.

His sister Elsie was a deeply compassionate woman who had never married; a nursing sister in her early years, she utilised her skills in looking after her father until his death in 1961, then Matthew, and finally their brother Ted, who died in 1996. Elsie died three years later of cancer.

Matthew Brinnand's death marked the sad end of a former police officer who, if his personal life had taken a different course, could doubtless have reached the highest rank.

CHAPTER 15

The Yokel

I do not believe that Gosling was the greatest of the officers who served on the Ghost Squad; in my opinion, that accolade goes to the cunning, artful Capstick with his painstaking, methodical way of meticulously assembling clues in order to arrest a murderer, as well as his ability to unerringly manoeuvre the best informants into the best situations to achieve the finest results, rather like a chess grandmaster. But Gosling ran Capstick a very close second; he *was* the Ghost Squad – he was present on day one and he lasted all the three years and ten months of its existence. He was there, running informants, keeping them safe, taking risks and cutting corners. When a job was about to come off, if it was too late to call in the Flying Squad or their Divisional counterparts, he would step in himself and he was often alone when he did so. He was charismatic, often loud, a great raconteur and a sound, fearless police officer.

After the death knell rang for the Ghost Squad, he was posted to Albany Street police station on 'D' Division. David Pritchard had been posted to the same station in 1952 as Police Constable 197'D' and described Gosling as 'legendary'. On one occasion, Pritchard was present when Gosling presented the station officer, Sergeant Slater, with a charge sheet already typed out, containing five names and addresses of men who, unbeknown to them, were going to be arrested and charged with stealing a lorry and contents, namely cigarettes, cigars and tobacco, valued at £50,000, an export order from John Players, Nottingham. Gosling asked Slater to ensure that the yard was cleared of the lost or stolen vehicles which were parked there, since when he returned he would be accompanied by one or two large lorries together with the prisoners. Pritchard was one of the officers deputed to push the cars out into the lane behind the station, and later that night Gosling returned complete with two lorries containing the property of John Player and five prisoners – their names corresponded with those typed on the charge sheet.

Pritchard also recalled that Gosling was in the CID office inspecting the books when a prisoner who was being charged with larceny suddenly dashed out of the charge room and into the CID office, picked up the heavy crime book and brought it down on Gosling's head with considerable force. Pritchard was in the charge room when Gosling dragged the prisoner in by the scruff of his neck and told the station officer to charge him with assault. The wording of the charge, irrespective of the rank of the officer involved, always read, 'That you did assault (name of the officer), a constable of the Metropolitan Police', so when the immaculately dressed Gosling stepped into the witness box the following day, after the prisoner, looking much the worst for wear, said, "Guilty, I'm very sorry," the magistrate asked Gosling if he had been in uniform at the time of the assault. Gosling coldly informed the magistrate of his identity and rank and produced the offending crime book as evidence of the assault. The magistrate apologised profusely, decided his powers were insufficient to deal with such a savage assault upon the head of such an obvious dignitary and committed the hapless villain to the Sessions for sentence, where he received twelve months' imprisonment.

"I found him to be a very pleasant and forthright senior officer, who always had time to speak to and advise junior officers," was Pritchard's opinion of Gosling. "A real gentleman."

This opinion was shared by Capstick's son David, for whom Gosling managed to acquire tickets for Wimbledon Speedway Track. "A big, booming voice," recalled Capstick. "Difficult to miss!"

Gosling spent four and a half years on 'D' Division – he was "getting Divisional experience," Gosling was told – during which he collected his last two commissioner's commendations, the first being for ability in a case of abortion. The circumstances of how the final commendation was acquired were far more interesting.

★ ★ ★

It is at this stage that the case of Tommy Smithson should be mentioned. Smithson had been born in Liverpool in 1920 but it was not long before he was brought to the East End of London. A former merchant seaman and fairground boxer, Smithson was known variously as 'Scarface Smithson' or 'Mr. Loser', and although the former nickname was certainly fitting, the latter seems hardly appropriate. An inveterate womaniser, Smithson was a strongarm man and gambler who worked for various gangs and was widely admired as one who would fight against sometimes insurmountable odds and never give up. His courage – or 'gameness' as East Enders referred to it – meant that Smithson was hero-worshipped, especially by two up-and-coming young tearaways from Bethnal Green named Reggie and Ronnie Kray. However, like his two young admirers, he was not the sharpest knife in the block. Smithson became involved in a gangland brawl in which he cut the throat of one Frederick 'Slip' Sullivan and promptly went into hiding. Unfortunately, his victim's brother, Sonny, was a member of the Jack Spot/Billy Hill gangland alliance. Betrayed by his employer, club owner George Caruana, who told him that a peace deal was being negotiated, Smithson unwisely attended a meeting in Mornington Crescent where, incredibly, Jack Spot actually persuaded him to hand over his gun. Although the gun was unloaded (Smithson had forgotten to purchase any ammunition) possession of the gun might have proved a useful bargaining chip had Smithson retained hold of it; but because he did not, he was seized by Spot and savagely 'chivved' by Billy Hill. At least three other members of the gang jumped out of a lorry and joined in the attack; apart from being cut in the face, Smithson was slashed all over his arms, legs and chest, kicked, then beaten with an iron bar, his arm was broken and the lorry was twice reversed over him before his unconscious body was thrown over a wall into Regent's Park. It seemed impossible that anyone could have survived such a frenzied attack; but Smithson did.

The following day, Gosling saw him in hospital. Smithson was in a sorry state; he had lost five pints of blood and was swathed in bandages. Gosling knew – as did everybody – who was responsible. In addition to mounting the attack, it was known that Billy Hill had been the brains behind the Eastcastle Street mailbag robbery, where £287,000 had been stolen, the previous year, yet nobody had been arrested for it. Jack Spot had been a thorn in the side of the police for several years and Gosling was exceptionally keen to arrest the pair of them. But first he needed a complaint from Smithson. Leaving the unconscious tearaway in the care of two detectives and warning them not to permit Smithson to receive any visitors or have any contact with the outside world, Gosling left the hospital to carry out another investigation. When he returned four hours later, Smithson, having had forty-seven stitches inserted in his face alone, was sitting up in bed and having finished a four course meal was lighting a cigarette; Gosling instinctively knew an approach had been made. Smithson suggested that Gosling was going to tell him to 'put myself in your hands'. "The last time I did that," commented Smithson, sourly, "I got three years in Borstal." Try as Gosling might, Smithson resolutely refused to tell him anything, and five days later he discharged himself from hospital. That is the official version. It was later rumoured – although it was certainly never confirmed – that Spot had remunerated Smithson to the tune of £1,000 for keeping his silence. In his memoirs, *Boss of Britain's Underworld* (Naldrett Press Ltd., 1955), Billy Hill – who referred to Smithson in the book, as 'Brownson' – commented, "But even while he was breathing what he thought was his last, he didn't sing. No, the cozzers tried everything to make him talk, but that Brownson just kept his mouth shut". However, as Smithson later remarked to Zoe Progl, a former girlfriend who was dubbed 'The Queen of the Underworld', he would have his revenge on his attackers; and perhaps he did.

In his memoirs Gosling made reference to an encounter with an informant named 'Hoppy Ted' and went to great lengths to describe him: a huge powerful man who had been a railway worker, who possessed an artificial leg and who had been disqualified from driving for life, having killed two people in a road collision. It was he who provided Gosling with some very pertinent information after a six-man gang had razor-slashed his face. Written fifty years ago, Gosling's private papers reveal that "this man ... was, and still is the terror of Hoxton". Although he does not directly say so, Gosling suggests in his memoirs that what followed was a Ghost Squad case, but it was not; it occurred four years after the Ghost Squad had ceased to function, in 1953 whilst Gosling was posted to 'D' Division; just about the time of the attack on Smithson.

Eight o' clock one evening saw Gosling – according to his memoirs – drinking with an informant in a pub on the borders of the City of London, when 'Hoppy Ted' entered, whereupon Gosling's snout made himself scarce. 'Hoppy Ted' offered to show Gosling the whereabouts of some stolen property in order to revenge himself on his attackers; however, he had had a great deal to drink and insisted on taking Gosling in his own car. With a great many misgivings Gosling agreed and described the drive which followed as 'a ride of death'. On the Southend Road, at Pitsea, Essex, 'Ted' stopped the car, pointed out some farm buildings in a valley and suggested to Gosling that he pay a visit the following morning. After an equally frightening drive back to the pub where his car was parked, Gosling did just that. Taking two officers with him, his search of the farm buildings revealed 2,000,000 Players cigarettes, a ton and a half of sweets, four British Road Service lorries in the process of being broken up to provide spare parts and five hundred empty cigarette cartons. The cartons were the part-proceeds of a warehousebreaking at Dover one month previously. The bonded warehouse belonging to H.M. Customs and Excise had had its doors blown off with gelignite, resulting in property, valued at £30,000 being stolen. The large number of Players cigarettes had been stolen by means of a warehousebreaking at Vicar Lane, Leeds, and there was a reward of £1,000 for the recovery of this property alone.

Gosling arrested the owners of the farm, two brothers who were later each sentenced to three years' imprisonment on their first conviction at Leeds Assizes. The court also commended Gosling, as did the commissioner, for ability and persistence. Sadly, as Gosling later remarked, this case which he described as being "out of this world" did not make him many friends. The Flying Squad was already keenly interested in this investigation and in fact, were working with two police officers from Leeds who had come down to London to assist in this case. However, to make amends Gosling ensured that another ten officers (all but one from the Flying Squad) were included in the commendation.

Whether or not Gosling acquired his information in the way which he describes it in his memoirs, his account raises the question as to whether Tommy Smithson was 'Hoppy Ted'. I think it highly probable, especially since Gosling became aware that the associates of 'Hoppy Ted's' attackers kept watch on the loss adjusters to see who collected the reward. In his private papers Gosling noted that it was not 'Hoppy Ted' who collected the reward, so it can be assumed that the services of a 'proxy snout' were utilised; highly understandable in the circumstances. It will be remembered that £1,000 was the sum on offer from the insurance company; the same amount that Jack Spot was supposed to have paid Smithson. It was not a matter which Spot could confirm or deny. However, whether or not Spot paid out a large sum of money to Smithson, because there was no prosecution it would appear that both Spot and Hill walked away scot free. Perhaps, perhaps not.

Later the same month, Spot was suckered into taking a call from a telephone box in Soho; as he emerged from the call box, a car-load of detectives drew up and arrested him for possessing an offensive weapon. At court, it was not thought desirable that someone with Spot's character should allege that honest police officers had planted the knife on him, so he pleaded guilty, invented spurious reasons as to why the knife was in his possession and was fined £20. Later he would allege that the knife had indeed been planted on him by the police and morosely placed the blame on "that cunt Sparks". He was unkindly referring to Detective Superintendent Bert 'Iron Man' Sparks, in charge of Soho's 'C' Division, and he was scarcely less scathing regarding the officer who had actually carried out the arrest. He was probably not to know that Detective Sergeant Charles Sydney Clifford Careless of 'C' Division had in the previous decade carried out arrests (as had Sparks) on behalf of the Ghost Squad.

And two months after the attack on Smithson, Billy Hill was arrested for inflicting grievous bodily harm on a former associate, Freddy Andrews, who, it was said, was 'getting too big for his boots'. With blood pouring down his face from a razor-slashing, Andrews named Hill as his attacker, and Hill spent three months on remand until at the Old Bailey Andrews realised that he had made a mistake and Hill walked away a free man.

So was that a salutary lesson – a humiliating climb-down and fine for Spot and three months deprivation of liberty for Hill? It depends how one looks at it; Spot did plead guilty and after Andrews stated in court that Hill was not his attacker, Hill was obviously not guilty, no more guilty that either he or Spot had been of the attack on Smithson, since he had named neither of them. Food for thought.

Whatever the origins of the £1,000, Smithson used the money to buy a share in a drinking club, but the word circulated that he was a police informant; it was sufficient for him to undergo another chivving, this time an attack which necessitated a further twenty-seven stitches. Three years after the initial attack, Smithson had one row too many; during an argument with some

Maltese gangsters he was shot dead. The underworld turned out in force to mourn the passing of the enormously brave, but singularly unintelligent tearaway, whose last words to a passer-by in the street were, "Good morning; I'm dying".

★   ★   ★

The commendation for the case disposed of at Leeds Assizes marked the last of Gosling's thirty-three commendations by the commissioner, alone. The number of District commendations, as well as those awarded by magistrates and judges, totalled almost one hundred.

And three weeks prior to receiving his final commendation, Gosling was transferred to C1 Department at the Yard, having been promoted to detective superintendent Class II.

In his memoirs, Gosling stated that he headed the Vice Squad (as did Fabian 'of the Yard' in 1949), but this is a misnomer; there was never any such animal. Fabian, as a detective inspector (second class), maintained an index and recorded incidents relating to vice and prostitution at Vine Street police station before World War Two, and later Clubs Office at West End Central police station dealt with the regulation of clubs in Soho. What Gosling dealt with in his department at the Yard were complaints regarding what was known as 'blue films' and whether they tended to corrupt and deprave anybody watching them. What was known as 'The Dirty Squad' was the forerunner of the ill-fated Obscene Publications Squad and the more successful (and rather ad hoc) squad under the ministrations of Bert Wickstead QPM during the seventies, and which culminated in the establishment of Clubs and Vice, under the supervision of the Assistant Commissioner of No.1 Area.

It was a task, his son Martin later told me, that he failed to relish. But Gosling's duties did not consist purely of writing reports regarding the frailties of public morality; he was introduced by Detective Constable John Swain to Commander Dave Reid and Lieutenant Tom Duvall, both of whom were attached to the United States Navy. A shortfall had been discovered in goods being delivered to American PX bases, and the truck in question was followed, with Gosling getting out of the office to participate in the case. Gosling's department possessed two underpowered Hillman Minx 10hp saloons; it became obvious that neither of them was able to keep pace with the truck, and Swain suggested to Gosling that the Flying Squad should get involved. This evoked a roar of disapproval from Gosling, who informed Swain that no thief "was going to take the micky out of him". Luckily, Swain utilised his motorcycle instead, the thieves were arrested and the thefts stopped.

During 1956 the curtain was coming down on some of the *glitterati* of the underworld. Jack Spot had by now fallen out with Billy Hill and on his way home to Hyde Park Mansions with his wife he was ambushed and attacked by a number of men; he required seventy-eight stitches in his face. Hill was impressively alibied; five of his associates were jailed for a total of twenty-seven years for the attack.

The following month, it was alleged that Spot had recovered sufficiently to launch an attack in Berkeley Square on a Hill associate, Big Tommy 'Bonz' Falco, who was slashed in the face; in July Spot was acquitted of the attack.

Then Billy Hill was beaten up, allegedly by Billy Howard, a south London club owner known as 'The Soho Don'. Much, much later, following their deaths, it was said that Hill, Howard and Moisha Bluebell (the latter having allegedly participated in the Mornington Crescent attack on Tommy Smithson) were all police informants. Were they? Difficult to say; no details of the true identities of informants would be kept at the Yard for many years to come.

As the gangsters drifted from the scene, so it was time for Gosling to call it a day. In his own words, "I felt I had had my share of sin and sorrow".

★ ★ ★

On 2 December 1956 Gosling retired, aged fifty-one, with over twenty-seven years' service, an annual pension of £570 3s 5d and an exemplary character assessment. Within months of leaving the Metropolitan Police Gosling returned, almost, to his roots. He embarked upon a house restoration at Mill House, Brantham, Suffolk, just across the border from Essex and a few miles away from his birthplace at Manningtree. The house at Hilbury Road, Warlingham was sold and the whole family contributed to a spring and summer during 1957 of hard work and building renovation. Gosling threw himself wholeheartedly into the project; and when it was eventually completed, he turned his attention to writing. Initially, this was with the encouragement and guidance of the late Tom Tullett, who at that time was chief crime reporter on the Mirror Group. Tullett had himself been a police officer, as had his father, whom Gosling remembered from his days on the beat. *The Ghost Squad* was a great success and during the period that followed there were interviews and articles in the newspapers, as well as television interviews. He collaborated on several books, one of which, *Death of a Snout,* was adapted for a film entitled *The Informers,* starring Nigel Patrick as the senior Yard detective who gets framed. It is a very good film that has stood the test of time, due undoubtedly to the fact that Gosling was technical advisor. The year following the publication of *The Ghost Squad,* Gosling followed this up with *The Shame of a City* (W.H. Allen, 1960), which he wrote in collaboration with Douglas Warner. It was with Warner that Gosling decided to work on a series of joint ventures for which he provided considerable information and anecdotes. However, Warner published *Death of a Snout* (Cassells 1961) under his name only and fled the country, ahead of expensive matrimonial difficulties; he subsequently published several pieces and scripts from Australia, without any reference to Gosling's material or the agreement they had made. This led to a prohibitively expensive action in the High Court, where, as usual, the only winners were the lawyers.

Following the attack on the Glasgow to London Mail Train at Sears Crossing, Buckinghamshire on 8 August 1963, where £2,631,684 was stolen, Gosling, in collaboration with crime writer Dennis Craig, wrote *The Great Train Robbery* (W.H. Allen, 1964) in which, "drawing on some of his best 'contacts'", he expressed his opinions on how the job had been planned and executed and how the money had been disposed of. Gosling and Craig visited Sears Crossing within days of the robbery taking place, to 'get the flavour' of the scene; unfortunately, their interest resulted in both of them being arrested. Gosling, in his normal subdued, tactful manner, managed to reassure the arresting officers of his innocence.

On the morning of 20 April 1966 Gosling was preparing to travel to London to discuss another project with a journalist whom he had known during his time in the police, when he suddenly died of a heart attack. He was aged sixty; his retirement had lasted less than ten years. The funeral was held at St. Mary's

Church in Mistley, where he had sung as a boy. It was where his father Walter was buried; he had died thirty-three years previously of pneumonia at the early age of fifty-nine. The church was full to overflowing at John Gosling's funeral. The turnout of Metropolitan Police officers was huge; and it is really not surprising that many of the Ghost Squad snouts turned up as well. In his obituary, the *East Anglian Daily Times* referred to him as 'one of the finest investigators in the history of police detection'.

Sadly, apart from some great memories, Gosling had little else to leave. Why this unfortunate state of affairs existed, nobody knows. Gosling had received £13,000 for selling the film and television rights of *The Ghost Squad* – approximately £182,000 by today's standards – as well as $10,000 from Columbia Pictures for the rights to his book, *The Great Train Robbery*. He received a substantial sum for being the technical advisor on the adaptation of *Death of a Snout* for Ken Annakin's 1963 film, *The Informers*, he had the royalties from his books, plus a superintendent's pension. It is quite possible that the costs of the civil action against his one-time collaborator, Warner, soaked up his assets; but whatever the circumstances, Marjorie was obliged to sell Mill House and move to a substantially more modest property, until her death, aged seventy-five, in 1983.

Gosling's story cannot end without a footnote. In 1969 Gosling's youngest son, Ben, was working as a checker for a forwarding company in Hadleigh, Suffolk. An incoming lorry was unloaded, and as Ben signed the accompanying paperwork the driver looked at his surname and asked if he had any connection with John Gosling. He then went on to reveal that Gosling had once arrested him and had 'put him away'. But he added that he had a great respect for Gosling, because whilst he was serving his sentence, Gosling ensured that his family 'didn't go short'.

"Perhaps that's how he groomed his snouts?" ironically suggested Gosling's eldest son, Martin, who recounted the story to me.

Having read everything about John Gosling's exploits, it's a question which doesn't require an answer.

CHAPTER 16

Nobby

I first became interested in the Ghost Squad even before I joined the Metropolitan Police in 1967. I had borrowed John Gosling's memoirs from the local library; then I read Norman Lucas and Bernard Scarlett's book on the Flying Squad, where there was a further mention of the Ghost Squad. During my service I heard other snippets of information about their work and then during my short period as staff officer to Commander John O'Connor, then heading the Flying Squad, I discovered further intelligence regarding that unit's activities.

I started serious research into the history of the Flying Squad in 1992, and this included the composition and the work of the Ghost Squad. As far as I was aware, all the members of it had long since died, and for the most part that was a correct assumption. There was no record of the death of Matthew Brinnand, but then he had not retired on pension and since he had obviously not become a member of the National Association of Retired Police Officers there would be no record of his demise with them. I made enquiries, and in 2004 Matthew Brinnand's son, John, got in touch. Had I known it, Matthew Brinnand was still alive at the time I commenced my research.

With regard to Henry Clark, I assumed that he too was dead. I had written to him via the Metropolitan Police Pensions Department (who refused to say whether he was alive or dead) but I heard nothing; either he was dead or had moved abroad, but in any event he had slipped underneath the radar. I had his address of 9 Conal Court, Streatham, but I found no evidence of its existence.

In 1996 I received a telephone call from an old friend and former police officer whom I had known him for many years and who, like me, lived in Upminster and had retired. He told me that his wife was a carer for an old man who had also been a police officer and who told her that he would like to meet and have lunch with rather more recent additions to the Metropolitan Police. Because my friend knew of my research into the history of the police, he thought that if he invited me along to the luncheon, I might be able to inject a few memories into the old chap and generally, keep the conversation going. I agreed, and asked the pensioners name. I was told it was Henry Clark. Clark is a common enough name, I thought, and I felt that it would be far too much of a coincidence for him to be *the* Henry Clark; after all, I knew that Clark, the former Ghost Squad officer, had retired over forty years previously, had been living south of the Thames and in all probability was now dead and buried. Which just goes to show you how wrong you can be. That venerable gentleman who had been born just yards away from my own birth-place, who had lived half a mile away from my parents' house, who had been married in the same church where I had been a choirboy, had for the previous nine years been living no more than one mile away from me, at 92 Hall Lane, Upminster, Essex.

* * *

Despite the fact that he was ninety-four years of age, Henry was lucid and voluble. He was charming and chatty and a great luncheon companion. As he poured out generous measures of Scotch, his hand was rock-steady, an attribute to be much admired. After Clark had left the Ghost Squad, he was posted to 'L' Division and stayed there for almost four years. His last posting was to 'P' Division and he retired from there on 5 December 1954, aged fifty-two, having served just over thirty-one years. He had been awarded a total of fifty-nine commendations. Despite his, perhaps grudging, promotion to detective inspector in 1945, from then until his retirement nine years later he was never further promoted. He was supremely capable, well informed and a hard worker. His last commendations were when he was serving on 'L' Division in 1948 and 1949, both for 'ability, perseverance and acumen' in cases of larceny and receiving. Clark's sister recalled that there was talk of further promotion when he received his final posting to 'P' Division, but nothing came of it. In those days (and for many years afterwards, before it was overtaken by diversity) Freemasonry was considered an extremely helpful adjunct to promotion. Not, however, in Clark's case. And no further commendations were awarded during his final years on 'P' Division; perhaps by then realisation had crept in that further promotion would not be coming his way. It was, I believe, a very short-sighted view on behalf of his senior officers. It did not appear to faze Clark, since, according to his sister, he never showed any bitterness. To him, she told me, "it was always a good job".

For ten years after leaving the Metropolitan Police, Clark worked for a local bookmaker, Max Parker (who, with his nephew Cyril Stein acquired Ladbrokes in 1956), and regularly visited racetracks in a security capacity; he also worked for Streatham Council until State retirement age. He and Ivy remained at Conal Court; Ivy's mother, Martha Elizabeth Ridgwell, had lived in Ilford, but in her later years, she moved into Conal Court with her daughter and son-in-law until her death, aged eighty-six, in 1971.

In 1986 Ivy's brother, Fred, died; he and his wife were living at 92 Hall Lane, Upminster. At around this time, the owner of Conal Court wanted to dispose of the property and Fred's widow wanted some company in the big house in Hall Lane; therefore it suited everybody for Henry and Ivy to vacate their flat at Conal Court and move into the upstairs of Hall Lane, which had been converted into a flat for them and where they lived for the rest of their lives, rent-free.

Henry and I talked about Capstick and Gosling and the Flying Squad of the 1930s; he was unable (so he said) to throw any light on the reasons behind Brinnand's departure, but when I suggested putting something down in writing about his experiences, he charmingly declined. I hesitated about pressing him, because I had no doubt that if I had done so, he would have been annoyed at my impertinence and that would have ruined the luncheon. In fact, I discovered I was wrong; if there was a question he didn't care for, it would be skilfully deflected, without any display of annoyance.

We met on a couple of occasions for lunch; both times, he was chatty and twinkling. The ladies at the Upminster Golf and Bowls Club would frequently come over and enquire after his health and wellbeing; they went away charmed by his replies. During a moment's respite, I asked him if the other members of the club had any idea of his former trade or calling. "I believe," he answered with a grin, "that they think I used to be a Bank Manager!"

But he steadfastly refused to allow me to commit him to paper, and he died a couple of years later on 2 September 1998 at the grand age of ninety-six. In his later years, Henry had developed cancer of the prostate but, as his doctor told him, "That won't kill you". It didn't; his death certificate shows that he died of 'old age'. His widow Ivy remained in the house a little longer but eventually she was unable to care for herself and moved to a care home, where she died a few short years later.

My enduring memory of Henry came as we sat back in our chairs and watched the elderly white-clad figures bend a creaking, arthritic knee as their bowls sped towards the jack, across the carefully manicured green at the bowls club. I put down my glass, turned to my companion and asked him the question which he, more than any other living person, would be able to answer. "Just why was it," I said, as casually as possible, "that the Ghost Squad came to an end?"

Henry Clark met my gaze unflinchingly, with eyes that never lost their twinkle. He shook his head, nearly imperceptibly. "Golden days, Dick," he replied with an almost dreamy smile. "Golden days!"

Bibliography

BEVERIDGE Peter, *Inside the CID* (Evans Bros. Ltd., 1957)

BURGESS P.H.E., *No Easy Way* (Privately published, 2009)

CAPSTICK John (with Jack Thomas), *Given in Evidence* (John Long, 1960)

DARBYSHIRE Neil & HILLIARD Brian, *The Flying Squad* (Headline Book Publishing plc, 1993)

DIBBENS Harold, *Dibbens' Diaries* (Privately published, 1989)

DONNELLY Mark, *Britain in the Second World War* (Routledge, 1999)

FABIAN Robert, *Fabian of the Yard* (Naldrett Press, 1950)

FIDO Martin & SKINNER Keith, *The Official Encyclopedia of Scotland Yard* (Virgin Books, 1999)

FIRMIN Stanley, *Scotland Yard – The Inside Story* (Hutchinson & Co., 1948)

FROST George 'Jack', *Flying Squad* (Youth Book Club, London, 1950)

GILLARD Michael & FLYNN Laurie, *Untouchables* (Cutting Edge Press, 2004)

GOSLING John, *The Ghost Squad* (WH Allen, 1959)

GOSLING John & CRAIG Dennis, *The Great Train Robbery* (WH Allen, 1964)

GRANT Denis, *A Fragmented History of the Flying Squad, its Transport, Drivers and Detectives* (Boxing Programme Notes, 1976)

HATHERILL George, CBE, *A Detective's Story* (Andre Deutsch, 1971)

HIGGINS R.H., *In the Name of the Law* (John Long, 1958)

HILL Billy, *Boss of Britain's Underworld* (Naldrett Press Ltd, 1955)

HOWE Sir Ronald, *The Pursuit of Crime* (Arthur Barker Ltd., 1961)

HOWE Sir Ronald, *The Story of Scotland Yard* (Arthur Barker Ltd., 1965)

INWOOD Stephen, *A History of London* (MacMillan, 1998)

JACKSON Sir Richard, *Occupied with Crime* (George G. Harrap & Co. Ltd 1967)

KIRBY Dick, *The Squad – A History of the men and vehicles of the Flying Squad at New Scotland Yard, 1919-1983* (Unpublished manuscript, Metropolitan Police History Museum, London, 1993)

KIRBY Dick, *Rough Justice – Memoirs of a Flying Squad Detective* (Merlin Unwin Books, 2001)

KIRBY Dick, *The Real Sweeney* (Constable & Robinson, 2005)

KIRBY Dick, *You're Nicked!* (Constable & Robinson, 2007)

KIRBY Dick, *Villains* (Constable & Robinson, 2008)

LEE Christopher, *This Sceptred Isle* (BBC Worldwide Books, 1999)

SCARLETT Bernard and LUCAS Norman, *The Flying Squad* (Arthur Barker Ltd 1968)

McCALL Karen (ed), *London Branch NARPO Millennium Magazine* (Orphans Press, Leominster, 1999)

McLAGAN Graeme, *Bent Coppers* (Weidenfeld & Nicolson, 2003)

MORTON James, *Bent Coppers* (Little, Brown, 1993)

MORTON James, *Supergrasses & Informers* (Little, Brown, 1995)

MORTON James, *East End Gangland* (Little, Brown, 2000)

MORTON James & PARKER Gerry, *Gangland Bosses* (Time Warner Books, 2005)

MURPHY Robert, *Smash & Grab* (Faber & Faber, 1993)

PAYNE Graham and MORLEY Sheridan (eds), *The Noël Coward Diaries* (Weidenfeld and Nicolson, 1982)

PROGL Zoe, *Woman of the Underworld* (Arthur Barker Ltd., 1964)

RAWLINGS William, *A Case for the Yard* (John Long, 1961)

READ Leonard & MORTON James, *Nipper* (MacDonald & Co, 1991)

SAMUEL Raphael, *East End Underworld* (Routledge & Kegan Paul, 1981)

SCOTT Sir Harold, *Scotland Yard* (Andre Deutsch, 1954)

SELLWOOD A.V., *Police Strike 1919* (WH Allen, 1978)

SWAIN John, *Being Informed* (Janus Publishing Co., 1995)

THOMAS Donald, *An Underworld at War* (John Murray, 2003)

THOMAS Donald, *Villains' Paradise* (John Murray, 2005)

Index

Abbreviations
ACC – Assistant Chief Constable
AC(C) – Assistant Commissioner Crime
CC – Chief Constable
CC(CID) – Chief Constable, CID
CI – Chief Inspector
Comm. – Commissioner
DAC – Deputy Assistant Commissioner
DCC – Deputy Chief Constable
DCI – Detective Chief Inspector
DCS – Detective Chief Superintendent
DDI – Divisional Detective Inspector
Dep. Comm. – Deputy Commissioner
DC – Detective Constable
DI – Detective Inspector
DS – Detective Sergeant
Det. Supt. – Detective Superintendent
Insp. – Inspector
HMI – Her Majesty's Inspectorate
PC – Police Constable
PS – Police Sergeant
SPS – Police Station Sergeant